nature's calendar

Collins

HarperCollins Publishers Ltd.
77–85 Fulham Palace Road
London
W6 8JB

The Collins website address is:
www.collins.co.uk

Collins is a registered trademark of
HarperCollins Publishers Ltd.

BBC and the BBC logo are trademarks of the British Broadcasting
Corporation and are used under licence. © 1996

First published in 2007

12 11 10 09 08 07
10 9 8 7 6 5 4 3 2 1

A catalogue record for this book is available from the
British Library.

ISBN 978 0 00 724646 5

Commissioned by Helen Brocklehurst
Edited by Kirstie Addis and Caroline Ward
Cover design and design layout by Emma Jern
Design by Bob Vickers
Proofread by Chris Turner
Index by Lisa Footit

Colour reproduction by Butler & Tanner
Printed and bound in Great Britain by Butler & Tanner

Contents

Acknowledgements and picture credits

The BBC wishes to thank everyone involved in the making of *Nature's Calendar*.

(T = top, M = middle, B = bottom)
Mapping © Collins Bartholomew 2007;
NHPA/Stephen Dalton p.8, p.36B, p.57T,
p.65T, p.67M, p.83M, p.119B, p.142,
p.157M, p.168, p.173M, p.180, p.186;
NHPA/Laurie Campbell p.11M, p.19 M&B,
p.21T&M, p.28, p.31T, p.35M, p.38, p.48,
p.60T, p.61B, p.75T, p.77B, p.81M, p.89B,
p.93B, p.95T, 101B, p.105T, p.128, p.131B,
p.134, p.139M, p.159T, p.179T&B, p.198T,
p.203T, p.205T, p.207T, p.211T, p.223T,
p.247M; NHPA/John Hayward p.60B;
NHPA/Iain Green p.50; NHPA/Mike Lane
p.11B, p.61T, p.100, p.121T, p.157T, p.179M,
p.198B, p.201T, p.211M, p.218, p.221B,
p.228; NHPA/Andy Rouse p.12T, p.25T,
p.59M, p.73T, p.76, p.78B, p.103T, p.135B,
p.235M; NHPA/Guy Edwardes p.13T,
p.67T, p.81T, p.114, p.117B, p.212, p.215T,
p.225T, p.241B; NHPA/Alan Williams
p.23B, p.25B, p.27T, p.31B, p.67B, p.70,
p.75M, p.97M, p.102T, p.113T, p.137B,
p.153T, p.173T&B, p.202, p.217T, p.236T,
p.237T, p.243T; Isle of Man Department
of Tourism p.23T; NHPA/Alberto Nardi
p.32, p.91T; Paul Rainsford, Exmoor Hotel
p.33T; Chris Moore, Sundial Guesthouse
p.33B; Ian O'Leary p.37T; NHPA/Paul
Brough p.35B; NHPA/Jordi Bas Casas
p.35T; NHPA/Lutra p.36T, p.176T;
NHPA/Jeff Goodman p.40; NHPA/Ernie
Janes p.41, p.51B, p.58, p.89T, p.92, p.108,
p.175B, p.181B, p.203M, p.216T, p.239B;
NHPA/Lee Dalton p.203B; NHPA/Joe
Blossom p.43T, p.71B, p.115B; Newcastle
City Council p.11T; Lough Neagh
Partnership p.12B; RSPB/Chris Gomersall
p.13B, p.193B, p.201B; Philip Newman
p.14; Glasgow City Council p.15; Lee Valley
Regional Park Authority p.17T&B; Scottish
Viewpoint/Iain McLean p.19T; NTPL/Joe
Cornish p.21B, p.37B, p.55T, p.71T, p.131T,
p.140B, p.151B, p.236B; Natural England/
Paul Glendell p.27B, p.51T, p.163B; Heligan
Gardens Ltd/Julian Stephens p.39T; Eco
Watch Limited p.39B; Mike Page p.43B;
Caerlaverock Wetland and Wildlife Trust
p.44, p,45B; Scottish Viewpoint/Allan
Devlin p.45T, p.237B; NHPA/Roy Waller
p.47T; Natural England/Peter Wakely
p.47B, p.73B, p.85T, p.119T, p.141B,
p.143T, p.215B; NHPA/Hellio and Van
Ingen p.53T, p.158T, p.208; Forestry
Commission/Isobel Cameron p.53B,
p.185B; NHPA/Manfred Danegger p.55B,
p.181T, p.185T, p.219B; Scottish
Viewpoint/Paul Tomkins p.57B; NHPA/
Ann and Steve Toon p.59T, p.143B; NHPA/
Jari Peltomaki p.59B; Ian Barthorpe (RSPB)
p.63T; NHPA/Roger Tidman p.63B, p.88,
p.132, p.133, p.158B, p.204; RSPB/Andy
Hay p.65B, p.193T, p.211B, p.217B, p.221T;
FLPA/Jim Brandenburg p.65M; NHPA/
Robert Thompson p.68, p.111all, p.159B;
Gordon Donaldson, Cowall and Trossachs
p.75B; Nicola Greaves and Jon Tainton
p.77T; FLPA/Winfried Wisniewski p.78T;
Douglas Buchanan/Woolston Eyes
Conservation Group p.79T, p.79B; NHPA/
Simon Booth p.81B, p.83T, p.93T, p.127T;
John Wilson/Whitelee Farm p.83B;
Natural England p.85M; Mike Dilger
p.85B, p.90, p.91B, p.97B, p.137T; NHPA/
Wayne Hutchinson p.86; Scottish
Viewpoint/P Tomkins p.95B, p.101T,
p.199B, p.207B; NHPA/Melvin Grey
p.97T, p.107B, p.121B, p.187B, p.194; Stuart
Abraham/Jersey.com p.99B; NHPA/Linda
Pitkin p.99T&M, p.136, p.146, p.182;
NTPL/Rupert Truman p.102B; English
Nature/Phil Holms p.103B; Forestry
Commission Wales p.107T; NHPA/Julie
Royle p.105B, p.163M; Broads Authority
p.118T&B; NTPL/Matthew Antrobus
p.176B; Mike Hartwell/Peatlands Park
p.177B; NHPA/B&C Alexander p.199T;
FLPA/Phil McLean p.188; Guy Huntington
p.191T&B; Matt Thomas p.191M; NHPA/
Alan Barnes p.110, p.130, p.140T, p.165T,
p.195B; Andy Davies p.113B; NHPA/Jean-
Louis Le Moigne p.113M, p.174; www.
walney-island.com p.115T; NHPA/Brian
Hawkes p.117T; FLPA/Richard Becker
p.122; NHPA/Gerry Cambridge p.123B,
p.177T; NHPA/NA Callow p.123T, p.125B;
West Kent Downs Countryside Trust
p.124, p.125T; Visit Herefordshire p.127B;
NHPA/Kevin Schafer p.135T; Mike Snow,
Wildlife Trust of South and West Wales
p.139T&B; NHPA/Martin Garwood p.141T,
p.161B; National Botanic Garden of Wales
p.144, p.145T&B; Andrew Davies for The
Royal Parks p.148, p.149T; NHPA/John
Jeffery p.149B; NHPA/Henry Ausloos
p.151T; NHPA/George Bernard p.153B;
RSPB/Mark Hamblin p.154; Scottish
Viewpoint p.155; NHPA/Bill Coster p.155B,
p.185M, p.245B; WWT/Martin Mere 157B;
NHPA/Jane Gifford p.161T; NHPA/David
Woodfall p.163T, p.195T; Cheddar Caves
and Gorge 165M&B; Martin Senior p.166,
p.167T; Anne and Chris Algar p.167B;
Shropshire Wildlife Trust/Ben Osborne
p.170, p.171T&B; English Heritage/Nigel
Corrie p.175T; NHPA/Matt Bain p.183B;
Forestry Commission/Forest Life Picture
Library p.187T; NHPA/S&D&K Maslowski
p.197T; Natural England/Julian Bateson
p.197B; FLPA/Gary K Smith p.205B;
NHPA/Rich Kirchner p.207M; Pamela
Tompsett/Helford VMCA p.213T&B; Janet
Sumner p.216B; Bristol Film Office p.219T;
Abbey Farm Organics p.227T&B; Forestry
Commission/John White p.225M; NHPA/
Yves Lanceau p.225B; NHPA/Dave Watts
p.230; NTPL/Nature Picture Library/
Laurent Geslin p.231T; FLPA/DP Wilson
p.231B; Lincolnshire Wildlife Trust p.233
T&B; Scottish Viewpoint/Richard Nicholls
p.235B; Jenny McMillan p.223B; NHPA/
Louise Campbell p.235T; FLPA/Richard
Brooks p.239T; Nicholas Cottrell p.241T;
Viktoria Gridley-Haack p.243B; Gigrin
Farm p.245T; NHPA/Andrea Bonetti
p.247T; Old Country House Farm p.247B.

Introduction

A jewel-eyed tigress brushes through a curtain of bamboo and slips into a predatory crouch. A frozen crowd of penguins huddle hard against a razor-edged hurricane. Tiny ants riot in a frenzied blur of a million legs and champ their jaws on the giant green carcass of a luckless caterpillar, and the massive bulk of a whale emerges from the big blue in an eruption of slow-motion salty spume, rolls over and crashes back into the wet world. And all this happens in our front rooms or kitchens. It happens in full colour and stereo on our televisions. We enjoy the most intimate insights into the natural world as we make and eat our dinner. We acquire a familiarity with a fantastic diversity of species without getting wet or cold, without picking up binoculars or a book, without travel, without cost, without investing any time. We tune into wildlife gold for the price of a licence or subscription and then we turn over.

Now, it might seem like great value, it's certainly entertaining, but there is a very significant catch. No smell, no touch, no sense of reality in time. No scope for expectation, no longing, no frustration, no wishing and no failure. And yet these are just a few of the essential components required to feel, yes feel, the wonder of the natural world. In truth, television is a good way to stimulate an interest in wildlife, but it is by no means a way to satisfy that interest. I'd rather spend ten minutes with a woodlouse on the palm of my hand than watch a tiger on TV.

Nature's Calendar aims to cure this condition. It aims to prove that fabulous encounters with wildlife are not the preserve of scientists, experts, wardens, life-long naturalists or film-makers and that you don't have to travel the world to revel in brilliant nature. It aims to invite you to publicly accessible sites to get close to shy, beautiful or large numbers of real life creatures. Critically, it doesn't come with a guarantee, but it is armed with solid and honest research. There's no fantasy because fantasy is always ultimately disappointing, and we know that disappointment is not on the modern agenda. We're not going to tease naturalists, especially young ones, with tales of otters at your feet, of eagles on the end of your nose or badgers giving birth. What this is about is getting up and going out to experience wildlife for yourself.

So why is that important? Well, it's a quality of life issue, it's about enrichment and enjoying what's on your doorstep. And it's about the development of a real and long-term affinity for all those creatures we share our world with. Without that, their care and conservation just won't matter enough to enough people and when they need help too few will feel impelled to give a pound or get up and do something. When you get dressed and set off to explore something wild and unpredictable and fail, and fail, and eventually succeed, it just means more to you – it has a personal value.

We live in an age when our children and young people are positively discouraged from exploring nature in the real world. We lock them up with sterilised computers and they never get stung, slimed, bitten, licked or excited first hand by the most immediately astonishing things in their world. We know that virtually all of the world's best naturalists are hooked before they are nine years old. When was the last time you saw a nine-year-old watching birds nesting, running about with a butterfly net or wrestling with a grass snake? I meet 'qualified' biologists who don't know common bird song because they've learned their trade in a library, and that is sad. All of our experts are getting old and the 'Great British Amateur Naturalist' is in danger of becoming extinct. So it's absolutely essential that we address the issue of putting young people in touch, literally, with wildlife. Of course the major wildlife charities do their bit, but they can only reach a relatively small number of kids. So it's down to you to make it happen. We cannot rely upon schools or the RSPB to introduce our kids to a love of life. Don't take them shopping this weekend – take them to feed a squirrel or catch a frog!

So come on, flick to a page in this book where you can find something you have always wanted to see, tell the kids to get their wellies on or ring the grandchildren and give them a 20 minute warning, grab something to eat and drink and get in the car, or on the bus, train or whatever. Go and get wet or sweaty, find a whole lot of surprising things that creep and crawl about and then revel in them! This book tells you where you can get so close to rutting deer that you can smell them, so close to dolphins that they splash you when they breach, so close to black-tailed godwits that you can see their eyelashes. Now, that's what I call wildlife!

Chris Packham

January

After the excesses of Christmas and the New Year, what better way to shed those few extra pounds than to go for a winter wildlife walk? What seems a cold, dark and unpromising month can in fact be an excellent time to see animals when they are forced to lose their inhibitions in their drive to find food.

Even in the depths of winter a woodland walk will reveal that the first botanical signs of life are stirring. The luscious greens of lichens show particularly well at this time of year and, if you look into the naked tree tops, January is the time when the courtship reaches fever pitch for the grey squirrels as they charge after one another through the leafless branches.

As cities may well be a degree or two warmer, they provide a welcome refuge for hungry birds and foxes, but, for a truly wild experience, little can beat an estuary in January when huge flocks of waders like knot can often put on a tremendous performance over the mudflats, which, in turn, attracts the attentions of local marauding peregrines and merlins. So, no excuses, get out there!

1 Northumberland Pools

Getting there:

Big Waters Reserve is located off the A1, close to Brunswick Village. Bus service 45 from Newcastle Haymarket.

Tel: 0191 2813833

Email: walker.riversidepark@newcastle. gov.uk

Opening times: Open daily; closed to vehicles after dusk

Charging policy: Not applicable. Small car park charge.

Disabled access: Varies for different pools. Big Water has level paths with good surfaces. Tape guide is available.

Find out more

Northumberland County Council – Eider Ducks
www.northumberland.gov.uk/vg/ eider_duck.htm

Northumberland Wildlife Trust
www.wildlifetrust.org.uk/ northumberland/

Newcastle City Council – Big Waters Nature Reserve
www.newcastle.gov.uk/core.nsf/ a/bigwaters?opendocument

Something peculiar is happening in the northeast countryside and it's turning out to be great for wildlife. There's a belt of coal that runs from County Durham to the coast at Druridge Bay, which for years it was at the heart of the coal-mining industry. But, when the mines closed and the pumps were turned off, the roofs of the mines caved in – and great pools formed on the surface.

These pools attract thousands of overwintering birds, from pink-footed geese to visiting ducks. There are plenty of pools to choose between, and many of them are now run as nature reserves. Among the best are Hauxley and Cresswell Pond near the coast and, one we heartily recommend, Big Waters near Newcastle, which is one of the largest subsidence ponds in southeast Northumberland. All of them are great places to go on a winter duck safari and as you start to pick out the differences you become aware that ducks are really, really interesting and that there are many more kinds than you might at first have imagined.

If you're lucky, you'll see the smew – a really elegant, small diving duck visiting from Scandinavia and Russia. It'll be here from December through to March. From a distance the males are black and white, but close up the feathers have a sort of 'cracked ice' appearance – it's seriously smart, a real Chanel bird of the duck world. The females are less immediately striking but have a punk-rock hairstyle which gives them a charm all of their own – they and the juveniles are appropriately known as redheads.

The smew belongs to a group of ducks known as sawbills. They have serrated beaks which help them hold on to the slippery fish that they hunt underwater. Another species of sawbill you might spot on these freshwater subsidence ponds is the goosander.

Goosanders breed in the UK (mainly in the north of England, Scotland and Wales) on fast-flowing upland streams and rivers. In the winter they move to lakes, gravel pits and reservoirs where they hunt in packs, working together to herd shoals of fish. Watching goosander go hunting is as fascinating as seeing lions in Africa – and the bonus is they're right here on your own doorstep.

The pools and lakes of Northumberland can support lots of different species of duck because of their varying diets and manner of feeding. Teal, for instance, are small dabbling ducks whose numbers are swelled in the winter by visitors from the Baltic and Siberia. The males have chestnut-coloured heads with broad green eyestripes and they're best seen in winter when they gather together in seriously large groups. Unlike

Big Waters in winter

the sawbills, teal eat seeds and small invertebrates which they dabble for on or just below the surface.

Another great dabbling duck is the shoveler. Now, this is one duck you really can't mistake – it's a comedy, cartoon version of a duck with an over-sized beak which it uses as a very effective sieve.

So we've got diving ducks and dabblers, but the great thing about this part of the world is that you can also see our final group of ducks – sea ducks – because lots of them use the pools just behind the coast at Druridge Bay. One of the most dramatic and easiest to identify is the long-tailed duck, a winter visitor from the Arctic Circle, which as its name suggests has greatly elongated tail feathers.

But you can't come to Northumberland without making a bit of an effort to see another sea duck which is the symbol of the coast round here – the eider duck, known locally as the cuddy duck. We had to cheat a bit to see this one by heading for the River Coquet near Amble. Apparently, eiders were protected by the patron saint of Northumberland, St Cuthbert, on the Farne Islands, but some locals say that's just because it was so cold there in winter that he wanted their feathers, still used today to stuff expensive duvets. Eiders begin their courtship in December, so this really is the best time of year to not only see them puffing up their apricot-pink chests and flirting with the females, but also to hear them. While the males give a musical 'coo-coo-coo!', the females make growling sounds. Once heard, an eider is never forgotten!

The female goosander

The eider duck, or cuddy duck

While we seriously recommend a wild duck safari in Northumberland, you might also like to know that this has to be one of the best places in the country to see otters in daylight. We were told we had a 98 per cent chance and yet we still couldn't quite believe it when we saw three otters, a mother and her two cubs, playing directly in front of the hide at Big Waters Nature Reserve. From the records in the hide log, if you're prepared to put in the time, you'll almost certainly be as lucky as we were. But remember to wear lots and lots of layers. Even properly dressed, we got so cold that our lips practically froze together – not the ideal way to make a programme that relies on presenters speaking to camera!

2 Lough Neagh, Northern Ireland

Getting there:

Oxford Island National Nature Reserve, Craigavon, Co. Armagh BT66 6NJ. Lough Neagh is one hour's drive from Belfast on the M1 or M2.

Tel: Discovery Centre – 028 3832 2205

Email: oxford.island@craigavon.gov.uk

Opening times: October–March, 10am–5pm (Monday–Sunday); April–September, 10am–6pm (Monday–Saturday), 10am–7pm (Sunday).

Charging policy: Not applicable.

Disabled access: Discovery Centre has disabled access and most hides, paths and facilities are wheelchair accessible

Flock of Whooper swans

Find out more
Lough Neagh
www.loughneagh.com/

Lough Neagh Partnership
http://loughneaghpartnership.com/

Ulster Wildlife Trust
www.ulsterwildlifetrust.org/

Ballyronan, Lough Neagh, in the snow

Now, you've got to be pretty keen to crawl out from under your duvet and venture out at 5am on a dark, freezing winter morning, even with the promise of seeing and hearing hundreds of Icelandic whooper swans coming in from their migration. But you'd be glad you made the effort, as we were on our visit to Lough Neagh.

An hour's drive from Belfast, Lough Neagh is the largest body of freshwater in the UK and a real mecca for migrating birds. The biggest of the migrants is the whooper swan and, if you visit in January, you'll get to see literally hundreds of them arriving at the end of their epic 1,300 kilometre journey from their northern breeding grounds in Iceland.

The whooper swan's call, after which it is named, is distinctive. But if you don't hear them call, it might be that you've confused them with another migrant, the Bewick's swan. The whooper is larger and longer necked than the Bewick's, but it's really the bill that distinguishes it. You need to look closely, because at first glance they both have similar yellow bills, but the whooper has a large triangular yellow wedge on its bill, compared to the smaller, rounded and more variable yellow patch on the bill of the Bewick's swan.

Whoopers usually leave Iceland and start heading for Britain and Ireland between mid-October and mid-November. We'll have them with us all winter until March or April when they begin the long haul back to Iceland once more. Interestingly, a small population of just over a thousand always stays behind in Iceland, as this is about the maximum number that can be sustained by the food supply in winter.

If you've made the effort to get up early to see the whoopers, it's worth spending the rest of the day checking out the other bird life on and around the lough. There are plenty of hides, as well as the Lough Neagh Discovery Centre, which has a café. There's even a 200 kilometre cycle track right around the lough, which is probably the best way to get a feel for the size and splendour of the place.

3 Belfast Lough, Northern Ireland

Getting there:

Located within the Belfast Harbour Estate. The two entrances are signposted along the A2.

Tel: 028 9147 9009

Email: belfast.lough@rspb.org.uk

Opening times: Two outdoor hides open all hours. Heated observation room 9am–5pm (Tuesday–Sunday). Rangers on hand daily except Christmas Day.

Charging policy: Not applicable

Disabled access: Good access to the observation room and one outdoor viewpoint. One hide inaccessible.

Black-tailed godwit; the main attraction

Find out more

Belfast Lough Nature Reserve
www.rspb.org.uk/reserves/guide/b/belfastlough/index.asp

Birding UK
www.birding.uk.com/links/Places-to-See-Birds-N-Ireland.html

Belfast Lough
www.blss.org/

Northern Ireland Tourist Board
www.discovernorthernireland.com/

Even on *Nature's Calendar* we sometimes stumble across a wildlife reserve that we've never been to before – and kick ourselves for not having gone there sooner. On the face of it, a wetland wedged between a busy airport and some of Northern Ireland's heaviest industry on the docks would do little to convince you that this is a top spot to visit. But, thankfully, appearances can be deceptive.

Walk into the RSPB's Belfast Lough reserve and you enter a different world, in which you can witness one of the greatest shows on earth. The reason? The birds are so close you can almost see your reflection in their eyes. It's that good.

Take a look out of the heated (yes, heated!) observation hide and you'll see ferries from Scotland and England, their human cargo oblivious to what they've just passed. What they've missed is a lagoon that is simply packed to the rafters with waders and wildfowl. They're not any old birds either. The main attraction is the black-tailed godwit. This is a bird that in its winter plumage is ghostly grey with a delicate, slender, pink bill. Come spring and their feathers will have turned the most vibrant shade of tomato-soup red, as they get ready to head up to Iceland to breed.

Black-tailed godwits are something of a success story. They were absent from our shores as a breeding bird for a century after much persecution and loss of habitat. It was only in the 1930s that the first ones were seen back in the UK. In the winter, however, they can be spotted at various coastal locations. And the views in Belfast are hard to beat.

In winter these birds are constantly on the go as they probe the grass and mud for tasty titbits. As they snake past at arm's length, fluttering their eyelashes, you have to remind yourself that these are birds that you'd normally need a telescope to see. Ask the staff to point out Ruby, a female godwit that's been ringed and returns to the reserve year after year. And, for goodness sake, remember to pack your camera.

Industry and wetland side by side

4 Hogganfield Park, Glasgow

Getting there:

Located 5km northeast of Glasgow city centre, bounded by Cumbernauld Road (A80) and Avenue End Road (B765). Regular bus services from Glasgow city centre.

Tel: Land Services General Enquiries – 0141 287 5108

Email: land@glasgow.gov.uk

Opening times: Open all hours, year round

Charging policy: Not applicable

Disabled access: Good wheelchair access with a tarmac path around the edge of the loch.

Find out more

Glasgow City Council –
Hogganfield Park
**www.glasgow.gov.uk/en/
Residents/Parks_Outdoors/Parks
_gardens/hogganfieldpark.htm**

Clyde Birds
www.clydebirds.com/

Wildlife Scotland
**http://wildlife.visitscotland.com/
unique/greaterglasgowclyde**

Glasgow Wildlife
**http://wildlife.glasgow.gov.uk/
13hg.htm**

Hogganfield Park is an urban nature oasis, five kilometres from the hectic centre of Glasgow and hemmed in on all sides by housing estates and trunk roads. To the visitor not tuned in to the ways of wildlife watching, the park is a place to take a break from the relentless churn of the city – or simply somewhere to just come and feed the ducks and swans. The park consists of 48 hectares of loch, a small island and a few boggy bits around the loch margins – doesn't sound much? Well, we were to discover that it was a little gem.

Arriving at the park, on first impressions, it has to be said it looks decidedly unimpressive – until we lifted our binoculars to see which birds had turned up for the Glaswegian 'white-sliced'. No sooner had we peered over the iron railing separating the birds on the loch from all the visitors standing at the edge of the car park, than we realised that we were looking at phenomenally close-up views of wild whooper swans jockeying for position with the resident mute swans. And the interest didn't just stop with the whoopers either, because, quite literally, ducking and diving in between the swans, tufted duck and goldeneye were to be found, also making a bid for the free bread handouts.

If asked to name the most secretive British bird, the jack snipe would come pretty close to the top of most birders' lists. A bird rarely encountered, and even more rarely filmed, this diminutive visitor from breeding grounds in Arctic Russia chooses to spend the winter months in remote habitats of the British Isles – such as far-flung marshes and flooded grasslands – or so we thought. We had arranged to meet up with the Clyde Ringing Group at the 'boggy bit' on the far side of the loch to see if we could catch this most elusive of waders.

The jack snipe is a bird about which very little is known, other than the fact that it spends a few short winter months with us and while here decides to pass its time

concealed in muddy vegetation, only deigning to reveal itself when almost trodden on by the unwary walker or birdwatcher not afraid of getting their feet wet.

It is actually possible to see the jack snipe in the wild if you spend a few hours at a known wintering site and stare at the mud waiting for a small bird to reveal itself, but we were keen to get a much closer view ... one in the hand in fact! So out we went with the Clyde Ringing Group and, as we duly unfurled a standard mist net, we were to find that it would be used to ensnare our prey in a rather novel way. Rather than erect the net vertically between two poles and retreat to see which birds flew into the fine-mesh wall, we adopted a much more proactive technique of holding the net horizontally and striding into the bog. When a likely jack snipe spot was reached, the net was placed onto the ground to see if we had trapped any of these bog-loving birds. As the first couple of attempts drew blanks, we began to suspect the little critters might have evaded us, so imagine our delight when a small, russet-coloured bird erupted out of the vegetation only to be ensnared by the blanket of the mist net!

In the hand, the jack snipe is a beautifully marked bird. Much rarer than the longer-billed, common snipe, this ultra-secretive bird is a master of disguise. Not only do its colour tones totally match the surrounding muddy vegetation, but the beautiful tan lines along its back also perfectly mimic the flattened reed stems. This is a bird that can melt into its surroundings far more easily than a needle in a haystack. In fact, so confident was our bird of its camouflage that, when finally placed back down on the ground, it didn't even fly off, but sat perfectly still hoping that we'd forgotten where we'd placed it – so if you catch one, watch where you put your feet!

Hogganfield Loch and island

Opposite: The secretive Jack Snipe

5 Lee Valley Park, London

Getting there:

Lee Valley Regional Park Information Service, Stubbins Hall Lane, Waltham Abbey, EN9 9EG. The park stretches almost 42 kilometres from Ware to Leyton. Nearest train station (to Information Service): Cheshunt.

Tel: Park information service – 01992 702200

Email: info@leevalleypark.org.uk

Opening times: Open daily. Park ranger service except Christmas Day. Information desk 10am–4pm.

Charging policy: Not applicable

Disabled access: Disabled access guide is available to be ordered from www.leevalleypark.org.uk/en/fe/brochure_request_s1.asp?nodeidl1=3&nodeidl2=10&level=3&nodeidl3=43

Find out more

Lee Valley Park
www.leevalleypark.org.uk/

Epping Forest District Council - Lee Valley Park
www.eppingforestdc.gov.uk/leisure_and_culture/tourist_information/lee_valley.asp

Lee Valley Park is London's green lung. It runs for 42 kilometres alongside the River Lee and is crossed midway by the M25. You can even reach the start of this 4,000 hectare park on the tube. Originally formed in 1967, Lee Valley encompasses five nature reserves and eight Sites of Special Scientific Interest. Although it's so close to London, Lee Valley has 32 different species of mammal, 500 types of flowering plant and 21 species of dragonfly. Even in winter you needn't worry that there will be nothing to look at as 10,000 waterbirds overwinter here, including nationally important numbers of tufted duck, pochard, goosander, great-crested grebe, coot, gadwall and shoveler. And one of the main reasons for visiting the park is that this is one of the most important sites in the UK for overwintering bitterns.

Bitterns have the three characteristics beloved of twitchers – they are secretive, elusive and rare. They're difficult to spot because they lurk around in the reeds, perfectly camouflaged with their buff-coloured plumage, covered with dark streaks and bars that beautifully mimic the shade of reeds in winter. If alarmed, they stand bolt upright, bill pointing upwards, even swaying slightly so that they look more reed-like than ever. What will give them away are their massive feet – once they start moving you'll be astounded at how large they are! During the breeding season in spring the males make a tremendous booming call, the loudest and lowest-pitched sound of any European bird, which can be heard for up to five kilometres. The bird's generic name, *Botaurus*, may be derived from the Latin *bos* for 'ox' and *taurus* for 'bull', referring to the bird's bellowing, bull-like call. The reason they can produce such a call is because, prior to the breeding season, the walls of the oesophagus strengthen, allowing it to be inflated and act as a resonating chamber. The extra muscle the birds build up can sometimes be as much as one-fifth of their entire body weight.

There are only around 50-100 birds in the UK in winter and only 20 or so males breed, making the bittern, sadly, a Red List species – one of our most endangered. As with many of our rare animals, they were once common: bitterns have been found preserved in the peat in England and Wales dating back to Neolithic times, indicating that once they were widely distributed. They were hunted for food, particularly during medieval times. When the Chancellor of England, George Neville, was made Archbishop of York in 1465 it was reputed that his meal included 400 swans, 2,000 geese and 204 bitterns. Even in the early part of the 19th century, they were common enough to allow shooting parties to kill 20–30 in a morning, and roast bittern was a frequent repast of fenland families, earning the bird the nickname, 'fenman's turkey'.

Two other winter visitors you might look out for in Lee Valley Park are the fieldfare and the redwing. The Spanish call fieldfares 'royal thrushes' because of their striking looks – they are slate blue and chestnut brown with creamy breasts smattered with black spots. They're about the size of a mistle thrush and travel in flocks. Once they've eaten their way through most of the rowan berries in Scandinavia, they head south to eat ours, arriving at the start of our winter season. They love holly, hawthorn and dog rose hips in particular, as well as windfall apples. Redwings have a burnt-orange, crescent-shaped patch under their wings. They also travel in flocks and have a thin, high-pitched whistle that the novelist John Fowles described in his journals as: '... glistening. Like a sudden small gleam of old silver in a dark room. Strange remote beautiful sounds.' As many as one million redwings, our smallest thrushes, come to the British Isles, but as they rarely visit gardens unless they're desperate for food in a particularly cold spell, Lee Valley Park is the place to see them.

The bittern, with its bill pointing upwards in alarm

Winter in Walthamstow, part of the extensive Lee Valley Park

6 Isle of Arran

Getting there:

Daily ferry from Ardrossan to Brodick year round. In summer there is an additional daily service from Claonaig to Lochranza.

Tel: National Trust Ranger Service – 01770 302462

Email: Ayrshire and Arran Tourist Board – info@ayrshire-arran.com

Opening times: Open daily.

Charging policy: Not applicable. Some charges for specific activities.

Disabled access: Varies depending on location. Contact 0845 2255121 (Visit Scotland), or tourist board

Find out more

Ayrshire and Arran Tourist Board
www.ayrshire-arran.com/

Isle of Arran
www.arran.uk.com/

Calmac – Hebridean and Clyde Ferries
http://www.calmac.co.uk/

Don't use the ferry journey across to Arran as an excuse to sit in the ship's galley and sip cappuccino. The crossing is only an hour long, so get yourself out on deck because you're in the right part of the world for bottlenose dolphins and some top quality seabirds too. Pick the right day and up to 30 species of bird could be seen gliding above or bobbing on the waves.

The tourist people will tell you that Arran is Scotland in miniature. Not that it's small of course, but that you get a replica of the highlands and the lowlands all on one island. So, if you're heading there with wildlife in mind, it means one thing – a great range and diversity of species.

We set out to Arran with two very different groups of birds on our target list. Both were going to be a bit tricky – golden eagles in the mountains, and red-throated, black-throated and great northern divers on the coast. To make things a touch more difficult, we only had a couple of days to find what we were looking for.

First up were the golden eagles. There's only a handful of birds on the island, so on the face of it, the chance of seeing one is pretty slim. But there's a spot on the mountainous northern side of the island where sightings are pretty much guaranteed. This is where eagle watching in a place like Arran comes into its own. Small numbers of birds on an island is a better bet than widely distributed birds in a big landscape on the mainland.

Being honest, though, for the first hour or so we were getting neckache looking into the sky. Golden eagles might be big, but they were nowhere to be seen. But, just as we were considering packing the camera gear away, not one, but two eagles floated into view.

February is also a good time to see these birds. This is when they're getting down to the business of nest building. You can often see them languidly soaring on the updrafts close to the mountains. Often they're just checking out possible new sites for their eyries, though they do stick to territories that have been used by generations of eagles.

Golden eagles mate for life and, if you're lucky, you might see a pair greeting each other after a few hours apart hunting in the uplands. This is when they perform a brief aerial display together, which is pretty magical to see. When the eagles greet, it looks as if they're about to crash into each other as they swoop, waggle their wings and drop their legs revealing those deadly talons. From a distance it looks like antagonistic behaviour, but in reality it's just the eagles saying: 'Hi, dear, had a good day?' Eagles cement their partnership in so many ways. It's been known for pairs of eagles

to hunt together – for one to chase the prey to exhaustion and for the second eagle to come in and complete the kill. That's what you call a husband-and-wife team!

If you come any later than February, you'll drastically reduce your chances of seeing these birds. By March, they'll have eggs in the nest and will be sticking a bit closer to their inaccessible nest sites.

Arran is not only good for golden eagles – hen harriers can be seen quartering along many of the upland valleys. You've also got a good chance of seeing them on lowland farmland, marshland and conifer plantations.

But what about those divers? Well, in winter they seek shelter close to the coast. The northern and western sides of the island are where you'll find most of them. What makes these birds so intriguing is that they're almost of another world. The American name for the diver species is 'loons', and it fits them pretty well. Sound recordists in Hollywood used the wailing sound of calling divers as a spooky effect in horror films.

These days what's really scary is how little time you get to see these birds. As their name suggests, they're constantly diving – so it takes a bit of time to locate them with your eye as they bob about in the swell. Then you've got to train your binoculars or scope on them. And just when you've focused, they've dived again. Oh, and in winter these birds don't have the distinctive red and black throat markings that normally make them easy to identify. Frustrating? Of course not – it's all part of the fun.

Isle of Arran – Scotland in miniature

Both black-throated and red-throated divers can be seen around the island

7 Isle of Wight

Getting there:

Car or high-speed passenger ferry services from Southampton, Lymington, Southsea and Portsmouth; routes connect directly with road, rail and coach links. The island has a network of buses.

Tel: 01983 813800

Email: info@islandbreaks.co.uk

Opening times: Open daily.

Charging policy: Not applicable. Some charges for specific activities

Disabled access: Varies depending on location; enquire when making booking.

Find out more

Island Breaks – Isle of Wight Tourism
www.islandbreaks.co.uk/

Hampshire and isle of Wight Wildlife Trust
www.hwt.org.uk/

Dinosaur Isle Museum
www.dinosaurisle.com/

UK Fossils
www.ukfossils.co.uk/iow.htm

Now, while most people don't really get excited about rocks, there's no way you could visit the Isle of Wight and walk in the footsteps of dinosaurs and not be amazed. The Isle of Wight is known as 'Dinosaur Island', and with good reason. Its many beautiful beaches are littered with the remains of creatures which roamed our planet millions of years ago. Winter is a good time to visit, as a few storms pounding the cliffs and beaches usually unearth all sorts of goodies.

One hundred and twenty million years ago there was no Isle of Wight as we know it. It was landlocked and part of a much larger continent. Dinosaurs roamed across marshy habitats leaving their footprints, and those that died were buried by mud and preserved as fossils. You can visit the Isle of Wight today and come away with your own genuine, small piece of dinosaur fossil – a pocket-sized bit of dinosaur bone makes a great souvenir – but you'll find other things here such as dinosaur footprints that, even if you were allowed to, you definitely won't be able to squeeze into your hand luggage!

We went down to Compton Bay near Freshwater and there, scattered all over the beach, found lots of weird, three-pronged sandstone boulders. It took only a few minutes to work out what on earth they were: the casts of giant dinosaur footprints. The imprints would have originally been made in soft mud, and then got filled in by sand. Since sandstone is much harder than mudstone, the casts are now being washed out of the mudstone cliffs by the sea and dumped on the beach.

If you're not sure you can identify fossils on your own, the Museum of Isle of Wight Geology (also known as Dinosaur Isle) leads field trips for all ages and will help you identify your finds – you're only a short step away from becoming a dinosaur hunter!

But ancient creatures are not all the island has to offer. The Isle of Wight is one of the last southern refuges of red squirrels. These are what we think of as our native squirrel. They came over to Britain about ten thousand years ago, just before the land bridge to Europe was washed away at the end of the last ice age. We caught up with them at Alverstone Mead Nature Reserve near Sandown and came closer to one than we would ever have imagined – all with the help of a bag of walnuts.

The plan was to set up some small static cameras on the front of the hide and then hold out one of the walnuts in our hand for a red squirrel, hopefully, to come and take. Now, bearing in mind that these are supposed to be very timid creatures, we didn't exactly have a lot of faith in our plan. But we were so intent on keeping perfectly silent and still that we didn't immediately notice a red squirrel running about around our feet and another poised on the edge of the hide, looking as if it was going to jump up onto our backs. They were obviously not as timid as we had thought, or maybe it was the fact that we were offering them banquet food that they just couldn't resist. They came up and took the nuts from our hands and gave us a perfect chance to observe them. They have gingery to reddish-grey fur on top, a lovely creamy-coloured underbelly and are topped off by beautiful long feathery ear tufts. It's this colour and the ear tufts that clearly distinguish them from the non-native grey squirrel. Being so close, we were even able to observe them doing that rather curious thing with the nuts – turning them over and over in their paws, assessing the weight and quality of each nut compared to the last one – and it turns out they were pretty good at it, because they never buried a dud nut!

Despite widespread decimation from disease of the red squirrel population, they have survived on the Isle of Wight. The reason for this is simple – it is an island and, so far, no grey squirrels, the carriers of the disease, have made it over from the mainland. Let's hope they never do!

Alverstone Mead Nature Reserve covers 18 hectares of ancient woodland so, apart from red squirrels, you'll see masses of woodland birds. In a nutshell – there's not much that the Isle of Wight doesn't have!

A real favourite: the red squirrel. The Isle of Wight is one of their last refuges

Pied wagtails – one of the many birds you can catch sight of on the island

The beach and cliffs at Compton Bay, Isle of Wight

8 Isle of Man

Getting there:

By plane to Ronaldsway Airport near Castletown or by sea to Douglas from Liverpool or Heysham, Belfast or Dublin.

Tel: Isle of Man Tourism – 01624 686801

Email: manxwt@cix.co.uk

Opening times: Open daily; ferry opening depends on operators

Charging policy: Not applicable

Disabled access: Varies depending on locations. Phone before you travel.

Find out more

Isle of Man Tourism
www.gov.im/tourism/

Manx Wildlife Trust
www.wildlifetrust.org.uk/manxwt/

Manx Bird Atlas
www.manxbirdatlas.org.uk/index.shtml

Isle of Man Birding
www.iombirding.co.uk/

RSPB – Chough
www.rspb.org.uk/action/species/casestudies/chough.asp

The chough is a bird with peculiar habits. This rarest of all our corvids has often been called the Celtic crow, because it only survives in all the areas of the British Isles where languages other than English still endure, including west and north Wales, west Scotland and the very western tip of Cornwall. But nowhere is it more abundant than on the Isle of Man, an island in the Irish Sea with a rich history of independence, and where the Manx language is still spoken in a few pockets.

According to recent counts, the Isle of Man boasts over 150 choughs, which, to put it in context, is about 30 per cent of all the choughs in Britain. Not bad, then, for an island that measures roughly 52 kilometres long by 32 kilometres wide!

The Manx people are proud not just of their choughs – they also have one of the most impressive hen harrier roosts in the whole of the British Isles. This wonderful bird of prey only began nesting in the Isle of Man in 1977, but found the habitat so much to its liking that over 40 pairs now breed on the high moorland areas in the centre of the island. Hen harriers can also be found roosting communally at certain sites in the winter. Ballaugh Curragh on the northwest of the island has recorded astonishing numbers – as high as 80 individuals – which turn up each dusk during the winter from the surrounding countryside to spend the night at the site. The best area, we were informed, to view this ornithological treat was actually on top of a specially designed hide in the middle of the bog itself, and indeed the view from the top gave us a fine panorama from which to film the harriers arriving.

The hen harrier is a bird that is sexually dimorphic, which basically means that males and females look completely different. Both sexes have the long wings and tail, features which immediately distinguish harriers from other birds of prey, but the female is larger and brown above with a distinctive white rump and black bands on her tail. Juveniles resemble females and because they, too, possess a white rump, both are collectively referred to as 'ringtails'. The male is smaller and pearl-grey above, with black tips to its wings and a pale belly.

We arrived well before dusk to set up our cameras, and, as we had to film in the depths of winter to catch the roosting hen harriers, you could describe the wait as 'long and cold' as the birds delayed their entrance. But, as dusk swiftly approached, all of a sudden a female ringtail was picked up drifting in off the moorland, closely followed by another and, then, another! The highlight of the visit was undoubtedly seeing a

beautiful pale, ghostly male drift right over our heads before dropping into the bog for the night. At final tally we had counted eight ringtails and two males!

The choughs were not to be outdone by their Manx hen harrier neighbours, though. The following morning we visited Castletown in the south. This small town used to be the old capital of the Isle of Man and has a long colourful history as the home of Vikings, kings and governments. The intertidal zone which fringes Castletown Bay is known as the premier spot for locating a large chough flock and, sure enough, upon arrival the flock was immediately located feeding among the seaweed. A quick count with binoculars revealed an incredible 40 choughs, and mixed in the flock were occasional hooded crows, with jackdaws and ravens to be seen flying overhead – what a crow-fest!

Few birders would disagree that the chough is the finest of all the crows. With its bright red bill and feet, glossy black plumage and wonderful 'kyeow' call it definitely stands out from the crowd. The bird is not just a pretty face either: as their broad wings and distinctive fingered primaries indicate, the chough is also a master of the skies. And as we watched the flock tumbling in the air and harvesting food from the beach with Castle Rushen as the backdrop, we realised that this was a view that the Vikings must have had as they watched these elegant and primeval birds from their longboats.

Flocks of birds near Castletown, the old island capital

One of the Manx choughs

9 Castlewellan Arboretum, County Down, Northern Ireland

Getting there:

An hour's drive south of Belfast, 6½ kilometres from Newcastle, County Down. From Newcastle take A50 to Castlewellan. At roundabout turn right to the top of the hill, turn left following signpost to Forest Park.

Tel: 028 43778664

Email: customer.forestservice@ dardni.gov.uk

Opening times: 10am–sunset daily.

Charging policy: Pedestrian forest access: Adult £2; Child 50p. Parking charges apply.

Disabled access: Variable terrain. Access for those with limited mobility.

Find out more

Castlewellan Forest Park
www.forestserviceni.gov.uk/our_ forests/castlewellan/castle_wellan. htm

Peace Maze
www.peacemaze.com/history_of_ the_park.htm

Woodland Trust
www.woodland-trust.org.uk/

Occasionally when out on a birding walk we have this tendency to mentally tick birds off: blue tit, seen that, treecreeper, seen that, nuthatch, tick, and so on. But everything slows down when you're filming wildlife. Indeed, sometimes there's so much waiting around while the camera crew get general views and backdrops of the landscape that you end up with a marvellous opportunity to stop birdspotting and start birdwatching. As a result, we've observed some fascinating bird behaviour that we might normally have walked right past.

It was on one of these occasions in January during a visit to Castlewellan Arboretum in Northern Ireland that we observed some robins. Everyone loves robins and every garden seems to have one. These birds were originally a woodland species and Castlewellan has them in abundance. Robins are extremely territorial and both the male and female have red breasts to warn intruders off their territory. In the arboretum, because there were so many so close together, they were constantly in action, bobbing about, flashing their red breasts and generally showing off. Several times they came right up to inspect us – one checked out the soundman's equipment and another flew right at us as if it was going to land on one of us. Robins seem to be one of the few birds that continue singing right through winter and, when they are not singing loudly to proclaim their territory, their little throats vibrate with a constant quiet murmuring, as if they're gently serenading themselves.

The robins were a bonus, because we'd really gone to Castlewellan to see some of the remarkable tree species they have in the arboretum. The arboretum is based around Annesley Garden, which dates back to 1740, and for this reason it contains some of the oldest existing specimens of trees in the British Isles, many of which are champion trees – that is, an example of the biggest or tallest of the species. Castlewellan also has Europe's longest continual hedge, the 'peace maze', which was planted by the people of Northern Ireland in 2001.

Now, where there are trees you'll find lichens, another thing most of us walk right past without noticing. Well, take our advice and stop for a closer look. They are fascinating. Lichens are a remarkable plant-combo to start with, co-existing in a mutually profitable 'symbiotic' relationship with fungus. The green algae photosynthesise and manufacture sugars to sustain the plant; the fungus provides shelter for the algae and stops them drying out, while also acting as a kind of scaffolding to determine the shape of the lichen.

The best way to appreciate lichens is to look at them through a hand lens. You'll be amazed at how what looks like a bunch of green stuff can turn into a tropical forest of cups on stalks, towers with horns, discs like tiny spaceships surrounded by hairs, often topped off by bright-red fruiting bodies. It's like looking at the set of a science-fiction movie. There are 1,355 British species, so plenty for you to have a go at. Just under half of them grow on shrubs and trees, and at Castlewellan our native lichen species have colonised even the exotic trees. On one particular ancient Japanese maple we counted at least seven different kinds – there could have been more. Lichens are not restricted to trees, they also grow on walls, gravestones, rocks and, even, grasslands and sand dunes. The number of habitats they have adapted to colonise is quite remarkable. Lichens do not have roots, they absorb water and gasses through their upper surface, and this makes them sensitive to atmospheric pollution. For this reason, you rarely find them in cities and they grow best in damp places. To get you started, there are three main types of lichen: flat, leaf-like and shrubby. The flat, encrusting types usually grow on rocks and there's a particularly wonderful one called map lichen. The leaf-like species grow in flat lobes (one called lungwort was used to treat coughs, asthma and tuberculosis, although who knows how effective it was). The shrubby types hang in tassels from trees. One known as oakmoss used to be ground up and used as a fixative in the perfume industry. So spare a thought for the poor old lichens when you're next out on a walk and don't pass them by.

Treecreeper with insect prey – something else to keep an eye out for at Castlewellan

Robins sing right through the winter

10 The Swale Estuary, Kent

Getting there:

Go through Oare Village, near Faversham, and take the right turn to Harty Ferry at the 'Three Mariners' pub. Continue 2 kilometres to the bank of the Swale estuary.

Tel: Kent Wildlife Trust and Oare Marshes – 0589 822412 (daytime only)

Email: info@kentwildlife.org.uk

Opening times: Elmley Marshes 9am–9pm, or sunset whichever is earlier (Wednesday–Monday); Oare Marshes 11am–5pm, or dusk (weekends and Bank Holidays).

Charging policy: Not applicable

Disabled access: Oare: disabled car parking 300m from hide overlooking the east flood and good views from the road. Elmley: two accessible hides

Find out more

RSPB - Elmley Marshes
www.rspb.org.uk/reserves/guide/e/ elmleymarshes/index.asp

Kent Wildlife Trust - Oare Marsh
www.wildlifetrust.org.uk/kent/ oare-info.html

Medway and Swale Estuary Partnership
www.medway-swale.org.uk/

Elmley Marshes on the Isle of Sheppey in North Kent is a huge, wet wilderness on the Swale Estuary and it can get very, very cold. Not somewhere you'd want to be in the middle of winter, you might think. But this is exactly the place to be if you want to see some of our wildest wildlife. The landscape is vast, flat and featureless, which means that there's nothing to get in the way when wigeon, teal and white-fronted geese descend in their thousands on the wetland meadows. This is also one of the best places outside Scotland to see our wintering raptors: hen harriers, marsh harriers, merlins, and up to twenty short-eared owls hunting over the bleak, windswept marshes.

A good spot to see the action is the RSPB's viewpoint at Capel Fleet. At dusk, it offers the spectacle of marsh and hen harriers as they gather for their large, communal winter roosts, often sharing them with merlins, the UK's smallest bird of prey and a real pocket rocket.

Marsh harriers are the largest of the three harriers we see in the UK, the others being hen harriers and the Montagu's harrier – a rare summer visitor to southern England. The marsh harrier is unusual for a raptor in that it has very good hearing due to its slightly disc-shaped face – like an owl – which helps to amplify the sound of its prey. It constantly looks down as it flies and uses both sight and sound to seek out small mammals and birds in the rushes and long grass. Sadly, this manner of hunting sometimes means the birds injure themselves, flying into things directly in front of them because they're too busy looking down. In 1971 there was just one breeding pair of marsh harriers left in the UK – not because of their clumsy hunting methods, but because of persecution and habitat fragmentation. To see them now overwintering at Elmley creates a warm feeling – which is about the only warm glow you'll experience at this location, so be advised and dress appropriately and remember to pack a flask and some sandwiches.

Now traditionally we think of owls as creatures of the night – but at Elmley you're equally likely to spot short-eared owls out hunting at dawn and dusk. In winter their numbers are swelled by arrivals from Scandinavia, Russia and Iceland and you've a good chance of seeing several of them hunting at once, a truly awe-inspiring sight. Perhaps the most distinguishing feature of the short-eared owl is its bright yellow eyes, each surrounded by a black eye patch which gives it a distinctive glare. If you don't get to look them in the eye, check out the underside of their wings in flight for black wingtips, a white trailing edge and a small black crescent about halfway along the leading edge of each wing.

To see so many raptors in such a wild and windswept environment is one of the great natural winter spectacles, ranking up there with penguins in the Antarctic and Canadian polar bears – and, yet, it's right here in Britain. It really is nature in the raw. But if you can't face such an expanse of wilderness, and the inevitable need to get out there and walk in the bitter cold, there's another internationally important reserve on the Swale Estuary that might suit you better. Oare Marshes is about half an hour's drive away from Elmley and is a small reserve with a road right through the middle of it. Here you don't even need to leave your car to see thousands of waders and ducks feeding in the mud just metres away from you. The reserve also attracts the same range of raptors, with merlins, hen harriers and short-eared owls, all regularly hunting across the marshes. It may be the soft option but, in winter, there's nothing wrong with that.

A short-eared owl takes a break from hunting

Mute swan nesting on Elmley Marshes

February

February is generally considered the coldest month, but it only takes a sunny day or two and the wildlife begins to stick its head over the parapet. In the southwest frogspawn can be seen as early as January, but February is the month that most people see the familiar jellied mass in their ponds. Wet dusks are perfect for the slightly later toads to march to their breeding grounds; upon arrival, the breeding resembles anything between a rugby scrum and an orgy!

Many of our resident birds will use this month to carve out their territory, and birds like blackbirds may already be sitting on eggs. Other birds are just at the courting stage, such as great-crested grebes with their weed dance. Badger activity at setts also picks up as the sows prepare for their underground births.

Towards the end of February the first signs of spring, such as cascading hazel catkins, appear, and the first flowers, such as sweet violet and coltsfoot, entice out insects such as queen bumblebees. Back on the water, wintering duck are looking at their finest and they too are courting like crazy before the majority fly north to breed elsewhere.

1 Buckenham, Norfolk

Getting there:

Buckenham Farm, Norfolk. Strumpshaw Fen is just under 1 kilometre southwest of Strumpshaw. Follow signs from Brundall High Street off the A47 east of Norwich. Nearest train stations: Brundall (2 kilometres) and Buckenham (limited service). Bus service from Norwich stops under one kilometre from the reserve on the Brundall to Strumpshaw road.

Tel: Strumpshaw Reserve – 01603 715191
Tourist information – 01603 727927

Email: strumpshaw@rspb.org.uk

Opening times: Daily, dawn-dusk.

Charging policy: Adults £2.50; Children 50p; Concessions £1.50; Family Ticket £5. Members free.

Disabled access: Disabled toilets available.

Find out more

RSPB Strumpshaw Fen
www.rspb.org.uk/reserves/guide/s/strumpshawfen/index.asp

BBC Science and Nature
www.bbc.co.uk/nature/animals/features/294feature1.shtml

Can you imagine what it must be like to experience the sight and sound of a hundred thousand birds flying en masse right over your head in a continuous swirling torrent of noise? Certainly the BBC team that headed off to Norfolk one cold day in February had never encountered anything like it. Well, certainly not in Britain. Our destination was Buckenham Farm, just a few miles east of Norwich, and our host was gamekeeper Joe Cullum. We'd come to see the great rook roost.

Rooks are among the most sociable of birds, unlike the solitary crow, hence the saying: 'A crow in a crowd is a rook; a rook on its own is a crow'. When feeding on the ground in groups they're quiet, but when airborne rooks raise a tremendous clamour. They are very vocal birds and each member of a pair keeps in constant contact with the other, so when there are several thousand flying, it's not surprising the noise is so loud. As with many birds, winter is the time to flock together for protection, and rooks may travel up to 40 kilometres from their daytime feeding grounds to their roosting site.

We'd been told that the Norfolk rook roost was an extraordinary spectacle, possibly the biggest in the world. Yet very few people know about it. This is no well-publicised event with organised trips that you can book online. Instead, even though it happens every night during the winter, there are rarely more than a handful of people to witness it.

We'd come to a vast landscape of sparsely populated, arable farmland. Among the great tracts of ploughed fields and stubble is a small woodland, part of Buckenham Farm, that for centuries has been the roosting site of tens of thousands of rooks.

Joe Cullum has lived in the hamlet of Buckenham all his life, and his house is just 300 metres from the roost. As a gamekeeper, he ensures that there are plenty of birds for people to shoot, but he would never let anyone harm the rooks. He considers himself the guardian of the roost, and never tires of the spectacle.

We were told to turn up at around four o'clock in the afternoon as the birds gather in the surrounding fields prior to the mass take-off towards the wood. The rooks will keep feeding in the fields as late as possible, poking their beaks into the soil for worms and grubs. We stood in the lane by Joe's house to await the birds' arrival. Large flocks began to fly in and we wondered if this was as good as it gets. But we needn't have worried.

Among the deep, rich sounds of the rooks are the bright squeaky calls of jackdaws. Jackdaws, like rooks, are sociable

Rooks roosting as the sun sets

A rook in flight

birds and they forage and roost together during the winter because they're both after the same kind of food – cereals and worms – and they're more efficient at tracking food resources if they stick together.

Just as it started getting quite dark, something triggered off the birds and the huge fly-in began. From one direction, coming right over Joe's house, a giant sardine-like shoal of birds headed our way, passing over our heads, then dropping into the tops of the trees. As we looked up, the sky was black, filled with thousands upon thousands of birds. The most extraordinary part was the sound. At first it was very noisy, but there was still individual bird sound. Then, as all the rooks and jackdaws called together, the noise became a giant, continuous roar – like a huge waterfall or river flowing. Fifteen minutes later and it was all over. What was left was the noise of thousands of birds clattering and cawing as they settled in the trees. The single roaring sound had gone.

To witness the rook roost, make sure you arrive at least an hour before it gets dark. The best time of year is February, when there is the greatest number of birds. Numbers start building in September or October. But don't leave it too late. Early in March, the whole roost leaves, except for 60-odd birds that stay to nest. By then, most of the rooks have paired up and dispersed to different parts of the country to raise chicks. Once again they nest colonially in rookeries at the tops of trees, but not in such vast numbers as the winter roost at Buckenham Farm.

2 Exmoor

Getting there:

Exmoor National Park Authority, Exmoor House, Dulverton, TA22 9HL. Snowdrop Valley is a privately run reserve. Take a special bus that leaves every 20 minutes from the small village of Wheddon Cross, southwest of Minehead.

Tel: Exmoor Park Visitor Centre – 01398 323841
Exmoor National Park Authority – 01398 323665

Email: info@exmoor-nationalpark.gov.uk
snowdropvalley@exmoor-nationalpark.gov.uk

Opening times: Open daily

Charging policy: Free entry to Exmoor. Bus from Wheddon Cross: adults £2.50; children 50p

Disabled access: A comprehensive guide is available from Exmoor National Park Authority

Find out more

Exmoor National Park official website
www.exmoor-nationalpark.gov.uk/

Wheddon Cross and Snowdrop Valley
www.wheddoncross.org.uk/

Exmoor Pony Society
www.exmoorponysociety.org.uk/

Straddling the counties of Somerset and Devon, the Exmoor National Park consists of 69,280 hectares of wonderful wilderness. In addition to being one of the places where you really feel like you're getting away from it all, Exmoor has to be the best location for seeing two of our biggest and most impressive mammals – the Exmoor pony and the red deer. It is perhaps the Exmoor pony that best epitomises this wild and remote habitat, because the National Park is the only location where the ponies can be seen roaming the moorland in anything approaching a wild state.

While many people's conception of Exmoor is that of mile after mile of open rolling moorland, it also has an abundance of ancient woodland that thrives in hanging valleys which run down off the moorland, many of which are in a near-pristine state. One such valley is near Wheddon Cross – one of the finest places to see snowdrops in Britain and aptly named Snowdrop Valley.

Back up on the moorland, it is thought that there may be only around 1,200 Exmoor ponies left in the wild. As a breed, they are considered to be truly prehistoric, having survived on the open moorland in a largely unchanged state since at least 60,000 BC.

The Exmoor pony has been endowed with a number of special features that enable it to survive the tough winter conditions. These include: a double-layered, dense winter coat with a fine insulating layer of springy hair and an outer waterproofing layer of hard greasy hair; a raised rim of flesh around the eye to prevent water from running down their face; and short hairs near the base of the tail that fan out to form a snow or rain chute. All these attributes combine to keep them warm and dry, whatever the weather.

The free-ranging Exmoor ponies we see on the moorland today survive with minimum intervention from man. However, they are neither truly wild nor domesticated, as all the ponies are owned, and every October they are rounded up and branded for release back onto the moor, or to be sold for pony-trekking.

Exmoor ponies are increasingly being used as a management tool on Exmoor and further afield, because their method of grazing, which consists of nibbling small amounts of vegetation at a time, prevents scrub encroachment on Sites of Special Scientific Interest. Filming the ponies grazing in the wild was a real treat and made us appreciate an animal that is perfectly adapted and totally in tune with its environment.

A mid-February daytrip to see the ponies on the moorland could easily be combined with a visit to Snowdrop Valley. The Exmoor National Park authority operates a park-and-ride scheme down into the valley from Wheddon Cross, which means you don't have to worry about negotiating the narrow country lanes that lead to the woodland. The moment we alighted from the bus and glanced at the woodland floor confirmed that we wouldn't have far to carry the filming equipment – the snowdrops were everywhere!

There is much debate as to whether the snowdrop is a truly wild species in Britain, or has become naturalised following introductions from the continent, but so white was the ground in Snowdrop Valley that some think that woodlands like this in the southwest are the most persuasive evidence that this is, indeed, a British native.

One of the more local names for snowdrop is 'snow-piercer', which exactly describes how the especially hardened leaftips are perfectly designed for breaking through the frozen ground. The snowdrops also provide an early feast for bumblebees, which in turn pollinate the flowers in a reciprocal arrangement that ensures the flowers put on a vibrant show year after year. Tip-toeing through the flowers gave us a wonderful reminder that spring was only just around the corner.

Just part of the Exmoor National Park in winter

Snowdrop Valley near Wheddon Cross

Opposite: One of the very few remaining free-ranging Exmoor ponies

3 Snowdonia

Getting there:

Snowdonia National Park Office, Penrhyndeudraeth, Gwynedd, LL48 6LF. National Park is south of Bangor and southeast of Caernarfon. Porthmadog is within driving distance south of the park.

Tel: Snowdonia National Park – 01766 770274
Snowdon Mountain Railway – 0870 458 0033

Email: parc@snowdonia-npa.gov.uk

Opening times: Open daily. Check train times with Snowdon Mountain Railway

Charging policy: Snowdon Mountain Railway: Adults £21; children £14 (return).

Disabled access: Some very steep slopes in upland areas and rough ground unsuitable for wheelchair users. Snowdon Mountain Railway has special carriages for wheelchair users.

Find out more

Snowdonia National Park
www.eryri-npa.co.uk/

Snowdonia Tourism
www.snowdonia.org.uk/

Snowdonia Society
www.snowdonia-society.org.uk/

Snowdon Mountain Railway
www.snowdonrailway.co.uk/

Driving into the Snowdonia National Park we were stuck by the very mountain from which the park takes its name – Mount Snowdon. At a challenging 1,085 metres, it is the highest mountain in Wales. Our favourite way to the top is on foot, but if you don't feel up to the climb the Snowdon Mountain Railway will take you right to the summit. There's a cairn at the top and, according to legend, this marks the burial place of the giant Rhita Gawr, who was so fearsome he wore a cloak made out of the beards of all the kings he had killed. Well, not much chance of us meeting him, but we did see giants of another kind – ravens.

In short, the raven is a big black bird, the largest member of the crow family. But you can easily tell it apart from its brethren with its wingspan of up to one and a half metres – that's bigger than a buzzard. Apart from its size, there are two crucial points to raven identification: it has a characteristic 'kronk-kronk!' call, best practised in the privacy of your own home, and a diamond-shaped tail in flight.

If you are just learning to identify birds, and this applies to any bird, it's worth taking note of the habitat around you. Ravens typically live and breed in mountainous areas, on inland and sea cliffs, and on moorland, most commonly in the north and west of Britain and in Ireland.

Ravens pair for life, return to a favourite nesting site each year, and increasingly add to the nest. The nest itself looks like a huge pile of twigs, but is often lined with sheep's wool. This is to keep both eggs and chicks warm, because ravens breed very early in the year (this can be as early as mid-February). They feed almost exclusively on carrion, so their nests are usually built in a place that offers a good vantage point over the surrounding area.

There are other large denizens of the mountains that you will certainly come across if you go to the Snowdonia National Park in winter – particularly if you visit the village of Beddgelert. Near there you might even find yourself in a face-to-face 'stand-off' with a Welsh mountain goat. There are more than one thousand of these feral goats within the park and in winter, when the going gets tough on the upper slopes, they descend into the valleys in search of food.

On arrival, we encountered several young billie goats standing by the side of the road. But, would you believe it, when we went out to film the next day – it was glorious sunny weather – they had all retreated onto the upper slopes. So we were faced with a veritable trek up the hillside, thrashing through rhododendrons, carrying all our camera and sound equipment, to try and get shots of a group of nanny goats and their kids. We really do try!

As much as we try to engage with nature, though, the best thing about North Wales is the 'in your face' landscape. It's hard to believe that the rocks here were laid down under an ocean more than 450 million years ago. Over time, titanic forces have crumpled them up into huge mountains, and since then nature has been doing her level best to grind them back down again. Wouldn't it be wonderful if we could press the rewind button, go back a few hundred million years and then fast forward through the changing landscape? What a movie that would make! The 'hard landscape' of Britain is changing all the time – it's just on a scale so incrementally small that we poor humans can't appreciate it. So, if you want a 'big nature' experience, get yourself out to Snowdonia in winter – but do remember to dress warmly and check the weather forecast before you head off up into the mountains.

Ravens are scavengers and will look for carcasses on which to feed

You will almost certainly come across Welsh mountian goats in Snowdonia

Snowdon Peak, from which the park takes its name

4 Lemsford Springs, Hertfordshire

Getting there:

Entrance to the reserve is on the west of the roundabout linking the B197 with the road to Lemsford village, and junction 5 of the A1M. No access from the motorway.

Tel: Herts Wildlife Trust – 01727 858901

Email: info@hmwt.org

Opening times: Access by permit only. Contact Herts Wildlife Trust.

Charging policy: Not applicable.

Disabled access: Disabled access to bird watching hide.

Freshwater shrimp – a welcome source of food

Find out more

Herts Wildlife Trust
www.wildlifetrust.org.uk/herts/
reserves/lemsford%20springs.htm

Field Studies Council
www.field-studies-council.org/

The Mammal Society
www.abdn.ac.uk/mammal/news.
shtml

A water shrew diving for food

Lemsford Springs is a little jewel. When we visited this nature reserve in February, it was as bright as cut glass, glimmering with frost. One of the surprising things about Lemsford Springs is that it's a completely artificial habitat. When digging out a floodplain in Victorian times, the workers discovered it had freshwater springs seeping through the chalk. This made it an ideal site for watercress beds because the plant needs very pure, fresh running water. Though no longer harvested commercially in Lemsford, watercress still grows wild, creating a unique habitat for a fantastic mixture of species.

One species that can only live in very clean water is the freshwater shrimp and these little morsels attract birds such as little egret, kingfisher, water rail, moorhen and grey wagtail.

The shrimps are a welcome source of food in winter, especially as the springs ensure the water never completely freezes over. The shrimps, and the fact that this is an old watercress bed, attract another resident – the water shrew. This is our biggest and fattest shrew, which, as its name suggests, lives alongside water. These little critters have white bellies and dark backs with bristles on the outer edges of their feet to help them paddle through the water, and on their tail to help them steer. As they dive, they look as if they've been coated in silver because their dense fur traps air bubbles and keeps them buoyant. They are also red-toothed – iron is deposited in the enamel on the tips of their teeth, making them that bit stronger. Water shrews eat small aquatic crustaceans, molluscs and small fish, which they locate with their whiskers underwater, as well as foraging on land for beetles and worms. It's a good job that the shrimps are so abundant – water shrews, like other shrews, have a high metabolism and have to eat half their own body weight (12–18 grams) every 24 hours in order to stay alive. These shrews are very unusual in that they have venom in their saliva, which helps them overcome small creatures. They will often leave spare, half-eaten, partly drugged creatures in caches – a rather ghoulish, walk-in larder for midnight snacks.

5 Hardcastle Crags, West Yorkshire

Getting there:

Estate Office, Hollin Hall, Crimsworth Dean, Hebden Bridge, HX7 7AP. A good base to explore the area is Hebden Bridge, 1 kilometre away – the town is well served by road, rail and canal.

Tel: Estate office – 01422 844518
National Trust Yorkshire Office – 01904 702021

Email: hardcastlecrags@nationaltrust.org.uk

Opening times: Open daily.

Charging policy: Gibson Mill: Adult £3, child £1.50, family £7.50.

Disabled access: The grounds are partly accessible but there are some steep slopes, loose gravel tracks and uneven paths. Braille guide.

Northern hairy wood ants building their nest

Find out more

National Trust – Hardcastle Crags
www.nationaltrust.org.uk/main/w-vh/w-visits/w-findaplace/w-hardcastlecrags/

BBC Bradford – Nature walk
www.bbc.co.uk/bradford/nature/walk1/06.shtml

Northern Hairy Wood Ant
www.arkive.org/species/ARK/invertebrates_terrestrial_and_freshwater/Formica_lugubris/

Hebden Water, Hardcastle Crags

Just above the town of Hebden Bridge is a stark landscape of millstone grit crags, rocky ravines, woods clinging to steep slopes and wide expanses of moorland bisected by paths that connect up to the Pennine Way. This is Hardcastle Crags, home to the northern hairy wood ant.

Wood ants are reddish in colour and the largest of all British ants. As for the hairy bit, you'd need very good eyesight, but they do have a long fringe of hair that reaches down to their eyes. There are about 400 nests on the hillside of Hardcastle Crags, each with around half a million ants. The nests extend well below ground, as well as above – up to two metres high – and look just like a huge heap of pine needles, earth and twigs, so you have to get your eye in.

We went to visit the ants in February, which can be a good time to see them as they slowly emerge from hibernation on sunny days. By sunbathing, they warm themselves and then transfer that heat back into the colony when they re-enter their nest. The ants have two main ways of sourcing food: the workers tend aphids, which exude a sugary substance called honeydew, and they suck sap from plants. They will also catch insects to bring back to the nest. One queen rules the colony and all the workers are female. At the beginning of spring the queen produces special unfertilised eggs, some of which become males. The larvae that are fed the most become new queens, instead of workers. In June, if you return, you'll see a haze of ants leaving the nests and engaging in a mating flight. These are the males and the reproductive females. Once they've mated, the males die and the females lose their wings and set up a new colony as a new queen.

Late winter is also a good time to get up early and listen to the dawn chorus. At this time of year, Britain's native male birds are staking out their territories and singing their hearts out to ward off rival males and attract females. The summer migrants have yet to arrive, which means that you can more easily separate the songs of our typical woodland species like the great tit, blue tit, goldcrest, robin, blackbird and song thrush.

6 The Lost Gardens of Heligan, Cornwall

Getting there:

Pentewan, St Austell, PL26 6EN. From St Austell, take B3273 towards Mevagissey and follow the brown tourist signs.

Tel: 01726 845100

Email: info@heligan.com

Opening times: Daily except Christmas Eve and Christmas Day. March–October 10am–6pm, November–February, 10am–5pm. Free parking.

Charging policy: Garden Admission: Adults £7.50; Senior Citizens £7; Children (5–16 yrs) £4.00; Children (under 5) free; family £20.00

Disabled access: Downloadable access guide available: http://www.heligan. com/downloads/access-guide.pdf

Find out more

Lost Gardens of Heligan
www.heligan.com/flash_index.html

The Great Gardens of Cornwall
www.greatgardensofcornwall. co. uk/

RSPB South West bird watching
www.rspb.org.uk/england/southwest /birdwatching/heligan.asp

Eco-watch
www.eco-watch.com/

No one who visits The Lost Gardens of Heligan can be anything other than delighted that they've been found. Heligan was the home of the Tremayne family for more than four hundred years. The 400 hectare estate, including walled vegetable garden, pineapple pit, glasshouse for peaches and ornamental gardens and woodlands, was functioning beautifully until the end of the 19th century. During the World Wars, the garden fell into neglect and disappeared under a tangle of brambles; the house itself was later divided up and sold as flats. But the discovery of a tiny room, buried under fallen masonry in the corner of one of the walled gardens, led John Willis to rediscover the garden. Along with Tim Smit, he began the restoration process in 1990. As well as the conventional large estate garden, they discovered hidden gems, such as the jungle – a narrow, steep-sided valley full of exotic plants like tree ferns, bamboos and bananas that survive in this warm microclimate.

The gardens now host Heligan Wild, run by Eco-watch. The team have hidden cameras throughout the woods to record the comings and goings of the many animals that live there. There are, for instance, cameras in the badger sett in the Lost Wood, as well as in a pipistrelle maternal roost. Spring is a fantastic time to visit, to see not only young badgers bumbling through bluebells, but also birds like goldfinches, blue tits and great tits rearing their chicks. The highlight for us, though, even in winter, was the barn owl. From the Heligan Wild hide we could see a female owl sitting on a nest box across the field. Having watched her on camera as she dozed inside until the light faded, we saw her emerge and tilt her beautiful, heart-shaped face towards the dying light. We were also able to watch video footage of her rearing her chicks the previous year. When we were there, she quartered the fields by her nest – this involves flying low over the grass, backwards and forwards, looking for small rodents. They could hardly have heard her coming because, on those moth-like

wings, she was able to descend silently upon them. This female made no sound, but barn owls – when they do call – don't hoot; they emit a long, eerie screech (hence its alternative name, the screech owl), as well as hissing, snoring and yapping!

The barn owl's face is adapted to help it hear the small noises that rodents make, because it funnels sound towards the ears. A ridge of feathers between its eyes splits its face into two dishes that collect sound waves, and the pattern of the feathers further scoops sounds towards the owl's ears. The ears are in different positions, too – the left one is higher than the right and points slightly downwards, whereas the right one is shifted upwards. This helps the owl to hear whether a noise is happening above or below its face, and thus helps it pinpoint its prey more effectively. We already knew that Heligan had a good diversity of prey for her because earlier that day we'd gone on a walk with one of the Heligan Wild team and trapped some small mammals, including a wood mouse.

The other winter resident we were privileged to see was a kingfisher. These birds nest in holes in the banks of streams and rivers, but tend to migrate to warmer parts of the country and overwinter on lagoons that are unlikely to freeze over. Fortunately for us, some had chosen to stay and fish in the ponds in the wood by the old charcoal furnace and it was a real treat to see a female flash by – that brilliant azure made bolder by the lack of foliage in the wood.

Heligan is well worth a visit: after all, where else could you see both bananas and barn owls in one spot?

The jungle at Heligan in winter

A real azure treat – the kingfisher

Opposite: The barn owl – one of Heligan's wildlife delights

7 Montrose Basin, Angus

Getting there:

Montrose is 48 kilometres north of Dundee; the Basin is 2 kilometres from the town centre – an easy journey by foot or bus.

Tel: Montrose Basin Wildlife Centre – 01674 676336

Email: montrosebasin@swt.org.uk

Opening times: Reserve open daily. Visitor centre mid-March–mid-November 10.30am–5pm; mid-November–mid-March 10.30am–4pm (Friday, Saturday and Sunday only)

Charging policy: Adults £3; Concessions £2; Children and Wildlife Trust members free

Disabled access: Level access by farm track to Montrose Basin Nature Reserve, with grass path to bird hide.

Find out more

Scottish Wildlife Trust - Montrose Basin
www.swt.org.uk/wildlife/montrosebasin.asp

Montrose Basin Tide Timetables
http://sites.ecosse.net/montrosebasin/BasinTide06.pdf

Angus and Dundee Bird Club
http://angusbirding.homestead.com/

There's a saying: 'Where there's muck there's brass'. For naturalists, though, it's more a case of where there's mud – there'll be birds. Nowhere is this truer than Montrose Basin, a giant tidal mudbath where the sticky gloop is more than nine metres deep in places. Now, you'd need a long beak to get to the bottom of it, but this is the very essence of life here – because the mud at Montrose is absolutely jam-packed with creatures.

In fact, you're actively encouraged to go out and get your hands dirty by going on a mud safari. There are regular events where you can venture out into the basin safely without the need to call out the mud rescue team (yes, there really is one). The great thing is, you never know what you might find. The ragworm was our favourite, even if the teenagers we'd roped in to help were squirming as it was handed over for them to hold. Be brave – you will survive your encounter with Mr Wriggly and live to tell the tale to your grandchildren.

If you need a bit more help, there's a cracking visitor centre that really does explain what's going on beneath the surface. You can even bring some of your haul back and have a peak at it under the microscope. Many of these creatures are small, but it's the quantity of life here that's staggering – one square metre of mud can contain hundreds of thousands of living organisms.

Montrose Basin is a restaurant that only closes when the tide comes in. Nutritious food is restocked and available twice a day as the tide ebbs and flows. Each species of bird that arrives here has a specially designed tool that enables them to make the most of this rich harvest.

Take three of our favourites. With its long down-curved beak, the curlew is a master at winkling out tasty morsels. How it does this is the stuff of science fiction. You might watch a curlew jabbing its beak into the mud and think that this is some haphazard underground fishing expedition,

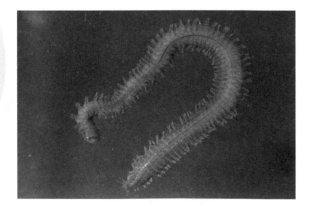

An oystercatcher uses its beak to break open the shell to find food

but how wrong you'd be. What makes the curlew so special is that its enormous bill is ultra-sensitive. When immersed – sometimes the whole bill gets pushed in – the curlew is able to detect the movements of its prey. It's then a case of taking the bill out and re-inserting it in the right place to catch a juicy titbit like a ragworm. Brilliant.

The oystercatcher is a different beast altogether. To many people, these are comical birds, and noisy too. But the oystercatcher is the bird equivalent of a safecracker. If you were ever planning to rob the Bank of England, then get an oystercatcher on the job. These birds can do something that mere humans can't: namely, open a cockle using brute force alone. We'd need teeth of steel to do this, but oystercatchers can find, open and consume a cockle every minute and a half. It's an amazing feat to watch as they ram their orange beaks into the cockle's weak spot using other stones as a point of leverage. All this from a bird that many take for granted.

The third Montrose expert is the eider. These are the crunchers. Take a walk along the foreshore at Montrose and you can witness the carnage caused by these birds on the local mussel population. They're experts at diving down and pulling up mussels, consuming them whole and regurgitating the broken shells. In a day, they can eat more than two kilos of shellfish. It's not something that endears eiders to some fishermen – but what a skill!

Keep your eyes peeled, too, for common seals. We spotted a small posse lounging on the mudflats at low tide. There were even a couple of inquisitive youngsters who came pretty close to see what we were up to. So take your camera – you never know what you might find. And whatever you do, don't forget your wellies.

• •

Opposite: A ragworm, one of the creatures you can find in the mud

8 Hickling Broad, Norfolk

Getting there:

6½ kilometres southeast of Stalham, signposted from the A149 Stalham-Great Yarmouth road.

Tel: Hickling Nature Reserve – 01692 598276

Email: admin@norfolkwildlifetrust.org.uk

Opening times: Reserve open daily, 10am–5pm.

Charging policy: Adults £2.75, children free; boat trips extra

Disabled access: Wheelchair access to visitor centre, toilets and boardwalk.

Find out more

BBC Norfolk – Hickling Broad
www.bbc.co.uk/norfolk/funstuff/360/hickling_broad_360.shtml

Norfolk Wildlife Trust
www.wildlifetrust.org.uk/norfolk/big%205/hickling.htm

RSPB – Crane
www.rspb.org.uk/birds/guide/c/crane/index.asp

Hickling Broad in Norfolk is the place to go to catch sight of one of our most spectacular birds – the common crane. This is our tallest breeding species and has a massive wingspan of up to 2.5 metres – similar to the white-tailed eagle. This elegant, grey bird with its bundle of tail feathers like a Victorian bustle has a sonorous bugling call that can be heard up to six kilometres away. And while it may once have been common – in England there are 300 towns named after the crane, such as Cranfield, Cranbrook and Cranmere – it is now, sadly, incredibly rare. Possibly the first recorded mention of a wild bird in Western literature is of the crane, whose clamorous calls as the species migrated were compared by Homer in the Iliad to the sound of armies advancing into battle. They were once roasted and served at feasts with a sauce of ginger, vinegar and mustard.

The first cranes to breed in Britain for four hundred years were at Hickling Broad in 1979. Their location was, and still is, kept a secret but over the next two decades or so their numbers rose to about 40, with 4 pairs of breeding birds. The time to see them is very early in the morning when they leave their (secret) breeding location and fly across the broads to feed in the nearby fields. We staked out Stubb Mill and saw them as they crossed above us, honking. What we were hoping to watch – and just caught the start of – was the courtship dance, something you can see between February and March. The birds mate for life and engage in a dance where the pair circle each other, bowing and hopping with half-open wings.

Although the cranes at Hickling Broad are a small, isolated population, barely hanging in there by their bills, the RSPB has plans to increase the numbers of cranes in Britain. They've launched a conservation project designed to breed cranes and re-establish them at a new site. A shortlist of sites has been drawn up and, with a bit of good luck, the first release will take place in 2009, with these British-born cranes breeding five years after that. Fingers crossed.

One of the more unusual residents at Hickling Broad are the koniks. These honey-coloured beasts are relatives of the now extinct tarpan, an Eastern-European wild pony. In the past, people used to manage the reedbeds by harvesting the reeds for thatching, but this has become uneconomical. The ponies now graze the fen, just as they did in the marshes of Poland where they came from. They're perfectly adapted to the job, minding neither the wet nor the cold in winter, and their coats are tough enough to deter the midges in summer.

Even if you don't manage to see cranes dancing, Hickling Broad is well worth a visit. It's one of the largest expanses of open water in East Anglia. Originally it was formed by digging for peat and is only about one and a half metres deep. As well as open water, there are also reedbeds and marshes, which are home to birds like bitterns and marsh harriers, a variety of butterflies, such as the swallowtail, and dragonflies like the Norfolk hawker (though not in February!). You can also see a wide range of aquatic plants only found here, like the holly-leaved naiad and three species of rare stonewort, a type of freshwater seaweed.

As well as walking through the marshes and reedbeds on raised walkways, there is a boat that allows you to have a coot's eye view of the broad. This will also take you to the tree tower, an observation hide that gives you a fantastic view over the water and across those big, expansive skies Norfolk is so justly famous for.

Common cranes at the Norfolk Broads

Hickling: the largest of all the Norfolk Broads

9 Caerlaverock, Dumfriesshire

Getting there:

Wildfowl and Wetlands Centre, Eastpark Farm, Dumfriesshire, DG1 4RS. Located 14 kilometres southeast of Dumfries. There is a limited bus service from Dumfries to Caerlaverock.

Tel: 01387 770200

Email: caerlaverock@wwt.org.uk

Opening times: Wetlands Centre open daily 10am-5pm. Closed Christmas Day.

Charging policy: Adult £4.40; Concessions £3.60; Child £2.70; Under 4s free; group and family rates available

Disabled access: Most areas suitable for visitors with disabilities – some muddy areas. Guide dogs welcome.

Find out more

Wildfowl and Wetlands Centre
www.wwt.org.uk/visit/ caerlaverock/

RSPB – The Barnacle Goose
www.rspb.org.uk/birds/guide/b/ barnaclegoose/index.asp

Dumfries and Galloway Tourist Board – Badgers
www.visitdumfriesandgalloway.co. uk/sitewide/events/

The Solway Firth is one of the UK's greatest estuaries. It drains into the Irish Sea and has Scotland on one side and England on the other. It's just 14 kilometres southeast of Dumfries in 'big sky country'. Caerlaverock means the 'castle of the lark', but we hadn't trekked all that way in search of larks. We went in February to witness the arrival of Britain's migratory 'super-goose', the barnacle goose.

Barnacle geese begin life high up in the Arctic. Every year they undertake a 3,200 kilometre migration south from Svalbard in the Norwegian Arctic, and large numbers of them overwinter from October to March on the Solway Firth. So what makes them super-geese? Well, it's not just the sheer length of their arduous migration across the hostile Norwegian Sea and North Sea, it's the fact that newly hatched young undertake this epic journey only three or four months after hatching out of the egg. Now, come on, most of us get frazzled on a short-haul flight to the Mediterranean.

We had to make the comparatively small sacrifice of getting up before dawn to get the best views of the barnacle geese, which bizarrely are so named because they were thought to originate from the barnacle shells that you find growing on rocks on the beach. Barnacle geese roost out on the mudflats of the Solway Firth at night, before coming in early in the morning to graze on the surrounding pasture land. The remoteness of the mudflats offers them protection from predators. During the day they graze like crazy on the leaves, stems, roots and seeds that they love in order to make up for all the muscle mass they have lost on their epic migration. In the frosty morning light, tinged with the pink of dawn, we sat shivering in a hide, watching packs of barnacle geese fly in over our heads. 'Pack' is a good word to describe them, because not only do they not fly in 'v' formation like other geese, but also they have a peculiar, almost dog-like, yapping or barking call.

Even if you disregard their amazing journey, barnacle geese are extremely attractive and

Caerlaverock Castle in the Solway Firth

charismatic birds. They have distinctive bright, creamy-white, shining cheeks, a glistening black neck and an almost Dior-designed black, white and grey striped body. Just substitute 'super-model' for 'super-goose' and you'll get the picture.

After you've spent the day watching the geese at Caerlaverock, there's one final treat in store for you at the end of your day. As the light fades, you can enjoy a 'stars and stripes' evening. A cottage on the reserve offers the unique opportunity to come within almost touching distance of badgers. You might have seen badgers in the wild, you might have seen them in daylight, but even we had never seen them this close before. Badgers usually amble away from their sett in search of food just after the sun has gone down. They are opportunistic feeders and will eat anything from earthworms, frogs, voles, mice, snails and wasps! They also munch on windfall apples, blackberries and even grass. Happily for the success of the 'stars and stripes' evenings at Caerlaverock, they are also rather partial to honey and nuts and it's these delicacies that bring them in so close. With a pane of glass between us and them, we didn't have to worry about keeping totally still and silent, a good thing if you're presenting a wildlife programme or aiming to produce gripping television. We had cracking views of the badgers and, for once, were able to talk freely and explain what we had been seeing without the stars of the show bolting off into the darkness. Badgers are creatures of habit and will use the same pathways to and from the sett. Once you've got your eye in, it's remarkably easy to spot these well trampled badger motorways and, while we wouldn't normally recommend that you go out and look for poo, badgers have elegant toilet habits and build neat latrines or earth thunder-boxes away from the sett. If you find the paths and find the loo, you've found badgers!

You can also see whooper swans

Opposite: Barnacle geese feeding themselves up after their long migration

10 Wembury, Devon

Getting there:

From the A379 at Elburton, follow the signs for Wembury and the beach. Beach is a 20 minute bus ride from the centre of Plymouth. National Trust car park.

Tel: Wembury Marine Centre – 01752 862538
National Shark Trust enquiry line: 0870 128 3045

Email: Wembury Marine Centre – info@wemburymarinecentre.org

Opening times: Beach open daily. Contact the marine centre for up-to-date opening times

Charging policy: Not applicable.

Disabled access: Wembury Beach has moderate disabled access.

Find out more

Devon Wildlife Trust
www.devonwildlifetrust.org/index. php?section=places:reserves& reserveid=23

Wembury Marine Centre
www.wemburymarinecentre.org/

Shark Trust
www.sharktrust.org/

You've probably never really given much thought to a crab's bottom, or ever examined one in detail for that matter! But that's one of the things we were faced with when we visited Wembury on the coast of South Devon, not far from the city of Plymouth. Well, it turned out to be a revelation. Do you know that you can tell a female from a male simply by the shape of her bottom? Well you can, at least in the world of crabs. Now, you don't have to go to Wembury to discover this amazing fact, but it's as good a place as any. You could describe it as a perfect beach – it's got sand, sea and rockpools – and slap bang in the middle of the bay is a ski-ramp-shaped island called Mewstone rock, which is an ideal place for nesting seabirds.

Like many people who grew up doing their rockpooling during the summer holidays, we were surprised to discover that it's just as much fun in winter – you just need to wear a few more layers. The really rewarding thing about rockpooling is that you have a 'trapped audience' – the inhabitants of the rockpool are not about to disappear off over the horizon, so if you look hard enough you'll find pretty much everything that's in there. We rolled up our sleeves and started turning over a few rocks (you have to remember to put them back as you find them) and before long had a collection of several shore crabs. That was when we learned how to sex a crab. One of the crabs had what looked like a mass of tiny orange berries on the underside. Like most sea creatures, crabs don't care for their offspring – instead they rely on producing large numbers of young to ensure at least some survive. Females may produce up to a million eggs in their lifetime, and this is where the bottom trick comes in. The eggs are carried under the flap-like tail on the underside of the crab. We noticed that the crab with eggs, which was a female, had a short, fat, triangular-shaped tail. The others we'd found, which were all egg-less, had narrow, much more pointed, triangular-shaped tails – they were all males. Once you've compared the two side by side, you'll always be able to tell them apart, and can impress your friends by instantly being able to sex a crab! One of the crabs also had what seemed to be a soft, rather spongy shell. The hard shell of a crab does not grow with it, thus, every so often, the crab has to moult and then, for while, it remains relatively unprotected while it grows a new bigger shell and waits for it to harden off. A couple of them looked as if they'd also been in the wars. One had a pincer and a leg missing, but this is not as serious as it may seem, because crabs have the rather nifty ability to grow new limbs.

Even easier to find than crabs are sea anemones – in fact, you won't even have to look for them. Out of the water, the commonest ones – beadlet anemones – look like round, red blobs of jelly. You'll probably remember giving them a prod as a child and watching them squirt out a jet of seawater. Hopefully, you're far more responsible now, and prefer to look for those that are submerged and have their tentacles out, waving gently in the water. One of the prettiest kinds is the snake-locks anemone, which is lime green with pink tips to its tentacles. The sea anemone's tentacles contain stinging cells which are used to kill or stun its prey: shrimps, worms and other small marine creatures. They can't sting us, but if you want to know what they feel like, put your finger very gently in the tentacles then pull it out – you'll feel the tentacles sticking to you. Arm yourself with a net and you'll be able to catch shrimps, prawns and small fish – you'll find it just as absorbing as when you were young.

Shore crab and beadlet anemones

If you've not done any rockpooling before, here's a trick to get you started. Save a piece of uncooked bacon rind for a couple of days until it's good and smelly, tie it to a piece of string and dangle it in a rockpool – you'll find the crabs just can't resist it. You can even use it to pull them out of the water and they'll still cling on!

Another thing you can do at Wembury is search among the seaweed on the shore for mermaid's purses. These are the empty egg cases of rays and sharks, and they come in all different shapes and sizes. The Shark Trust in Plymouth will be happy to help you identify any you've found, and add your finds to their database.

Wembury beach

March

March can feel like it is still the middle of winter one day and almost T-shirt weather the next, but, this is the month when spring has undoubtedly started. By the end of the month there are more hours of daylight than of darkness, giving the wildlife their cue to get busy flowering, mating and migrating.

The key spectacle to look for in March is that of boxing hares. This can happen in virtually any month, but, with the vegetation short, this is the best time for an unimpeded view. While many of our resident birds are well into the swing of the breeding season, March is the month when the advance party of migrant birds arrive: wheatear are best looked for on headlands, chiffchaffs belting out their monotonous song in southern woodlands and sandmartins hawking for insects over a lake.

Waders, wildfowl and winter thrushes make the arduous journey to their northern breeding grounds in March. Woodlands resound with the drumming of greater-spotted woodpeckers and, in some locations, daffodils, lesser celandines and then primroses give the woodland floor that yellow feeling.

1 Northward Hill, Kent

Getting there:

Located 6 kilometres north of Rochester in Kent; follow signposts from High Halstow. Nearest railway station: Strood (8 kilometres).

Tel: North Kent Marshes team – 01634 222480/222489
Tourist information – 01634 843666

Email: info@kentwildlife.org.uk

Opening times: Public footpaths and heronry open daily.

Charging policy: Not applicable.

Disabled access: Limited: though some paths are level, there are also fields; it is just over one kilometre to see the herons.

Find out more

RSPB
www.rspb.org.uk/reserves/guide/n/northwardhill/

Birds of Britain
www.birdsofbritain.co.uk/bird-guide/grey-heron.htm

Kent Wildlife Trust
www.kentwildlife.org.uk/

The grey heron is without doubt one of our most familiar birds. With a wingspan almost as large as that of a golden eagle, the heron is our most widespread predatory bird and is seen as often feeding at an urban pond as it is on a remote windswept estuary. Invariably it seems the grey heron is the most solitary of birds, preferring its own company as it stands in lonely vigil waiting for an unwary fish to come within a neck's length of its dagger-like bill. But the grey heron does have a sociable side too, which it saves for the spring when they come together to breed in large treetop colonies, known as heronries.

Northward Hill is a reserve managed by the RSPB on the North Kent coast and consists of 291 hectares of grazing marsh, farmland and oak woodland. The ancient wood is home in spring-time to the largest colony of grey herons in the UK; the most recent count of active treetop nests stands at an impressive 155.

The grey heron is an early breeder and both sexes arrive back at the heronry as early as February to build a nest, or add to a construction from a previous year. As the stick nests are tended and eggs laid, the heronry becomes a very noisy place as the pairs assert their rights over particularly prized locations. In the centre of the colony, the nests can dominate the canopies in certain oak trees and on our visit we counted six nests in one tree alone. The crescendo of noise continues to increase throughout the spring as chicks hatch, grow and become constantly vocal in their perennial pursuit of food.

March is a good time to visit as the nests are more visible before the trees are covered in leaves. Early May is also a particularly fine time to go, as the young herons begin to resemble adolescent teenagers with spiky hair. By this time, many have hopped out of the nest and stand around on the branches of their tree looking disconsolate as they wait for their parents to arrive back from another fishing trip.

The other thing to bear in mind at heronries is that they are not the cleanest of nesting places. We were given permission to enter the heronry to help the

Some of the oak woodland that makes up Northward Hill

warden conduct a census of the nests, and the stench of rotting fish from their pellets, half-digested meals and dropped food is enough to make your eyes water! Everywhere we looked the heronry was a bustling hive of activity, as adults constantly wheeled overhead as they flew to and from the estuary. Watching the scene unfold above our heads, it didn't require too much imagination to picture that this is what watching pterodactyls must have looked like sixty-five million years ago!

Dotted in among the heronry and often slightly lower in the trees were smaller nests which belonged to the new kids on the block, the little egrets. These first bred at Northward Hill in 2000, when two pairs raised young, and by 2006 numbers had rocketed to around 50 pairs, an increase which has mirrored a rapid expansion and colonisation across the UK of this very welcome immigrant from the continent.

Grey herons at nest

Little egrets in breeding plumage are very dandy-looking birds in spring, with their snow-white plumage, breeding plumes on their chest and two very long plumes on their hind-neck. Their black legs contrast with their yellow feet, which makes the egrets look like they have just been standing in a bowl of custard! Although not as vocal as the more numerous and larger grey herons at Northward Hill in spring, the little egrets do produce an assorted range of gurgling and croaking noises not heard at any other time of the year.

With both grey heron and little egret numbers on the increase, the future looks bright for our two nesting herons. Let's hope that the full-board accommodation offered at places such as Northward Hill continues to provide a sanctuary for this noisy and characterful duo.

Opposite: A heronry

2 Thetford Forest, East Anglia

Getting there:

Travel from the M11 from London, the A11 from Norwich/Newmarket and the A14 from Cambridge/Ipswich. High Lodge Forest Centre: enter the forest drive from the B1107 Thetford to Brandon Road and follow it for about 2½ kilometres.

Tel: Forest centre – 01842 810271

Email: e.anglia.fdo@forestry.gsi.gov.uk info@thetfordtourism.co.uk

Opening times: Thetford Forest daily. High Lodge Forest Centre winter: 10am–3pm (weekdays), 9am–4pm (weekends and school holidays); summer: 9am–6pm.

Charging policy: Forest toll: car £5, motorbike £2, minibus £10, coach £20, annual season ticket £30

Disabled access: Disabled parking and toilets available.

Find out more

Forestry Commission - Thetford Forest
www.forestry.gov.uk/thetfordforestpark

Visit Norfolk
www.visitnorfolk.co.uk/norfolk/breckland.htm

BBC Norfolk
www.bbc.co.uk/norfolk/

BBC Suffolk
www.bbc.co.uk/suffolk/

Thetford Forest in the heart of East Anglia is the biggest lowland pine forest in the UK. On the border of Norfolk and Suffolk, this is a modern working forest, planted in the 1920s to supply commercial timber. These days it's very much geared up for leisure as well, with lots of cycle tracks, signposted walks and a visitor centre with that all-important café.

Thetford has a wide mix of habitats: conifer trees, heathland and broadleaves, which mean that it attracts some brilliant wildlife. There are four types of deer to be spotted – muntjac, roe, fallow and red – and a glorious range of birds. If you're lucky, you may come across a stripy brown bird called a woodlark, with its characteristic white eyestripe meeting behind the neck. In flight, the woodlark is smaller than the skylark with shorter wings and tail. Also, whereas the skylark's tail sides and wing trailing edges are white, the only white to be found on the woodlark's wings and tail is confined to the tail tip. It is important to tread carefully and keep to the paths because, in late February or early March, woodlarks can start nesting on the ground. The preferred habitat for this fastidious bird is where trees have been clear-felled with mainly short, open vegetation and the occasional taller tree for a singing post. The male has a flute-like descending song, which has been described as one of the finest in Britain, and, like the skylark, will sing during flight.

This is also a good time of year to see one of the classic forest predators, the goshawk – a hawk almost the size of a buzzard with bright yellow eyes and a distinctive white eyebrow. Most of the year goshawks are hard to see, as they keep clear of humans and hunt through conifer forests, but in spring an established pair will begin to sky dance, displaying from mid-March through to April.

The goshawk and the woodlark are both characteristic Breckland birds, but another species that has found Thetford to its liking is the crossbill. Resembling a budgie or a small parrot, the crossbill is a colourful, chunky member of the finch family, which lives up to its name – the upper mandible crosses over its lower mandible – and enables it to prise open fir cones to access the seeds. The male crossbill is largely a vivid red colour while the female is a yellowish-green, and this exotic colouring means that crossbill flocks are quite easy to spot. You may not even have to stray far from the visitor centre because crossbills can often be found drinking from nearby puddles, a consequence of the obviously thirsty work of seed eating! Crossbills will often feed acrobatically, flying from cone to cone so, if you're hit on the head by a fir cone, look up! Numbers of crossbills will fluctuate according to the size of the cone crop, and native birds sometimes have their numbers swelled by immigrants from the continent.

There are lots of other finches to look out for too. The hawfinch is our largest finch, but it's a devil to see as it's so shy. Early spring is probably your best bet, when the leaves have yet to cloak the broadleaved trees it so favours. Its massive, thick beak is designed to crack open the toughest seeds, such as the wild cherry. The siskin is much smaller and, like the crossbill, makes a meal largely of fir-cone seeds. This member of the finch family is about the size of a blue tit and is a lively, yellowy-green colour. The male is particularly dapper with a black cap and a black patch under the chin contrasting beautifully with yellow flashes on his tail and wings. The siskin has a more delicate-looking, long, narrow beak than the crossbill, which it uses to tease out the cone seeds, rather than scythe the cones open.

Thetford Forest covers around 19,000 hectares – an area about the size of Nottingham – so we'd recommend starting at the High Lodge visitor centre near the village of Brandon. You will have to pay a small forest toll but it's worth it for such a wonderful woodland experience. The range of walks are colour-coded (depending on length and ease of access). We recommend the orange route, a trail of one and a half kilometres with a small hide at the end that offers the chance to see some of the deer species.

The differing colours of the female and male crossbill

Thetford Forest – a modern working forest

3 Orford Ness, Suffolk

Getting there:

Orford Quay is 16 kilometres east of the A12 (on B1094/1095) or 19 kilometres northeast of Woodbridge (on B1152/1084). Nearest train station: Wickham Market (13 kilometres). Regular boat crossings to Orford Ness.

Tel: Orford Ness NNR – 01394 450900 Havergate Island Nature Reserve – 01394 450732

Email: orfordness@nationaltrust.org.uk havergate.island@rspb.org.uk

Opening times: Contact for up-to-date opening times.

Charging policy: Orford Ness non-members (incl. Ferry crossing) £6, children £3. Under 3s free. NT members pay for ferry only. Group rates available

Disabled access: The nature trail on the island is unsuitable for wheelchairs.

Find out more

National Trust – Orford Ness National Nature Reserve
www.nationaltrust.org.uk/main/ w-vh/w-visits/w-findaplace/ w-orfordness/

The Royal Society for the Protection of Birds
www.rspb.org.uk/reserves/guide/h/ havergateisland/index.asp

Orford Ness National Nature Reserve is a bizarre place with a history to match. Described as 'half wilderness, half military junkyard', the peninsula has been managed by the National Trust since 1993 and is the largest vegetated shingle spit in Europe. The spit is linked to the mainland at Aldeburgh and stretches south along the coast to Orford, from which it is divided by the River Alde.

The raw material that has built Orford Ness emanates from further north along the Suffolk coast. Although the spit is currently about 16 kilometres long, it is very much a dynamic structure as its size and shape fluctuates over time. The spit was formerly owned by the Ministry of Defence, which used it for conducting secret military tests during both World Wars. The Atomic Weapons Research Establishment also had a base on the site and many of the buildings, such as the distinctive-looking pagodas which are clearly visible from Orford Quay, were specially designed to collapse in the event of an explosion.

As a result of having been closed to the public for many years, Orford Ness has become a haven for a suitably eclectic range of wildlife, which is rarely bothered by aesthetics and thrives both on the peninsula and on neighbouring Havergate Island.

This lack of disturbance and a paucity of predators has meant that numerous hares have thrived on the spit. Normally the habitat most associated with hares would be the large arable farmlands more commonly found in the east of England. However, on Orford Ness, abundant numbers of hares are constantly seen running over the shingle from one sparse vegetation patch to the next. Spring is an excellent time to go hare-watching, as this is when they are most often seen indulging in their energetic courtship action. On the spit, we were able to observe them particularly easily because there is so little cover in which they can hide.

The lack of a human presence throughout most of the 20th century has meant that the hares are much more tame, and we frequently passed as close as ten metres from them hopping over the ridges, a stark contrast to the timid hares on the mainland.

The main food of the hares on the spit seems to consist of sea campion, which grows in huge rafts over the shingle, and sea pea, a very uncommon plant and another shingle specialist, which is found on the seaward side of the peninsula. During spring, the sea pea produces very striking purple, pea-like flowers which, when pollinated, eventually form into small brown pea pods. There is a story that, during a 17th-century famine on this part of

the Suffolk coast, villagers collected and ate the peas to ward off starvation.

Of course the most famous resident along this part of the Suffolk coast is the avocet. This stunning-looking wader, and logo of the RSPB, first bred at Havergate Island in 1947 after an absence of just over a hundred years, leading to the island becoming a reserve just two years later. The island has now become nationally important for avocets, with up to 100 pairs breeding here each spring, accounting for up to a quarter of the UK breeding population. The island is only a stone's throw from both Orford Ness shingle spit to the east and Orford Quay to the west and it is the only island on the whole Suffolk coast. The numerous small mud islets on the north of this small island are a perfect nesting habitat for the avocets, and the surrounding brackish lagoons and estuary make excellent feeding grounds. Combined with a constant presence of wardens to protect the birds during the breeding season, the island makes for five-star avocet accommodation.

As we watched these beautiful birds with their pied plumage, blue legs and delicate upturned bill, we were delighted that they had given the UK a second chance.

Orford Ness and the pagodas in the background

Spring is the time to see the brown hare

4 Falls of Clyde, Lanarkshire

Getting there:

New Lanark World Heritage Site, South Lanarkshire, ML11 9DB is located 1 kilometre south of Lanark, off the A73. Follow signposts. Bus service from Lanark.

Tel: Falls of Clyde – 01555 665262 New Lanark World Heritage Site – 01555 661345

Email: fallsofclyde@swt.org.uk

Opening times: Open daily 8am–8pm. Visitor centre: March–December (except Christmas Bank Holidays) 11am–5pm.

Charging policy: Adults £3; Children free; Concessions £2. Some activities cost extra.

Disabled access: Fully accessible.

Find out more

Scottish Wildlife Trust – Falls of Clyde
www.swt.org.uk/wildlife/fallsofclyde.asp

New Lanark
www.newlanark.org/fallsofclyde.shtml

Visit Scotland
http://walking.visitscotland.com/walks/centralscotland/wildlife_falls_clyde

When we're filming, sometimes a few things go wrong and end up on the cutting room floor. But just occasionally the opposite happens, and something lovely occurs, we keep the cameras rolling and it ends up on film. That is what happened when we went up the Falls of Clyde in March.

The Falls of Clyde Wildlife Reserve is situated near the New Lanark World Heritage Site, a beautifully restored 18th-century cotton mill village. It's a woodland reserve running along the River Clyde gorge, with four spectacular waterfalls. The waterfalls alone are worth seeing, but the woods and gorge are packed with birds: there are dippers, herons, kingfishers, warblers, tits and wrens. There's even a pair of nesting peregrine falcons.

The peregrine is the fastest-moving bird on the planet, and dive-bombs its prey in the air at speeds of up to 350 kilometres per hour, though you won't see a turn of speed like that at the nesting site – things are much more sedentary. We spotted the female sitting on guard at the end of a ledge and beside her were four fluffy, grey-white bundles of feathers. They were her chicks: three females and a smaller male. Peregrines were an endangered species in the UK, having been persecuted by gamekeepers and targeted by egg hunters, but they have been recovering since the 1970s. We found ourselves hoping that all three of these chicks would survive and contribute to the growing numbers of this raciest of birds.

But our visit to the peregrines had to be in the nature of a pit stop. We had come to see badgers, and, to maximise our chances, we had to make sure we were in the right place at the right time. The badgers' underground sett was high up in the woods, and we needed to be in position, on the bank and downwind, before they came out in the early evening. Badgers have an excellent sense of smell and very good hearing, and while they may not have the sharpest of eyes – we were within about ten metres of the sett, a wide area with many holes and mounds of earth – we still had to keep very quiet and also very still. We had hardly arrived and set up to film when our wildlife cameraman nudged and pointed. Two small, and what appeared to be juvenile, badgers had already ventured out of the sett. They were foraging around and playing with each other. We were caught rather on the hop, to say the least. Suddenly, there were the badgers and there were we, giving a whispered running commentary of their actions. Because badgers are nocturnal they are rarely seen (other than by mammal enthusiasts and BBC camera crews sitting in woods late at night!), but they are quite numerous. They like woodland, especially when it borders onto pasture land.

We had come to the right place to see them, because life centres around the sett and a single family of badgers will occupy it for generations. They burrow tunnels many metres long, create chambers on different levels, and have several different entrances. This whole labyrinth is kept immaculately clean by both the boar and sow, who bring in clean bedding and drag out the old, which we could see piled in mounds around the entrances. All around the sett were well-defined pathways. As the dusk deepened, we watched the parents come out and join their young, and then the whole family went stumping and snuffling off into the gathering gloom to go grubbing for earthworms, their favourite food. We packed up our cameras and left the rest of the night to the badgers.

Badgers are best seen in the early evening

One of the waterfalls in the River Clyde gorge

5 Farndale, Yorkshire

Getting there:

Hutton-le-Hole is 3 kilometres north of Kirbymoorside. Take the A170 west from Pickering. Moorsbus network runs every Sunday Easter-October. 'Daffodil Bus' runs from Hutton-le-Hole every Sunday in April and over the Easter weekend.

Tel: English Nature – 01904 43550 Information centre, The Moors Centre, Danby – 01439 772737

Email: york@english-nature.org.uk moorscentre@northyorkmoors-npa. gov.uk

Opening times: Moors Centre: November-February 11am-4pm (Saturday, Sunday); March 11am-4pm (daily); April-October 10am-5pm (daily).

Charging policy: Not applicable.

Disabled access: Facilities available for disabled visitors.

Find out more

North York Moors National Park
www.moors.uk.net/

English Nature - Farndale
www.english-nature.gov.uk/special/ lnr/lnr_details.asp?C=o&N=&ID=153

Ryedale Council - Hutton-le-Hole
www.ryedale.co.uk/ryedale/ villages/huttonlehole/huttonlehole. html

Undoubtedly the best time of year to visit Farndale is the spring. Farndale is set in a deep valley, interwoven with narrow lanes and dotted with tiny, chocolate-box hamlets. One of the most picturesque villages is Hutton-le-Hole, which has a stream running through the middle, and a wide expanse of moorland above the fields and drystone walls. But what attract visitors to this part of North Yorkshire at this time of year is the daffodils. Their old name of Lent or Easter lily gives us a clue. In April, there are literally thousands of them blooming on either side of the River Dove. Their profusion and their sunshine-yellow colour really do bring a smile to even the most miserable curmudgeons. Smaller than our garden variety, these are wild, not cultivated, daffodils.

One reason why there are so many is because this area has never been farmed, so has never been subjected to high levels of fertiliser. Another reason is that, after flowering, sheep grazing alongside the river deadhead the daffodils, which means that the leaves put more nourishment back into the bulb instead of spending energy setting seed. There is a traditional daffodil walk, which we took, starting in the small hamlet of Low Mill, gently strolling three kilometres to High Mill, where there's the conveniently sited Daffy Caffy, before ending in the tiny hamlet of Church Houses. Unfortunately, wild daffodils are now much less common and this decline has occurred relatively quickly since the nineteenth century. No one really understands what has caused their mysterious demise. Lovely though this part of Farndale is, with its clouds of golden marsh marigolds growing in the streams and adding to that yellow covering, we also recommend a walk up on to the moor above it.

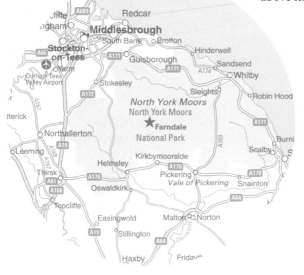

The glorious colours of the lapwing

These moors, like Spaunton, part of the North York Moors National Park, are home to a number of upland birds, such as meadow pipit, golden plover, curlew and lapwing. Lapwings are particularly beautiful birds – although they look black and white from a distance, they have glorious iridescent, bottle-green plumage on their back and wings, flecked with bronze and royal purple patches. And that sweeping crest is extremely chic. Lapwings probably have more colloquial names than any other British bird – from green plover, after their striking plumage, to peewit, because of their call, to the oddest, tieve's nacket, its Shetland name, meaning, somewhat unfairly, 'thieves' imp'. In spring, the lapwings begin their courtship, the males carrying out a looping sky dance, an aerial ballet of zigzags, dives and rolls, to show off to females and warn other males away. The bird's Latin name, *Vanellus vanellus,* means 'little fan' and refers to its slow, flapping flight with its round-edged wings. Lapwings have declined in numbers significantly as a breeding bird over the last 25 years, but the UK still plays host to almost two million birds in the winter. Their eggs were prized as a delicacy and eaten in inordinate quantities, served still in their shells in a moss-lined basket. Fortunately, this practice was outlawed in 1926. In recent times, changes in agricultural practice have caused problems: autumn-sown crops are often too high by spring to enable lapwings to nest successfully.

One of the birds' more intriguing characteristics has evolved as a way to protect their chicks. If they spot a threat, one of the parents will drag its wings along the ground as if injured and call in an agitated manner to try and lure the predator away from the nest.

Upland birds such as the golden plover ...

and the curlew

Opposite: Daffodils that decorate Farndale in spring

6 Rathlin Island, Northern Ireland

Getting there:

Ferry service (late spring and summer) or private boats for charter from Ballycastle Harbour. No cars permitted on the island; there are taxis and a minibus service, or go on foot or by pushbike.

Tel: Antrim Net – 028 2177 2100 Ballycastle Tourist Information Centre – 028 2076 2024.

Email: rathlin@nacn.org info@antrim.net

Opening times: Visitor centre April–August. Contact warden prior to visit: 028 9049 1547.

Charging policy: Ferry: Adult return £8.60; Children (5–16) £4.30. Family ticket also available.

Disabled access: Limited wheelchair access.

Kittiwakes nest on the cliff face

Find out more

Antrim Net
www.antrim.net/rathlin/

RSPB – Rathlin Island
www.rspb.org.uk/reserves/guide/r/rathlinisland/

Caledonian MacBrayne ferries
www.calmac.co.uk/

Rathlin Island might be just 10 kilometres off the north Antrim coast, but it's a world away from anything you'll find back in Northern Ireland. With a population of around 80 people, Rathlin is a beautiful, unspoilt and tranquil location.

Most visitors come for the wildlife and especially one must-see natural wonder. It's over an hour's walk – or a short cycle or minibus ride to the west lighthouse which, from spring through to mid-August, is just alive with the sight, sound and smell of tens of thousands of seabirds. If you want to see kittiwakes, fulmars, razorbills, guillemots and puffins, then this is the place to head for.

The view from the cliffs does little to prepare you for the assault on your senses. Once you're on the viewing platform, the sound is overwhelming as the birds launch themselves off the sheer cliff face and whirl around the magnificent sea stacks. Then, there's the smell. It's not exactly a top *eau de cologne*, but after a while your stomach will settle down.

This is Northern Ireland's biggest seabird colony, and during spring and summer there are volunteers on hand to point out the different bird species. What we liked most was the feeling of being surrounded by birds. It's a huge rock amphitheatre, with birds above, below and right in front of you.

But there's more than birds to hold your attention on Rathlin Island, and we urge you to keep your eyes peeled for a top mammal. It's a creature that has developed almost mythical status. The Irish hare is different from the lowland brown hare, with smaller ears, and lacking the black mark on the upper surface of the tail and the brown hare's mottled coat. They're a relative of the Arctic hare and are arguably Northern Ireland's oldest surviving mammal. We spotted some hares in farmland close to the harbour, where we watched around a dozen galloping through the long grass.

Then word reached us that there were a couple of highly unusual hares to be seen from the road on the way to the west lighthouse. When we arrived, what can only be described as a hare the colour of a ginger tomcat popped out of the heather. We'd found the 'Golden Hare of Rathlin'. Some people think it's a bit of a genetic mutant, others believe the colour is rare but natural for a creature that relies on speed, not stealth, for protection. Whatever the truth, it was a truly stunning moment.

The Irish hare – one of the spectacles on Rathlin

7 Muncaster Castle, Cumbria

Getting there:

Muncaster Castle, Ravenglass, Cumbria, CA18 1RQ. From the south take the A5092, then the A595 to Muncaster. From the north take the A595 to Cockermouth, and then Muncaster. Nearest train station: Ravenglass (1 kilometre).

Tel: 01229 717 614

Email: info@muncaster.co.uk

Opening times: Gardens, Owl centre, Meadow Vole Maze open daily 11am–4pm (or dusk if earlier); Castle open Sunday 2pm–4pm; Heron Happy Hour daily 3.30pm.

Charging policy: Castle, Gardens, Owl centre, Meadow Vole Maze adult £8, children £4; under 5s free; family ticket and season ticket available. Car parking free.

Disabled access: Wheelchairs for loan. The main areas of the gardens, Owl Centre and Meadow Vole Maze, and ground floor of the castle have wheel chair access. Induction loop for castle tour. Disabled toilets available.

It's difficult to see tawny owls in the tree but keep looking, they're there

Find out more

Muncaster Castle
http://www.muncaster.co.uk/

World Owl Trust
http://www.owls.org/

BBC Cumbria - Muncaster
http://www.bbc.co.uk/cumbria/web cams/muncaster/index.shtml

Set in the rolling hills of the English Lake District, Muncaster Castle, home to the Pennington family for 800 years, is a whole lot more than a stately home. It is also the headquarters of the World Owl Trust and the host of a quite delightfully eccentric British wildlife event, 'Heron Happy Hour'.

The owl centre at Muncaster has one of the largest collections of owls in the world. They have an established captive breeding programme, and there are owls of all shapes and sizes – from massive eagle owls down to diminutive pygmy owls.

We whiled away much of the morning with the owls, until in the afternoon 'Heron Happy Hour' was announced. It's a bit of a crowd puller, and rounding the back of the castle we could see why. There must have been about 40 herons, all lined up in the trees surrounding the back lawn. The food was put out and the herons flocked down, followed by the most disgraceful display of squabbling. Strangely, even though the food was clearly visible to them in the short grass, they did not immediately grab it, but behaved just as they do in the wild. They stalked the food, often standing motionless before stabbing down with their dagger-like beaks. When two males were after the same piece, they would rear up, chests out and heads back, flapping their wings forward to beat off their adversary, generally setting up a din and making a spectacle of themselves. But, like most domestic tiffs, it looked rather more dramatic than it actually was – a lot of posturing and showing off.

We could tell that most of the herons at the feeding site were males, using a little trick we learned. The saying is: 'lipstick, powder and comb'. In spring – and this only works in spring – the female's bill turns a lovely rosy pink, that's the lipstick; the powder is the soft down that she grows on her front to keep the eggs and chicks warm; and the comb is an extra claw which she grows on her foot to keep the soft, powdery down in order. Remember the saying and you'll easily be able to tell them apart.

A grey heron

8 Minsmere, Suffolk

Getting there:

Minsmere Reserve, Westleton, Saxmundham. Follow brown tourist signs from A12 to Westleton, then take Dunwich road. Turn left at crossroads for reserve entrance track then left at Scotts Hall. Nearest train station: Darsham (8 kilometres).

Tel: 01728 648281

Email: minsmere@rspb.org.uk

Opening times: Reserve open daily 9am-dusk (or 9pm if earlier); Visitor centre 9am-5pm (or 4pm November-January). Closed on Christmas Day and Boxing Day.

Charging policy: Adults £5, children £1.50, concessions £3, family £10. Free to RSPB members.

Disabled access: Reserve has a mixture of surfaces; see www.rspb.org.uk/reserves/guide/m/minsmere/specialinfo.asp.

Find out more

RSPB
www.rspb.org.uk/reserves/guide/m/minsmere/index.asp

BBC Suffolk
www.bbc.co.uk/suffolk/dont_miss/restoration/minsmere/minsmere.shtml

To birds, Minsmere is the equivalent of a four-star bed and breakfast. Set on the Suffolk coast, on a line between Norway and France, it is an ideal spot for birds migrating between Scandinavia and Europe. Minsmere is one of the RSPB's first reserves, established over 50 years ago, and is one of the most popular birding locations in the UK. There's a huge variety of birds to see – 350 different species pass through or are resident, and in spring you can see 100 different species in a day without breaking into a sweat. Classic birds to look out for are the avocet (the RSPB's logo) since about 100 pairs return in spring to breed, as well as small numbers of bittern. A third of the UK's bitterns breed on this reserve and it is said to be just about the best place in Britain to hear them booming. In later spring, you'll also be treated to that wonderful, mellifluous song of the nightingale, singing from the scrub right next to some of the paths through the reserve, as well as other warblers, like the Dartford warbler, which recolonised the reserve in 1996 after an absence of 60 years. And even for those of you who don't make it past the tearoom, you'll be able to watch sand martins nesting in the car park as you sip your coffee.

Minsmere is the ultimate reserve for seeing something at quite literally any time of the year, including black-tailed godwits, wigeon, teal and Bewick's swans in the winter, and a wide number of passage migrants in spring and autumn. We were particularly excited about spotting marsh harriers, with their lazy wing beats, almost lolling on the breeze as they crossed the reedbeds. One female suddenly went into overdrive and impressively snatched a large dragonfly on the wing right in front of us. But our hearts were in our mouths as we watched a brood of moorhen chicks sitting right out in the open beneath the harrier as their parents struggled to round them up and usher them into the comparative safety of the reeds. Marsh harriers are the largest of all our harrier species – they have big, broad wings, a heavy build and, unlike other harriers, no white rump. Females are easy to tell apart from the males because they are larger and have creamy heads. The turbulent history of the marsh harrier starts off in a familiar vein: harriers were persecuted by gamekeepers as well as egg collectors and their numbers sank to just a few pairs in Norfolk in the 1870s. In 1915, a keeper at Hickling Broad came across a nest containing five eggs – the first breeding attempt for 20 years. Unfortunately, the eggs didn't hatch and the pair didn't try to breed for another six years. During the 1960s, the birds were affected by organochlorine pesticides and had the unenviable reputation

of being our rarest bird of prey. By 1971, the population was down to just one single breeding pair and that was at Minsmere. Fortunately, there is a happy ending: the birds' numbers have dramatically increased since these pesticides were phased out and there are currently 360 breeding females.

Minsmere is great for both beginners and advanced birders alike. If you're starting out, it's a good place to ask questions – the RSPB regularly run guided walks and also have a guide-in-a-hide scheme. It was also the first reserve where bird hides were pioneered just after World War II. One of the reasons why Minsmere is so popular with birds and birders alike is because it has five main types of habitat: reedbeds, semi-natural woodland, lowland wet grassland, shingle and lowland heath, which help to promote a real diversity of wildlife. In addition, the RSPB actively manages these ecosystems and creates new ones, such as scrapes – shallow pools with raised mudflats – exactly the kind of habitat avocets like.

Minsmere – a bed and breakfast for birds

A female marsh harrier feeding

9 Sperrin Mountains, Northern Ireland

Getting there:

Sperrin Mountain is 90 minutes drive from Belfast; Gortin Burn is just above the village of Gortin. Sperrin Rambler Service no. 403 operates Monday-Saturday between Magherafelt and Omagh.

Tel: Sperrins Tourism - 028 8674 7700 Sperrin Heritage Centre - 028 8164 8142

Email: info@sperrinstourism.com

Opening times: Heritage Centre Easter–October 11.30am-5.30pm (Monday-Friday), 11.30am-6pm, (Saturday), 2pm-6pm (Sunday).

Charging policy: Gold panning 80p. Charges for other specific events.

Disabled access: All areas suitable for wheelchair users, apart from the gold panning.

Find out more

Sperrins Tourism
www.sperrinstourism.com/

Discover Northern Ireland
**www.discovernorthernireland.com/
destinations_sperrins.aspx**

Water Wildlife
**www.fortunecity.co.uk/safaripark/
fish/66/CADDISFLIES.htm**

There's gold in these hills. For thousands of years, it's been taken from the rivers and streams that run through the Sperrin Mountains. Even today there's still a bit left and you can have a go at finding it in the stream that runs close to the Sperrin Heritage Centre. We had a go, but we won't be giving up our day jobs just yet.

The Sperrins are one of Northern Ireland's gems. The locals will tell you that they've been too quiet about this place for too long. It's a rugged patchwork of mountains, bogland and rivers, and streams that are so clean they contain the building blocks for a top-rate ecosystem. We based ourselves close to the Owenkillew river, one of the main water courses through these mountains. Our task was to leave the gold behind and look for a very different kind of treasure.

We joined a couple of kids from the village of Gortin, where they've got a great community project going bringing both Catholic and Protestant children together to explore their local environment. The youngsters go and get their hands and feet wet in the Gortin burn, a tumbling stream that runs into the Owenkillew river. And the kids have become pretty good at it. One of the best techniques is 'kick sampling', where you place a fishing net just a few inches downstream of an area that you disturb with your feet. You'll be amazed at the living creatures you can find.

First up were stonefly nymphs. Now, we urge you to get into these little critters. Take a look at one under a magnifying glass and you're looking at a great piece of insect architecture. These creatures spend their lives under stones in streams. Find these and you know that the water is clean: they're one of the first creatures to disappear when there's pollution. They're really primitive and were among the first insects to develop flight. These larvae or nymphs will later emerge as adult stoneflies - but the vast majority of their lives are spent underwater. The smaller nymphs spend their time consuming algae and detritus, while some larger species are carnivores. By the way, you'll know it's a stonefly by its characteristic two tails, as mayflies have three tails.

The real treat was getting our hands on some caddis fly larvae. These are the house builders of the stream. There are nearly 200 species of these remarkable creatures in the UK. What makes them so special is that many build a camouflaged home out of gravel, grit or plant material which they hold together with silk. They do this to protect themselves from the numerous predators below the surface.

It's impressive stuff - and it was a niche that was spotted by an artist who's even used caddis fly's ingenuity to make jewellery. He took the insects out of their natural cases and provided them with jewels instead of gravel. The industrious insects busily reconstructed their protective coverings with these brightly coloured stones. Then the insects were removed and the decorative and unique pieces of jewellery were sold on to the rich and famous. Diamonds truly are a caddis fly's best friend. Not all caddis fly larvae build homes, however. Others are free-flowing insects and live a naked and precarious existence in the river.

Of course, where you find these insects you may well be able to notice other predators too. These streams are also spots where you'll find young trout and salmon. Due to the very clean nature of the water, the rivers in the Sperrins are among the best fishing rivers in Ireland. We joined a team from the Loughs Agency, who monitor the health of the fish population by electrofishing. This is where a small electrical current is passed through the water to temporarily stun the fish. They're then scooped out of the water so their size and weight can be recorded before being returned back. Now, it's not a thing ordinary Joe Public can do – but if you get in contact with your local university, electrofishing is often done by research students. Give them a ring – you might be able to tag along and get cracking views of fantastic fish.

The Sperrins – one of Northern Ireland's gems

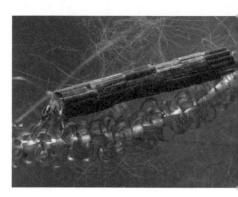

Caddisfly larva with a case made of reed stems

We weren't lucky, but you might be

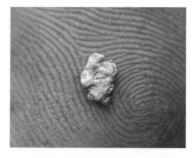

10 Portland, Dorset

Getting there:

Portland Bird Observatory, The Old Lower Light, Portland Bill, DT5 2JT. In Portland cross the causeway with Chesil Beach on your right and follow the signs to Portland Bill. Nearest train station: Weymouth (16 kilometres).

Tel: 01305 820553

Email: obs@btinternet.com

Opening times: April–September (excl. Saturdays) 11am–5pm, open most Sundays in winter. Accommodation can be booked at the field centre; telephone for availability.

Charging policy: Accommodation charges apply; free access to paths.

Disabled access: Limited disabled access; there is a ramp leading to a patio area at the Observatory.

Find out more

Portland Bird Observatory
www.btinternet.com/~portland birdobs/

Dorset Wildlife Trust
www.wildlifetrust.org.uk/dorset/

Natural History Museum – Plants – Portland Bill
http://flood.nhm.ac.uk/cgi-bin/ fff/glob.pl?report=pcfllist&group= &sort=&inpostcode=DT5

Everyone longs for the start of spring and one of the first signs that it has arrived is when you hear the song of the chiffchaff – the clue to the song, of course, being in the name. Although a few hardy souls spend the winter in Britain, the majority of these olive-brown warblers disappear to the Mediterranean or neighbouring North Africa, flying back across the English Channel in March to set up breeding territories. That's what they're doing in the still bare trees as they sing 'chiff, chaff, chiff, chaff!' becoming one of the first migrants to arrive on our shores.

If you want to see spring literally flying into the British Isles, then one of the best places to do so is on a piece of limestone rock that juts out from the Dorset coast into the English Channel. It's called Portland Bill on the Isle of Portland and, for hundreds of thousands of birds that have spent the winter in warmer places, it may well be the first land that they see at the end of their epic journey back to Britain. The great thing about Portland is that you stand an excellent chance of seeing them as they stop off for a rest and a feed. In spring, a walk along the cliffs by the lighthouse is an avian adventure. If you're really lucky, you'll see birds that very few people in the British Isles will ever see – species that are not breeding but that have overshot the continent – but even the ones that are considered common have some amazing stories to tell, and many have achieved journeys which put humans to shame.

If you can, check out the excellent website run by the Portland Bird Observatory and Field Centre before you visit. It'll give you a good clue as to what is about and you can find out if the weather conditions look right for a bumper arrival from the continent. The Observatory was started in the 1950s and is one of 16 recognised bird observatories in the UK that study migration and bird movements. It has recorded nearly 200 species of bird in and around the gardens, which have been specially planted to attract the birds to land. Mist nets are used to catch migrants, which are then ringed by volunteers. It is because of work like this that we know so much more about migratory patterns.

The Observatory records for March confirm that, like the chiffchaff, wheatears are a common early migrant to our shores, flying in from West Africa, south of the Sahara desert. The males migrate a week or two before the females, some of them leaving their wintering grounds as early as January and taking their time to rest and feed on the way. Just a little bit bigger than a robin, the male wheatear is a real looker, with black eye mask, black wings, a soft grey head and back, pale

The limestone rock of Portland Bill

A species of thorn moth

underparts and a white rump and tail feathers - the height of elegance. Most of them are on their way to the north and west of the UK, choosing to breed in rocky and stony places, such as upland pastures with dry stone walls, or moorland

Portland is a great place to try out a bit of sea-watching. You'll find people with telescopes gazing out to sea in all weathers, counting the passing seabirds. Common scoters, gannets and divers pass by either singly or, if you're lucky, in groups of several hundred. From here you can see Manx shearwater arriving from South America: not only do they make long journeys at incredible speed, they're also amazingly long-lived - one bird preparing to breed off the north coast of Wales was found to be about 50 years old!

And if all that's still not enough, then visit the cliffs at night and you'll find some hardy people out moth-trapping with lamps, because it isn't just birds that migrate. And, once you start to look, some moths have some terrific migratory stories to tell as well.

For the uninitiated, Portland itself is probably more famous for its quarries than its wildlife. Portland Stone was used to build St Paul's Cathedral after the Great Fire of London, not to mention The British Museum, The National Gallery and the Bank of England. The island is attached to the mainland by a single road and Chesil Beach - a stretch of shingle about 29 kilometres in length and a world famous geological feature. Famous too for its prison, Portland can sometimes look a little bleak - but for a bird coming back to breed, and for the thousands of birdwatchers who make the journey every year to see them, this is a destination that never disappoints.

Chiffchaff, an early migrant

April

You are spoilt for choice for wildlife watching in April, because everything begins happening everywhere, all at once. Freed from the winter straitjacket, wildlife has one thing on its mind – sex!

This is the month when the majority of our migrants arrive and it is always a seminal moment when the first swallow of the year is spotted in mid- to late April. Another red-letter day is when the first cuckoo of spring is heard, but seeing these shy and retiring birds is a different matter entirely. Baby badgers may well emerge above ground for the first time and moles, or more usually the mess they make, are much more in evidence, the only time these antisocial creatures meet up to mate.

The first reptiles may come out to bask on a sunny day and it is not unusual to find adders or slow worms in post-hibernation congregations as they warm up for the breeding season. Hedgerows become alive with male orange-tip butterflies on their never-ending search for virginal females to mate with, and, near the end of April, who could forget to check out the bluebells – surely the UK's greatest botanical spectacle!

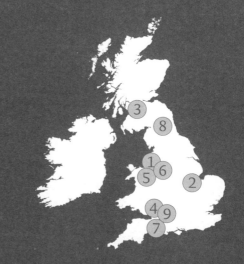

1 Formby, Liverpool

Getting there:

Pinewoods and Red Squirrel Reserve, Victoria Road, Freshfield, L37 1LJ. From Liverpool, follow signs to Southport until the A565. Follow the brown signs from the north end of Formby bypass. Nearest train station: Freshfield (1 kilometre).

Tel: 01704 878591

Email: formby@nationaltrust.org.uk

Opening times: Daily during daylight hours, closed Christmas Day. Part of the beach car park closes at 5.30pm (March–October) or 4pm (November–December).

Charging policy: Car park charge applicable.

Disabled access: Ample parking facilities and access to the squirrel viewing areas for wheelchairs. Braille guide.

Find out more

National Trust - Formby
http://www.nationaltrust.org.uk/main/w-vh/w-visits/w-findaplace/w-formby/

BBC - Science & Nature - Wildfacts - Natterjack toad
http://www.bbc.co.uk/nature/wildfacts/factfiles/482.shtml

Forestry Commission - Red Squirrels
http://www.forestry.gov.uk/forestry/Redsquirrel

The beach at Formby near Liverpool is a glorious stretch of golden coast. It's also home to a rare, but cute, creature. There are 200 red squirrels living in the pine woods alongside the beach. The pines were originally planted to stop the coast eroding at a time when the squirrels were plentiful. Now that there are only 20–30,000 of these animals left in the UK, with most of them in Scotland or northern England, Formby is a welcome haven for them, and for us.

You can buy nuts to feed the squirrels at Formby, a necessary treat for them since each one needs to eat the seeds from 20–40,000 pine cones to survive each year. They will also snack on nuts, berries, fungi, buds, shoots, flowers, bark, lichen, and insects in summer. The best way to see them is to choose a spot, scatter some seeds or nuts and then sit quietly, and that way you should be able to entice them to come quite close to you. We visited in April and, at this time of year, you might see them gathering moss to line their dreys, which are the large, ramshackle nests that they build out of twigs. Baby squirrels are called kittens – they're born with their eyes closed and have no hair or teeth, but within seven weeks they are mini versions of their parents and ready to leave the drey. Red squirrels live for up to four years and have, on average, three young in March or April. In a good year, they might also produce a second litter in June or July.

The red squirrel originally migrated to Britain about 10,000 years ago during the last ice age. Since the grey was brought over from America in the 19th century, the red has steadily declined. There have been a number of theories regarding why the grey has been able to displace the red: one reason is because the greys are better able to digest tannins in seeds like acorns, while the reds are much better adapted to conifer forests containing trees like the Scots pine. But the real killer for the reds has been the parapox virus, which the grey harbours, but isn't affected by. Sadly, the disease is almost invariably fatal to reds.

The wonderful coastline of Formby

You can tell the difference between the two species because, of course, the red has a rusty-coloured coat whereas the grey is, well, grey. Red squirrels are also slightly longer and more slender than greys, with tufted ears; they weigh up to 300 grams; greys can reach up to half a kilo. And you can impress your friends by pointing out that reds have double-jointed ankles!

Just eight kilometres away, at Ainsdale, is another rarity that is good to look out for at this time of year. This is one of the best places to hear natterjack toads calling. This little beast, although smaller than the common toad, is claimed to be the loudest amphibian in Europe. In April, the males call to attract mates and their chorus of croaks can carry for several kilometres. Natterjacks are mostly nocturnal, so we joined a toad walk just as the sun was setting and headed out into the dunes. It's a really magical experience standing by the side of a pond, the jet-black surface shimmering with the moon's reflection, the sea whispering on one side, as all around toads sing their throaty songs.

Natterjack toad with its distinctive yellow stripe down the back

We managed to see some, not just hear them. They have fairly flat bodies that are warty brown, olive or grey (the males can lighten or darken their skin in order to camouflage themselves better) and they have a distinct yellow stripe that runs all the way down the back. The males have nuptial pads – hard patches on the inside of their forefingers, which they use to grip the female during mating, and large vocal sacs. They also have glands that can secrete toxins. They're not very good at jumping, only doing it if they are alarmed. Instead they run – a bit like a lizard – and, surprisingly for an amphibian that likes water, they're poor swimmers and can drown in deep water.

Opposite: You might see a red squirrel at Formby

2 Rutland Water, East Midlands

Getting there:

From the west, take the A6003 from Uppingham or Oakham. From the east, from Stamford the A606/A1. Nearest train station: Oakham (3 kilometres).

Tel: 01572 770651

Email: jfisher-robins@lrwt.org.uk

Opening times: Egleton reserve daily 9am–5pm (4pm November–February). Lyndon Reserve Easter–October 10am–4pm (Tuesday–Sunday); November–Easter: weekends and Bank Holidays only. Both reserves closed Christmas and Boxing Day.

Charging policy: Adults £4; OAPs £3, other concessions £2. Afternoon prices (November–February) £1 off normal prices. Group/Four-day rates available.

Disabled access: Bird Watching Centre has hearing induction loop; wheelchair access restricted to ground floor. The *Rutland Belle* can take wheelchairs and has a hearing induction loop.

Find out more

Rutland Water
www.rutlandwater.org.uk

Rutland Osprey Project
www.ospreys.org.uk

Leicestershire/Rutland Wildlife Trust
www.lrwt.org.uk/

Rutland Water is one of Europe's largest man-made reservoirs. It is set in the beautiful county of Rutland in the East Midlands, and is home to a remarkable comeback king. We set off in April to unravel the story of how ospreys have been returned to Central England by a hardworking group of enthusiasts.

The osprey disappeared from Central England roughly 150 years ago. When Rutland Water was created in the 1970s, it seemed like the perfect locality for this magnificent bird to breed. However, there was a problem – ospreys usually return to breed in the place where they were born. So a decision was made to translocate a number of ospreys from Scotland to Rutland and hope that they would 'stick'. Between 1996 and 2001, 64 young ospreys were translocated. They were fed from platforms around the reservoir to keep them in the area, and nesting platforms were built to encourage birds to breed in the vicinity. Well, that all seemed straightforward – get the birds imprinted on the area and encourage them to breed. But ospreys migrate. In late August and early September, ospreys start to head for West Africa and don't return until March. Nobody could be sure that the Rutland ospreys would come back to the reservoir and breed.

Although the first ospreys were translocated in 1996, they take three or four years to reach breeding age, and it wasn't until 2001 that success was achieved – the first pair of ospreys came back and one healthy chick was raised. It was a slow start, but from that beginning the ospreys at Rutland Water have gone from strength to strength.

The exact nesting site at Rutland Water is kept secret for fear of the eggs and chicks being stolen, and because too many visitors might scare the birds. But we wanted to give you the whole osprey story, so we were given special permission to go up to the nest. It was a huge construction of branches forming a large, flat platform on the top of a dead tree, and there, right in the middle, was an osprey sitting on her eggs, and perched next to her on a branch was the male, keeping guard.

Even the most novice birdwatcher cannot fail to identify an osprey. The white head and black eyestripe clearly distinguish it from all other native raptors. The male keeps guard over the nest and brings food to the female while she incubates the eggs for anything up to six weeks. They usually lay three eggs and often all will hatch, but successful fledging of all three chicks only occurs when there is an abundant food source (two is more usual).

Although the nest site is kept private, this should not affect your chances of seeing an osprey at Rutland Water. By far and away the most exciting views of ospreys are to be had on the reservoir itself. Ospreys feed almost exclusively on fish, both fresh- and saltwater species, and seeing them dive for and catch a fish is a must on any birder's tick-list. With this behaviour in mind, we boarded the good ship *Rutland Belle* with a group of other eager osprey spotters and headed out onto the water.

Osprey cruises run on certain dates in spring and summer. The birds have known favourite fishing sites, so your chances of seeing them in action are pretty good. On this occasion we weren't lucky enough to see an osprey diving and plucking a fish out of the water in front of us, but there was a grand finale to our day. Flying straight towards the boat came an osprey carrying a fish almost as long as its body. They have specially adapted talons, with two facing forward and two facing back, which allow them to carry fish in the most streamline, aerodynamic position – like a torpedo – and we had a perfect view as it flew right over our heads.

Ospreys are not the only thing Rutland Water has to offer. There are good numbers of breeding wildfowl, including tufted duck, garganey and pochard, and there's also a large breeding colony of cormorants at the western end of the lake.

If you're lucky, you'll see an osprey fishing at Rutland

The reservoir of Rutland Water in spring

3 Queen Elizabeth Forest Park, Stirlingshire

Getting there:

From Glasgow take the M8, from Stirling the A81, to Aberfoyle.

Tel: 01877 382383
Visitor Centre – 01877 382258

Email: cowal.trossachs.fd@forestry.gsi.gov.uk

Opening times: Grounds open daily; Visitor centre March–December (daily), January–February (Thursday–Sunday).

Charging policy: Visitor centre £2.

Disabled access: Some remote and hilly areas, some wheelchair friendly pathways – check website for details.

Find out more

Forestry Commission – Queen Elizabeth Forest Park
www.forestry.gov.uk/qefp

Visit Scotland
www.visitscotland.com/aboutscotland/explorebymap/features/queenelizabethforestpark

RSPB Scotland
www.rspb.org.uk/scotland/

The Raptor World Centre, Scotland
www.raptorworld.co.uk/index.html

Queen Elizabeth Forest Park has pretty much got it all. It's handy to two major cities (an hour's drive from Glasgow and not much more than Edinburgh); its scenery of mountains, lochs and forests is breathtaking; and it is home to some of Scotland's most charismatic animals. On top of that, the layout of the park is fantastic and designed to make it as easy as possible to see the wildlife.

The 20,000 hectare forest park is part of the Loch Lomond and Trossachs National Park, described as a place where the Highlands meet the Lowlands. Here is some of Scotland's finest scenery and a rich variety of animals and plants, including carpets of bluebells in spring. But the forest park is probably most famous for its birds of prey, and here they have done everything they can to help you see them.

For a start, there's a 50 kilometre bird of prey trail that is the link between the park's hilltop visitor centre at Aberfoyle, from where you get panoramic views, and a red kite feeding centre just outside the park. On this trail, there's a chance to see most of Britain's birds of prey or 'raptors', as they're also known. There's kestrel, merlin, peregrine, sparrowhawk, red kite, osprey, buzzard, hen harrier, even golden eagle, plus all of Britain's owls except the little owl. There are cycle and walking trails and plenty of viewing points.

Let's face it, though, even if you're in the right place at the right time, birds of prey aren't always easy to identify. Views can be brief, distant or just silhouettes against a dull sky. It may also be difficult to work out size because there's nothing to give you a sense of scale. To be an eagle-eyed raptor spotter you need to focus on wing shape, wing position, head size, tail shape and the manner in which the bird flies. There's a leaflet available with silhouettes of each bird of prey on offer so that when that magnificent creature soars over your head, you've got a real chance of working out that it is a particular raptor rather than just a large gull!

Of all the birds of prey in the park, during spring and summer there's one that you've got the best chance of seeing, and it is also one of the most exciting.

The osprey returned to Scottish skies in 1954, after decades of persecution led to its extinction in 1916. Famous for its taste in fish, it can often be seen over the park's lochs and rivers. Perhaps the best place of all is over the Lake of Menteith, the only major body of water in Scotland known as a lake, rather than a loch. When we turned up on a warm day in spring, we must have seen osprey flying over the lake seven or eight times in an hour, circling, and rewarding us just once with a spectacular dive to catch fish.

Female osprey, best viewed over the Lake of Menteith

The bird has a wingspan of over 1.5 metres and is dark brown and pale below with long wings that are bent at the 'wrist'. But it can, from certain angles, resemble a buzzard or red kite. Of course, buzzards fly in a shallow 'V' and red kites have that distinct forked tail but there are ways to be sure it's an osprey. It's the only raptor in the park to dive for fish, and the only one with white underparts.

But if it's wet and cold and you simply aren't in the mood for a walk, then in spring you can still get great views of these birds. At the Aberfoyle visitor centre, called the David Marshall Lodge, the Forestry Commission Scotland and RSPB have cameras beaming up-to-date pictures from nests of buzzards, peregrines and osprey. You might even see the female osprey feeding her chicks with a big, juicy trout that she's just plucked from the Lake of Menteith.

If that still isn't enough, you can join the Forestry Commission's rangers as they take buzzard and tawny owl chicks from their nests to ring them – all part of a project to monitor the populations of the birds of prey. Seeing a downy white tawny owl chick, blinking, seemingly unperturbed at being held in the hand, is a quite unforgettable experience.

One of the Park's 'raptors' – a buzzard shows off its wings

The scenery is breathtaking at Queen Elizabeth Forest Park

4 Forest of Dean, Gloucestershire

Getting there:

The Forest of Dean district is within easy access of the M4 (M48), M5 and M50. Nearest train stations: Lydney, Chepstow and Gloucester.

Tel: Dean Heritage Centre – 01594 822170

Email: tourism@fdean.gov.uk

Opening times: Heritage Centre open daily, summer 10am-5.30pm; winter 10am-4pm. Closed Christmas Bank Holidays.

Charging policy: Adult £4.50, Concession £3.50, Child £2.50, Family ticket and group rates available.

Disabled access: Guide available at www.visitforestofdean.co.uk/documents/Accessibility_Guide.doc.

Find out more

Royal Forest of Dean
www.fweb.org.uk/dean/

BBC Gloucestershire
www.bbc.co.uk/gloucestershire/

Visit Forest of Dean
www.visitforestofdean.co.uk/

British Wild Boar
www.britishwildboar.org.uk

Usually when we're asked to go off and film something for *Nature's Calendar*, it's because there's a pretty good chance of getting to see the wildlife in question. However, when we set off to The Royal Forest of Dean in Gloucestershire in April to film one of Britain's most elusive mammals, which is apparently making a comeback, we really did feel as if we'd been sent off on a wild boar chase!

You don't have to go off the beaten track to find the field signs for wild boar. There are lots of trails through the forest, just keep your eyes peeled as you stroll around. Here are a few tips for what to look out for. Wild boar regularly visit puddles in wet ground and create a large muddy hollow as they wallow around to keep cool and remove parasites. If you come across a likely looking patch, examine the area around it carefully for footprints. The footprint of a wild boar is very distinctive. They have two prongs, called dew claws, which are set low down on the sides of the foot. These are used to dig into the ground, producing a cloven footprint with two deep stab marks on either side – it's unmistakeable once you learn what to look for. Close to the wallow there's likely to be a rubbing tree. Look for a tree which is smeared and coated in dried mud over the bottom of the trunk. A rubbing tree helps the boar to remove more parasites, and also allows them to scent mark an area. If you find a rubbing tree, check for the solid gold proof of boar. We had to grovel around at bit, but we did strike gold - or rather hair! Wild boar have a thick, bristly coat, made up of two distinctive types of hair: long, coarse guard hairs, which classically have very split ends; and clumps of fine, almost woolly, underhair called pelage – again, unmistakeable once you've seen it. The other thing to look out for on trees is scores and notches in the bark. These are made by the sharp tusks of the male and probably mark out his territory. At about two years

Lea Bailey Wood with a ground cover of anemones

of age the males grow two sets of tusks, both curving upwards. The top tusks are hollow and act as whetstones, constantly sharpening the lower tusks. You could be forgiven for thinking that wild boar are pretty ferocious and quite scary things. Well, they can be aggressive towards each other, especially females protecting their young, but essentially they are reclusive, very shy animals – and since they are nocturnal, the chances of actually seeing them in the wild are slim.

We didn't really feel that we could do a film on wild boar without at least trying to bring you some pictures of them in the wild. To do so, we had to resort to some cunning tactics: a local wild boar expert volunteered to go to a known foraging site a few days before filming and put out some grain to entice them. We built a camouflaged hide up a nearby tree and put Plan Wild Boar into action. The cameraman set up some small, remote cameras at ground level and we shimmied up the tree. The rule of thumb for watching wild boar is nil-by-mouth – complete silence and total stillness. Perfect, just like a game of hide-and-seek! It was torture, with the tension only heightened by an approaching thunderstorm. However, barely before we had a chance to get cramp, we heard the rustle of leaf litter and the soft grunting of wild boar. A couple of juveniles checked out the clearing from every angle, before the lure of free food proved too much for them and they barged in and started snouting for the grain. Once the coast seemed clear an adult female joined them. Wild boar have a matriarchal society, and she lost no time butting the youngsters out of the way.

With lightning approaching, we launched into the softest running commentary ever, but sadly even this was too much – there was a drumming of tiny feet and they were gone.

It's wonderful that wild boar are back breeding in our forests after such a long absence and, while you might never actually see one, you can still have loads of fun looking for evidence of them in the wild.

If you visit in spring, you'll see carpets of bluebells – a wonderful sight

Opposite: One of Britain's oldest big mammals – the wild boar

5 Ruabon Moor, Wrexham

Female black grouse

Male black grouse in breeding plumage

The black grouse is a bird that has been in long-term decline throughout large parts of the UK. But not all is doom and gloom because a group of conservationists in northeast Wales have decided to turn around the grouse's fortunes.

Recent surveys of populations are based on counting the flamboyant males as they display at ancestral 'leks', or breeding grounds. According to current estimates, Wales has a small but significant 213 males, the core population being centred on Ruabon Moor, of which Llandegla forest forms a substantial part. So important is this site that half of all the Welsh black grouse are thought to live within a mile of it.

The spring spectacle of a group of male black grouse displaying to attract the attentions of a female is something you simply have to experience. For a few short weeks in March and April, the males gather at an ancestral lek in an attempt to impress, and then try and mate with, as many females as possible.

The male black grouse in all his breeding plumage is a fine sight to behold. When puffed up, he is about the size of a very large football with black glossy plumage, a red wattle over his eyes, white wing bars and a black lyre-shaped tail with a white rosette of feathers underneath. But seeing this display is only half the story; the males also produce a far-carrying call like that of a pigeon, 'cook-roo', and a strange sound similar to the screech a cat would make if its tail was being trodden on!

Because there is such demand from birdwatchers to visit leks, a hide has been set up on the edge of Llandegla forest where they can be observed without disturbance.

The birds only display for a short period around dawn, so to maximise our chances of filming them we arrived for 4am. The first male turned up just as it started getting light, and soon other suitors arrived and what a wonderful sight it was as we counted up to eight males strutting around like turkeys on steroids. After two hours of drama, the birds eventually melted back into the forest; their morning exhortations had been in vain, as not a single female had even turned up to view the spectacle.

6 Woolston Eyes, Cheshire

Getting there:

Leave the M6 at junction 21, take the A57 (signposted Warrington) and, after 200m, turn left down Weir Lane to park by Woolston Weir.

Tel: Woolston Park Rangers – 01925 824398

Email: rangers@warrington.gov.uk

Opening times: Public footpath from end of Weir Lane to Thelwall Lane open daily. Access to other parts of the reserve and hides by permit; apply at www.woolstoneyes.co.uk/permits.php

Charging policy: Not applicable for Reserve. For group visits or to get on to the islands £8 per person; book in advance

Disabled access: Designated parking at Woolston Park. Good network of paths to the east and a wheelchair accessible picnic area.

A spring highlight: black-necked grebe

Find out more

Woolston Eyes Bird Reserve
www.woolstoneyes.co.uk/

BBC Manchester
www.bbc.co.uk/manchester

Cheshire Biodiversity
**www.cheshire-biodiversity.org.uk/
bird-bngrebe.htm**

This top spot deserves a prize for being one of the most unusual habitats in the UK. Like so many of our 'wildlife hotspots', it is in fact a man-made creation. It sits alongside the Manchester Ship Canal and for years it was used as a dumping ground for dredgings from the canal. Today, it's a 220 hectare site that consists of four large beds filled with water, surrounded by grassland and scrub, all managed by the Woolston Eyes Conservation Group.

Its great claim to fame is that it is the stronghold for one of our rarest breeding birds, the black-necked grebe. It's thought there are about 50 pairs in the country and latest counts indicate that almost a third of the UK population breed here at Woolston Eyes. No surprise, then, that this spot acts as a magnet for birders. Armed with scopes and bins, people will travel hundreds of miles just to get a glimpse of this little beauty. And you can see why.

Visit 'The Eyes' in spring and you'll have a great chance of seeing the grebe's beautiful, golden-feathered cheeks and fiery red eyes. Really lucky birders may witness its magnificent courtship display: male and female birds appear to almost stand up in the water with their chests puffed out, before rushing across the water side-by-side. Believe us, it's just one of those rare examples of animal behaviour that you really should observe at first-hand.

If your luck runs out and you fail to spot the black-necked grebe, fear not, as more than 220 species of bird have been recorded at this one location. The abundance of scrub surrounding the beds means you should spot a variety of breeding warblers, including sedge, grasshopper, willow, whitethroats and blackcaps.

Although the black-necked grebes are best viewed in spring, 'The Eyes' are worth visiting at all times of the year. Check out the breeding black-headed gulls (whose heads aren't actually black) and the little gull, the smallest bird in the gull family. Keep an eye out for teal, pochard and tufted ducks in the beds. You've also got a chance of spotting peregrine falcons, marsh harriers, merlin and hobbies taking advantage of the abundance of breeding birds and insects that this wonderful site supports.

Woolston Eyes reserve

7 Kingcombe Meadows, Dorset

Getting there:

Located 21 kilometres west of Dorchester, near Toller Porcorum, northeast of Bridport. Small car park at Pound Cottage visitor centre; additional parking at Copse Close. Nearest train station: Maiden Newton (6 kilometres).

Tel: Paul Comer – 01305 264620

Email: Kingcombe Centre – kingcombe@hotmail.co.uk

Opening times: Grounds open daily.

Charging policy: Not applicable.

Disabled access: Limited.

Find out more

Dorset Wildlife Trust
www.wildlifetrust.org.uk/dorset/ reserves/kingcombe.htm

BBC Dorset - Kingcombe
www.bbc.co.uk/dorset/content/ articles/2004/12/07/wildlife_diary _dec_feature.shtml

The Hardy Orchid Society
www.hardyorchidsociety.org.uk

To come here in late spring is to walk into a landscape that looks as though it was painted by the French Impressionist artist Claude Monet. The Impressionists wanted to create emotional excitement by exploring new ways of showing colour and light. With its green meadows dotted with splashes of yellow, purple and red, that's what the reserve at Kingcombe achieves quite naturally for its visitors.

It is, though, very much an English landscape – England as it used to be before the industrialisation of agriculture. Kingcombe is still managed as a working farm, but its small fields, ancient hedgerows brimming with wildlife, and unimproved grassland are farmed primarily for wildlife. And it works. The hay meadows are packed with so many species of orchid you could almost lose count – from early purple orchids in April to heath spotted orchids in May, not forgetting pyramidal orchids, fragrant orchids and, best loved of all, the insect-mimicking bee orchids.

Look beyond the orchids and there are hundreds of fascinating wildflowers to explore. The reserve at Kingcombe is a botanist's paradise. Four hundred and thirty different flowering plants and ferns have been recorded, many of which, because of the way our farming practices have changed, are in severe decline across the British Isles.

Their names alone seem to transport you back to the days of Dorset's most famous rural writer, Thomas Hardy. There's lady's smock, also known as the cuckoo flower, ragged robin, meadow saxifrage and yellow rattle – a plant often used by wildlife trusts to help recreate flower-rich hay meadows because it is partly parasitic and its roots fix to those of grasses, weakening the grasses and allowing other flowers to set seed. Yellow rattle gets its name from the fact that the seeds rattle in the husky capsules when it ripens. Birdsfoot trefoil is also named after its seed – the seed head is said to resemble a bird's foot. It is, though, also known as 'eggs and bacon' after the yellow and red colour of the flower. If you want a name that really trips off the tongue, then spring is a great time to get to grips with the corky-fruited water dropwort and its relation the pignut, both members of the carrot family. Pignut roots are much loved by badgers and even the occasional wild boar. In fact, the area around Kingcombe Meadows and Powerstock is known locally as the Valley of the Pigs, and there is said to be a population of 20–30 wild boar – descendants of escapees from farms – which are occasionally spotted at Kingcombe. They're shy creatures, so you are very unlikely to see them, but you may see signs of where they've been rooting around for the pignut roots, which incidentally used to be eaten by country folk just like lady's smock was once used in salads.

If you can tear yourself away from the flowers, then the star species at Kingcombe has to be the strikingly patterned marsh fritillary butterfly. Come in late spring and there's a good chance you'll be able to get some close-up views of this quite sedentary and increasingly rare butterfly. The marsh fritillary has declined in almost every European country and is extinct in Northern Belgium. In Britain it's declining at a rate of ten per cent a decade, but Dorset is something of a stronghold. Its caterpillar lives on the locally abundant devil's bit scabious, another plant with some interesting folklore. Legend has it that the short stubby root of the devil's bit scabious was caused by the Devil trying to bite the root off and so kill the plant because he was envious of the plant's uses to man. He might also have been envious of its usefulness to butterflies, because in summer the purple flowers seem to attract more than their fair share of them. In fact, 36 of the UK's 56 native butterfly species have been recorded on the flower-rich meadows of Kingcombe, including the earliest butterfly of spring, the bright yellow brimstone, and the striking orange-tip, whose caterpillars feed on lady's smock.

Kingcombe is also a great place to spot mammals – there are lots of dormouse boxes and visitors can occasionally join in walks when the boxes are checked by someone licensed to handle dormice. Look out, too, for signs of foxes because spring is a great time to spot the cubs out playing. A trail of chewed feathers is a good indication that a fox has been about, or you may see areas where the grass has been compressed by youngsters playing, or well-used trackways leading to a hiding place or den.

Kingcombe also has a field studies centre run by a charitable trust – so if you're really into your wildlife, then sign up for a course and pick up some skills while at the same time experiencing a unique piece of English countryside.

Ragged Robin – one of Kingcombe's floral sights

You might just catch a glimpse of a fox, or signs that one has been about

The stunning flowers of the early purple orchid

8 Whitelee Farm, Northumberland

Getting there:

Whitelee Farm, Byrness, Otterburn, NE19 1TJ. From the A68, turn off towards Chattlehope, and Whitelee Farm is located next to Catcleugh Reservoir, within the Northumberland National Park.

Tel: 01830 520530

Email: Online enquiry form at www.whiteleeholidaycottages.com/contact/index.htm

Opening times: Year round, accommodation must be booked in advance.

Charging policy: Accommodation charges apply.

Disabled access: Some disabled access, telephone regarding specific needs.

Find out more

Whitelee Cottages
www.whiteleeholidaycottages.com/index.htm

Whitelee Farm
www.whiteleefarm.co.uk/

RSPB – Swallow
www.rspb.org.uk/birds/guide/s/swallow/index.asp

Whitelee Farm is perched on a steep hillside surrounded by miles of moorland. But instead of hearing the keen moaning of the wind sweeping across the heath, the tranquillity is broken by the farm's resident peacocks whose raucous calls can be heard right across the valley! Whitelee, run by John Wilson, has open access and John actively encourages wildlife. If you rent one of his cottages, you can sit with a glass of wine and watch CCTV images of a barn owl rearing her chicks on the television, as well as the resident badgers' comings and goings. However, if you're just here for the day, there's another local whose activities are equally interesting.

Swallows usually arrive in Britain at the end of March and through April from Africa, where the lucky things spend their winters. Thanks to increasingly warmer winters, they occasionally get here as early as February, having flown a staggering 9,000 kilometres. They're abundant at Whitelee Farm because of the plethora of insects. Swallows are one of the few blue species of bird we have; in the UK only the kingfisher is bluer. They're a joy to watch – there's their chattering, twittering call, for a start, and then their flight, which naturalist Richard Mabey describes as 'looping playfulness'. They are the smallest species to incorporate gliding into their flight. Originally swallows used to nest in caves, but they've now commandeered the eaves of our houses. At Whitelee, they often roost inside the barn and John has cut holes in the barn doors allowing them easy access to their nests. It was incredible seeing them fly through a tiny space, barely a palm's length across, at great speed. These nests, which are constructed out of mud and spit, can be reoccupied for ten to fifteen years! Each female lays about four to five eggs, and in good years the pair can rear two or even three broods. Although both sexes are practically identical, you can impress your friends by pointing out that on arrival the male has ever so slightly longer tail streamers than the female (later they become abraded).

The moors surrounding Whitelee Farm are partly composed of blanket bog. They're very damp, yet sited on the tops of the hills. The reason for their bogginess is down to the geology of the landscape: impervious rocks are the foundation for these hills and, as they were eroded by glaciers, they left dips, which trap water and have filled up with water-loving plants. Amazingly, although some of these blanket bogs are thousands of years old, they're only a metre thick, so pretty fragile. If you visit in June, the cotton grass will be in flower: glorious swathes of bobbing, white rabbit-tails stretching across these otherwise bleak moors.

It's prime habitat for two delightful little birds too. From a distance, they're your archetypal LBJ – Little Brown Job – which twitchers love to tick off their lists. But get up close to them and you'll be able to see the differences between these two chats – the whinchat and the stonechat. The two used to be referred to as 'furze chats' by locals because of their similarity and their penchant for hanging out in gorse. The rarer whinchat is a summer migrant, is less patterned than its cousin and has a white eyestripe, which the stonechat lacks. The resident male stonechat is a little more distinctive with a white half-collar, black face and peachy-chestnut chest. Males like to sit on top of bushes and other prominent posts. The females of both species are fairly hard to tell apart because they're much dowdier than the males, needing to be camouflaged for the serious business of rearing chicks. The name refers to their clacking tongue – like two stones being tapped together, but they can really go for it, producing harsh, scolding cries when they're disturbed. WH Auden is said to refer to the stonechat in his poem, *The Wanderer*: 'Or lonely on fell as chat, By pot-holed becks A bird stone-haunting, an unquiet bird.' Richard Mabey thinks he's referring to the ringing chat of another LBJ, the wheatear, and, if you're lucky, you might just get to hear these as well in the valley below.

A whinchat and its distinctive white eyestripe

An adult swallow feeds its young in a barn

Whitelee Farm is surrounded by moorland

9 Cricklade, Wiltshire

Getting there:

North Meadow, Cricklade, SN6 6HA. Located 20 minutes walk northeast of Cricklade town centre. Roadside parking available within 300 yards of the meadow.

Tel: English Nature Site Manager – 01380 726344

Email: Wiltshire@english-nature.org.uk

Opening times: Open daily.

Charging policy: Free public access to the footpath.

Disabled access: Disabled access gate to the reserve but site can be very wet.

Find out more

English Nature – Cricklade
**www.english-nature.org.uk/
special/nnr/nnr_details.asp?nnr_
name=North+Meadow,+Cricklade
&C=0&Habitat=0&natural_area=
&local_team=0&spotlight_reserve
=0&X=&NNR_ID=120**

Botanical.com – Snake's Head Fritillaries
**www.botanical.com/botanical/
mgmh/f/fritil33.html**

Cotswold Water Park
**www.waterpark.org/leisure/
north_meadow.html**

A walk around North Meadow National Nature Reserve near Cricklade is like stepping back in time. The site, which covers 44 hectares of glacial flood plain between the Rivers Thames and Churn, is one of the finest examples of a lowland hay meadow in Europe. It is also famous among British botanists as the location of an incredibly impressive 80 per cent of the UK's population of snake's-head fritillaries. During a small window of opportunity between Easter and the beginning of May, it is possible to see up to two million blooms of this striking and nationally rare flower, which give the meadow a wonderful purple haze.

A few hundred years ago, meadows like North Meadow must have been abundant along the Upper Thames. Unfortunately very few remain today, as they have been drained, ploughed and 'improved' for agriculture, or simply been bulldozed to oblivion for gravel extraction. However, this meadow has been saved by the simple fact that it has been managed by the people of Cricklade for over 800 years in a very traditional manner. Natural England now own most of the meadow and they work closely with the Court Leet, an ancient judicial court which still sits today, and local residents to ensure that the time-honoured system of land tenure that has so benefited the flowers continues into the future.

During winter, the rivers often flood the meadow and this is a vital and integral part of the yearly cycle for all the meadow's flowers. During spring and early summer, a hay crop is grown which is sold to local farmers. The hay is always cut after 1 July, when the wildflowers have set seed, and the crop has to be removed by 12 August before the ground becomes too wet for the tractors. Traditionally, the whole meadow was split up into strips under different ownership and ancient carved stones can still be seen embedded in the meadow which mark the boundaries of the different 'hay-lots'. Following the hay crop, the meadow then becomes a common for the Cricklade residents to graze their livestock until 12 February of the following year, after which the meadow is rested for that year's hay season.

This traditional regime is perfect for a whole array of early flowering species. Flowers such as marsh marigold, which give the meadow a series of yellow splashes in the wetter patches, are very much in evidence in spring, as are pink cuckooflowers, so called because their flowering heralds the arrival of the cuckoo. The undoubted attraction is, though, the fritillaries with their purple nodding flowers, which cannot be mistaken for any other flower. When seen up close, the petals are

North Meadow, Cricklade

The beautiful snake's-head fritillary

And one of the completely white flowers

actually minutely chequered maroon and white, giving the appearance of a chequerboard or, without too much imagination, the scales on the head of a snake.

Interestingly, we noticed a small proportion of fritillaries with completely white flowers. These are thought to be a naturally occurring version of the much more abundant purple flower, and on close inspection the familiar chequerboard pattern was still present; however, on the white flowers it looked like a watermark!

North Meadow doesn't just put on a spectacle of flowers, though. For the whole time we were filming at the site, we were serenaded by skylarks that would burst out of the flowers on their upward journey, singing all the way as they climbed to an end point anywhere between 25 and 50 metres above the centre of their territory. Once at the top, they would hover while delivering a virtuoso performance. At any one time throughout the whole day, there must have been at least a couple of males delivering their towering performance and, as they tired after a couple of minutes and plunged back down to the fritillaries, we wanted to stand up and applaud for the bird, the flowers and the sheer delight that spring had well and truly arrived.

May

The breeding season is at its height, birds are singing and flowers are blooming. With the temperature rising in May and an abundance of nectar and pollen on offer, insects begin to emerge, in turn providing food for broods of chicks and insectivorous mammals.

May is the month for enjoying the dawn chorus in full swing. Reed and sedge warblers provide a constant chattering noise in the reedbeds, occasionally punctuated by the loud yet liquid song of Cetti's warbler or the foghorn boom of the bittern. May is also the time for the ultimate songster, the nightingale, a short-lived visitor to our woodlands.

Hawthorn is also known as 'may blossom' so it is no surprise to find that hedgerows turn white this month. Rural roads also become flanked by the frothy flower heads of cow parsley, while, on acidic and upland soils, the yellow of gorse is the colour that dominates.

May is a time for specialist butterflies too, such as the pearl-bordered fritillary, a rapidly declining visitor on western woodland rides. And, if you are moth-trapping this month, expect huge numbers of cockchafers or May bugs!

1 Breckland, East Anglia

Getting there:

From the A11 or A134, follow the signs off the road between Hockwold and Weeting. Parking at the site. Nearest train stations: Thetford, Bury St Edmunds and Kennet.

Tel: Norfolk Wildlife Trust – 01603 625540
Visitor Centre – 01842 827615

Email: admin@norfolkwildlifetrust.org.uk

Opening times: April–September 7am–dusk (daily), Visitor Centre April–August (daily). Public access restricted to pine belt and hides.

Charging policy: Members free.

Disabled access: Wheelchair access to visitor centre and hides.

Find out more

English Nature – Weeting Heath
www.english-nature.org.uk/about/teams/team_photo/Weeting heath.pdf

Norfolk Wildlife Trust
www.wildlifetrust.org.uk/norfolk/big%205/weeting.htm

BBC Norfolk – Stone-Curlews
www.bbc.co.uk/norfolk/nature/stone_curlews.shtml

Breckland is an area of heathland on the Norfolk/Suffolk border. We went there to find one of the UK's strangest looking birds – the stone-curlew. This summer visitor breeds on poor soil in East Anglia and Wiltshire, and one of the easiest places to see them is the Norfolk Wildlife Trust Reserve at Weeting Heath in Breckland.

The reserve is surrounded by a rabbit-proof fence – designed to keep the rabbits in. They graze the scrubby growth to a length that then allows the stone-curlews to scrape out shallow hollows on the ground where they nest, relying on their camouflage to avoid predators. They are about the size of a crow, with long yellow legs. In spring, they spend most of the day on the nest, so the legs are hidden and their stripy feathers blend in perfectly to the sandy soil and small flints. The only telltale sign is their big yellow eyes, developed for vision in low light. These birds are active after daylight hours, often feeding on insects at neighbouring, open-air pig farms.

Because they are difficult to see, allow yourself plenty of time at the reserve – if you can only visit for an hour at lunchtime, you'll be lucky to see them. We went there several times during our visit in May, including dusk and dawn. The evening is a great time to hear them calling: 'kur-lee'. It is similar to the curlew's call, but that is the only connection – the species are not related. The name of the stone-curlew comes from the call and their love for stony nesting sites.

Just after dawn, we were rewarded with a fabulous view of a pair of stone-curlews. This pair had nested, but had been disturbed – possibly by a stoat or a fox. This was not good news for the birds, but it was a spectacle for us birdwatchers. A third bird joined them and together they put on an extraordinary courtship display, known as parallel walking, whereby the male and female strut along as a pair and then the male makes a presentation of a worm as a gift, and the female responds with a bit of false nesting to illustrate

Breckland at sunrise

what the courtship is leading to! This is not a common sight, but Weeting Heath is the only place where you can be sure you can watch in peace without any risk of disturbing the birds. There have been sightings of them nesting in all sorts of places, such as in gardens and in crop fields, but confine yourself to Weeting Heath. Stone-curlews are protected because they are rare and very easily disturbed; if disturbed they will abandon the nest even if they have eggs.

This part of East Anglia is one of the driest areas of the country. The dry, sandy ground is what the rabbits love as it's easy for the females to dig their burrows. Rabbits are not top of the list for naturalists, but they have a crucial role in this habitat. Their constant grazing creates a fine, short turf, perfect for stone-curlews and plants that can't compete with long vegetation.

The ground is perfect for rabbits

Rabbits were introduced by the Normans in the 12th century to be farmed for their meat and fur. The land was divided into warrens, and warreners were employed as gamekeepers. The warrener's lodge at Thetford still stands, a large, flint, fortress-like building dating from the 15th century. It shows just how important the rabbits were to the Breckland communities. Rabbits can breed from January to August, producing a litter of three to seven young per month. The young can then breed at four months old, but 90 per cent die in their first year, the vast majority taken by foxes or stoats. Wherever you see rabbits, you may see stoats. We saw several at Weeting Heath, but, as is often the way with wildlife filming, the camera wasn't running!

Opposite: The great camouflage of stone-curlews, and their nesting site

2 The Lizard Peninsula, Cornwall

Getting there:

Take A3083 to Lizard town from Helston and follow tourist signs. Car parking at The Lizard and in Lizard town.

Tel: National Trust – 01326 561407
Lizard Countryside Office – 01326 561 407

Email: lizard@nationaltrust.org.uk

Opening times: Daily access to paths and external views of lighthouse.

Charging policy: Lizard Lighthouse: Adults £2.50; Concessions £2; Students £1.50; Family £6.50.

Disabled access: Wheelchair friendly path to The Lizard and overlooking Lizard Point. Some terrain unsuitable. Lighthouse access for wheelchair users at ground floor level.

Find out more

BBC Cornwall – Lizard Lighthouse
www.bbc.co.uk/cornwall/photos/ winterscenes/27.shtml

The Heritage Trail – Lizard Lighthouse
www.theheritagetrail.co.uk/ industrial/lizard_lighthouse.htm

National Trust – The Lizard and Kynance Cove
www.nationaltrust.org.uk/main/ w-vh/w-visits/w-findaplace/ w-thelizardandkynancecove/

There is something wonderful about the extremities of the UK in that they always deliver memorable wildlife days and are usually well worth the sometimes considerable effort it takes to get to them. Botanically speaking, there is no finer extremity than the Lizard Peninsula, the 'second toe' of Cornwall and the southernmost and almost westernmost part of England. Put simply, you can find more rare plants in half an hour on the Lizard than you can anywhere else in the UK. This is due to two factors: its southerly position, and its underlying geology, consisting of a special type of rock called serpentine, which is very rich in magnesium and calcium and found nowhere else in Cornwall. So abundant are the rare plants in some parts of the Lizard that the famous Cornish botanist, the Rev C A Johns, completed his famous 'hat trick' in 1847 when he succeeded in throwing his wide-brimmed hat over three species of rare clover, plants which to this day are found only on the Lizard.

For the filming trip, we took the coastal route between Mullion Cove and Lizard Point, a walk of about 13 kilometres taking in some breathtaking scenery. Along the way, we were able to get to grips with some of the typical flowers that make our coastal areas so distinctive in spring. The clifftop edges were a riot of colour and plastered with the pink cushions of sea thrift, blue swathes of spring squill and yellow clumps of kidney vetch. We couldn't afford to spend too long admiring these flowers, though, as we were on a hunt for rare Lizard plants and one in particular that would be instantly recognisable to those with a passion for cooking – the wild asparagus.

Kynance Cove is a beautiful location, the mid-point of our walk and one of the classic sites famed for its rarities. As we dropped down to the cove surrounded by the plant Cornish heath, it was easy to be blasé about a plant so ubiquitous on the Lizard but found nowhere else. Down at the cove, the coastline was simply

Lizard Point, Cornwall

stunning and consisted of a number of small islands and stacks with names such as Lion Rock, Bishop Rock and Asparagus Island. The vegetation around the cove itself is a great place to look for rarities and, with the help of Pat Sergeant, a local botanist and expert on the Lizard, we were able to find special Lizard plants with wonderful names such as Babington's leek, fringed rupturewort and western clover right next to the footpath.

Asparagus Island can only be reached at low tide because at any other time it is, as its name suggests, an island. Having previously checked the tide timetables we had picked our window of opportunity carefully and were soon scrambling over the top of the steep island, itself no bigger than half a football pitch, in pursuit of our quarry. And all of a sudden as we turned a corner, poking through the grass was indeed a bunch of asparagus tips! Unlike the cultivated variety, this rarity grows in a prostrate form in the wild, no doubt as a counter-measure to the relentless buffeting from the wind. The actual spears, though, looked identical to those that you would find in the vegetable section of your local supermarket and would probably be just as tasty – but collecting these plants is definitely off the agenda for such a five-star rarity! Our time with the asparagus had unfortunately to be limited to ensure we weren't cut off by the rising tide, a situation that would be untenable with about five more kilometres still to cover until we reached our final destination, Lizard Point.

For the last 100 metres of our journey, we were accompanied by the Lizard Point's most famous residents, one of only two pairs of breeding choughs in the whole of England. Since re-colonising Cornwall in 2001 from the Continent, one pair has bred annually and they have only recently been joined by a second pair along these famous cliffs. We hoped, as we watched them feeding away along the clifftops, that they appreciated the rare flowers while digging for worms!

Wild asparagus can be found on Asparagus Island

Opposite: Sea thrift on the cliff edge

3 Bempton Cliffs, North Yorkshire

Getting there:
Take the cliff road from Bempton and follow the B1229 from Flamborough to Filey. Nearest train station: Bempton (2 kilometres).

Tel: RSPB – 01262 851179
Tourist information – 01262 673474

Email: bempton.cliffs@rspb.org.uk

Opening times: Reserve open daily. Visitor centre March–October 10am–5pm (daily); November–February 9.30am–4pm (weekends). Closed Christmas week.

Charging policy: Car parking £3.50; free for members.

Disabled access: Wheelchair access to the nature reserve and picnic area.

Find out more

RSPB - Bempton
www.rspb.org.uk/reserves/guide/b/bemptoncliffs/index.asp

UK Fossils
www.ukfossils.co.uk/seco43a.htm

Gannet Colony Report
www.rspb.org.uk/eng/and/north/action/mixed.asp

We arrived at Bempton Cliffs RSPB Reserve on the Yorkshire coast on a misty morning in May to witness surely one of Britain's most accessible seabird spectacles. Approaching the clifftop, it became clear that there were plenty of birds here. There was a cacophony of noise coming up from below. Then, as the sun started to burn off the mist, almost on cue the spectacle we had been promised was slowly revealed. We were looking down on towering white chalk cliffs and the air was filled with thousands, yes thousands, of wheeling birds.

There were so many that it looked like a snowstorm of dense fluttering white flakes. For a long time we just stood and watched, making no effort to identify the birds, but just looking at the vast swirl of activity and wondering how on earth there were no mid-air collisions. At first it all looked random, but when we started to take things in, a sense of order emerged. The cliffs, which are the largest chalk sea cliffs in eastern Britain, were acting as a sort of high-rise city to the quarter of a million seabirds nesting on them. There were puffins nesting in the soily banks near the top, then kittiwakes on ledges at the top the cliffs, and below them, massed ranks of guillemots. There was constant noise and motion, birds leaving the nest and heading out over the sea, birds arriving back, landing, and jostling. We tried to give you a sense of this with sound and pictures, but the one thing we cannot give you is smelly-vision! With so many birds, there's a lot of guano generated and that in turn can produce a huge pong!

The bright white gannets with their black wingtips flying out over the sea were easy to pick out, being the largest birds there. But we had to walk a little way along the cliff top to get a good view of the gannet colony. Bempton has the largest mainland breeding colony of gannets in the UK, and we were looking down on roughly 3,500

The white chalk of Bempton Cliffs

pairs. And what a spectacle these impressive and elegant birds make. For a start, there's something very pleasing about their stark black and white body, and the buttery-yellow head and beak and the beady blue eyes, all beautifully outlined in black. In fact, one of the ways you can tell males from females is to look at the head. Males have a slightly darker yellow head, which you can see quite easily looking at a pair on a nest.

Gannets are fabulous fishermen, so it's wonderful to watch them folding their wings back and plunging into the sea like daggers. They're specially adapted to do this, having little fluid-filled sacks in their heads that function rather like car airbags and prevent brain damage. They have endearing social habits, too, with pairs often seemingly affectionate to one another and indulging in 'bill-fencing' when one returns to the nest after an absence.

The nest itself is a large, clumsy affair of sticks and seaweed, but the male always goes out of his way to please his lady, bringing back coloured string and rope which he knows she will use to adorn her ramshackle nest.

The gannets, along with the other seabirds, are at Bempton Cliffs from April to August. The RSPB reserve stretches about three miles along the cliffs, but you can also have a sea-level encounter with Bempton's seabirds. A boat goes out daily in the summer from the nearby town of Bridlington, and this will take you right up to the base of the cliffs. You'll be among all the noise and bustle and surrounded by birds – the most wonderful 360-degree birding experience.

Kittiwakes nest on cliff ledges

Opposite: The noise and spectacle of a gannet colony

4 Moray Firth, Scotland

Now, scoring a winning goal in extra time in the FA cup final? That's pretty hard to beat. Watching a bottlenose dolphin for more than an hour while it feeds just a few metres away? Absolutely impossible to beat. Yet, this is what we experienced on the Moray Firth near Inverness during our visit in May. What's more, almost every single day people have encounters like this at the UK's top dolphin hotspot. Indeed, some believe it's the best place in Europe to see these terrific animals.

You've got two great opportunities to see dolphins – from land and from sea. There are a number of dolphin-watching boat trips, and we joined one operating out of the historic village of Cromarty.

Setting out in a rigid inflatable boat – the kind of vessel used by the military and the Royal National Lifeboat Institution – we bounced out into the Firth. Sightings over the previous week had been good, and the weather was on our side. The sea was reasonably calm, meaning it would be easier to spot a dolphin breaking through the waves. It also wasn't too sunny, which is good because the glare from the sea can make dolphin-watching difficult (if you're out on the water on a sunny day, take some polarising sunglasses – they'll really help).

Sarah, the captain, knows these waters well, and it only took about half an hour for her to spot a group of dolphins in the distance. We approached with caution, because the last thing we wanted was to get too close and distress them. After cutting the engines, the dolphins came to us. There are believed to be around 130 dolphins in the Moray Firth colony. It's the most northerly resident population of bottlenoses on the planet and, to combat the cold waters of the North Sea, the dolphins grow much bigger than others that live in tropical waters – some can grow up to four metres in length.

As we bobbed about in the sea – only a hundred metres or so from the land – around ten dolphins put on a remarkable display. They really did come and check us out. It must have been a comical sight as we tried to film them. One moment they were on the port side, the next they were over on starboard. While Sarah held the boat steady, we swivelled around this way and that trying to get as many shots as we could. We had no idea how long they would stay with us, so we filmed everything. Thankfully, the dolphins were pretty accommodating and topped off their display with a series of leaps clean out of the water. This, though, isn't a theme park. These are top of the food chain predators that are living in the wild under pressure – but watching from the boat you can only marvel at them taking time out to play. On this occasion, our contact with the dolphins lasted only ten minutes or so, and they moved off and we left them alone. There were high-fives all round after a remarkable experience.

If boats aren't your thing, you can get equally impressive views from land. The place to head for is Chanonry Point near the village of Fortrose on the northern side of the Moray Firth. It's here by the spit of sand near the lighthouse that people gather every day throughout spring to see dolphins. Now, there's no absolute rule about if and when these wild animals will turn up. But the more time you put in, the more opportunities you'll have of seeing of them – and the greater the chance of watching them close up.

Dolphins leaping in the Moray Firth

It was six in the morning and misty when we met up at Chanonry Point with Charlie Phillips, a photographer who works with the Whale and Dolphin Conservation Society. Charlie knows these dolphins better than anyone. He's identified scores of animals, giving each a number and name. The shape of their dorsal fin is as personal to them as our faces are to us.

We were out early because an incoming tide was due, and Charlie knew that this would maximise our chances of seeing dolphins really close to land. There's a deep underwater trench close to the point, which is used by salmon and sea trout. Twice a day it brings the fish in almost like a supermarket conveyor belt – and the dolphins are there waiting to ambush them. One of Charlie's favourites, a female, was already surfacing close by. The sea was like a millpond when a sea trout leaped out of the water just a few metres in front of us. Almost instantly it was followed by the dolphin. The fish conveyor belt was up and running. Within ten seconds, she'd caught the fish and she then spent the next hour playing with her catch before manoeuvring so that it slipped down her throat headfirst. (If it was to go down the other way, the fish's fins could catch in her throat.) It was an amazing event to witness – all within a few metres.

One of the boats that will take you to see the dolphins on the Moray Firth

And that wasn't all. As the morning went on, scores of dolphins moved down through the Firth following the fish. They would return later when the tide came in again. As well as bottlenose dolphins, you can also see harbour porpoises, and common and grey seals. The birdlife's not bad either, with a full range of seabirds nesting here or passing through. All in all, it's a top spot – but we must remember there's a delicate balance to be struck between watching these creatures while not damaging the environment in which they live. Marks out of ten? It has to be an eleven!

5 The Llangollen Canal, Clwyd/Shropshire

Getting there:

Colemere is located approx 5 kilometres southeast of Ellesmere. Wood Lane Nature Reserve is less than 1 kilometre walk down a country lane from the canal.

Tel: British Waterways – 01606 723800

Email: enquiries.wbc@britishwaterways.co.uk

Opening times: Open daily.

Charging policy: Colemere, Woodland and Mosses NNR are all free to enter throughout the year; other charges may apply.

Disabled access: Good access to the canal.

Find out more

BBC Shropshire - Colemere webcam
www.bbc.co.uk/shropshire/content/panoramas/ellesmere_colemere_360.shtml

Waterscape - Llangollen Canal
www.waterscape.com/Llangollen_Canal

Wood Lane Nature Reserve
www.woodlanereserve.co.uk

The Llangollen Canal is one of the most popular waterways in the UK and boasts incredible engineering, scenic beauty and great wildlife spots in equal measure. Beginning near Llangollen in the foothills of Snowdonia, the canal gently winds for more than 70 kilometres, passing through the abundant lakes in the Shropshire countryside and finishing just north of Nantwich at the Shropshire Union Canal in rural Cheshire.

Taking a cruise aboard one of the many canal boats that navigate the waterway in spring offers an unparalleled opportunity to see wildlife as it would have been seen in Georgian Britain. We were particularly keen to explore the ancient water-logged landscapes of Shropshire, which were formed at the end of the last ice age. Passing through Ellesmere towards Colemere, the canal travels through a watery landscape peppered with very unusual lakes called meres; these meres have virtually no water running out of them, making them of huge interest to wildlife.

Only a stone's throw from the canal is Wood Lane Nature Reserve, a site that is presently a sand and gravel quarry but also home to a rather wonderful colony. As the quarry is active, the location is not the quietest corner of Shropshire to go birding, but the diggers and bulldozers have inadvertently created the perfect habitat for sand martin colonies in the newly exposed quarry faces. One ten metre high sandbank, in particular, has become the focus for what must surely be one of the largest sand martin colonies in the UK with over 400 active nests.

Slightly smaller than the swallow with uniform brown upperparts, white underparts and a distinct brown band across the chest, the sand martin is one of our earliest migrants to arrive back in Britain from sub-Saharan Africa. They can often be found hawking for insects as early as mid-March in the blustery cold wind above lakes and reservoirs.

Sand and gravel quarries serve as the most important breeding sites for this bird in the UK, and the most amazing thing of all was that the martins were completely unphased by all the industrial noise in the background with juggernauts rumbling past a mere 20 metres away!

The sand martin is by far the most sociable of all our hirundines and at the top of the sandbank we could see systematic rows of burrows marking the entrance to a tunnel of 60–90 centimetres in length. All the burrow entrances seemed to be in neat lines and often no further than 15 centimetres apart; this was definitely a high-rise flat! The colony was a constant hive of activity as parents ferried insects which had been caught over the meres back to the hungry mouths of the chicks down in the burrows. Occasionally the martins would all take flight above the sandbank and circle above the colony in a large flock while twittering to each other, which was a wonderful sight against a blue sky backdrop.

On the other side of the road, less than 100 metres from the sandbank, is a series of shallow, water-filled scrapes, created during the extraction process and these provide a welcome home for another specialist bird. The little ringed plover first bred in the UK in 1938 and since then it has been gradually colonising England and Wales. This dainty little wader with its black neckband and golden eye-ring has consistently plumped for nesting sites that could at very best be described as 'works in progress'. Here at Wood Lane Nature Reserve, a couple of pairs breed amid the bedlam and we were able to see one of the chicks, no bigger than a cotton wool bud with a pair of cocktail sticks for legs, following one of its parents on a feeding expedition along the water's edge.

Unfortunately, we had to tear ourselves away from the birds as we had a date back with our canal boat. We did so, however, secure in the knowledge that the owners of the gravel pit, the Tudor Griffiths Group, were fiercely protective of their martins and plovers and would provide a sanctuary for the birds for many years to come.

The dainty little ringed plover

Sandmartins at the entrance to their burrow

The hundreds of burrow entrances

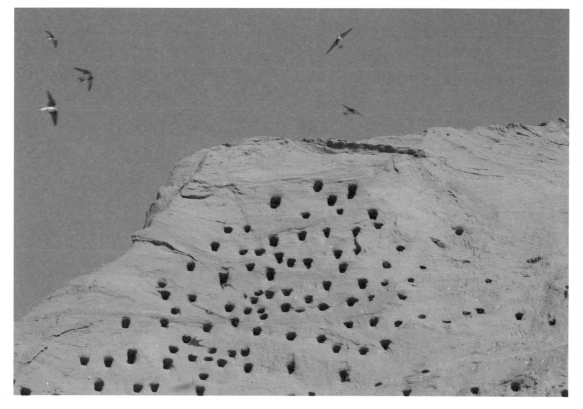

6 Jersey, Channel Islands

Getting there:

Several airlines offer regular scheduled flights from the UK; Condor Ferries operate a car and passenger service from Weymouth, Poole and Portsmouth.

Tel: Jersey Tourism – 01534 500700

Email: info@jersey.com

Opening times: Open daily.

Charging policy: Charges apply for travel and accommodation.

Disabled access: Detailed information available at: www.jersey.com/content_page.asp? id=566&lan=

Find out more

Jersey Tourism
www.jersey.com/

BBC Jersey
www.bbc.co.uk/jersey/

Tarka Sea Trips
www.tarkaseatrips.com/index2.htm

Jersey Sub-Aqua Club
www.jsac.org.uk

If you're cursed with a bit of an adventurous streak and want to explore nature from a completely different perspective, diving is thoroughly recommended. We took the plunge during our visit to Jersey in the Channel Islands and, quite literally, jumped in feet first – oh boy, was the water cold!

If you're a decent swimmer and don't mind a bit of cold water, diving is easy. You can do a course and become qualified in just two weeks – well worth the effort because it opens up a whole different world. Once at neutral buoyancy, you can glide, soar and hover weightlessly over a landscape that is laid out before you – it's wonderful and the closest you'll ever come to being able to fly.

The Channel Islands are geographically closer to France than Britain and so enjoy a pleasantly mild climate. Jersey is the southernmost of the islands and has one of the best sunshine records in the British Isles. It is also surrounded by shimmering, crystal-clear waters.

Now, while diving is lots of fun, it's a bit of a palaver getting into the kit. A neoprene-rubber wetsuit needs to fit snugly and you can go through considerable contortions to get into one. Over that goes a buoyancy jacket, a huge, heavy tank of compressed air and, to add insult to injury, a belt of lead weights. By the time we'd got all this on and staggered down to Bouley Bay on the north coast of Jersey, we were dripping with sweat and positively looking forward to cooling off in the water. With mask and flippers on, we sank beneath the waves, feeling the blissfully cool water creeping up the legs and arms of our wetsuits. The water was remarkably clear and as we finned off towards a rocky outcrop, all the discomfort of being a diver on land left us and we entered into a world which we were now equipped to explore and enjoy.

Just like on land, spring is the time for mating underwater and we were on the hunt for fishy-courtship. Our first find was a black-faced blenny which, as the name suggests, has a black head, but which is coupled with a beautiful, canary-yellow body. We watched him doing his figure-of-eight courtship dance around the drabber-looking female and were reminded of old school discos! Finning a little further, we encountered a corkwing wrasse. The male was sporting his most vivid spring colours – a rusty-red back and yellow underbelly, decorated all over with a filigree pattern of white and turquoise. Unlike the blenny, this fish chooses to entice his mate by building a perfect nursery. He builds a fishy nest out of seaweed, and, if the female is impressed, she'll lay her eggs there for him to fertilise.

By now, after nearly half an hour underwater, the pleasantly cooling waters of Jersey had started to feel uncomfortably cold. We started to fin back to shore, and then we saw it. We couldn't work out what 'it' was at first – a kind of rippling, swimming, torpedo-shaped creature – but as we approached it puffed out a cloud of black ink, and then we knew: it was a cuttlefish, a relative of the squid. It just goes to show, you think you've seen it all and yet still you can be constantly surprised by nature, even at home.

The black-faced blenny

May is the time when cuttlefish lock together, head to head, to mate. If you ever see them, you can spot the male because he's smaller and more vividly coloured. The females mate only once and then die after the eggs are laid; their remains are washed up on the beach as cuttlefish 'bones', which often end up stuck through the bars of bird cages.

Corkwing wrasse

Now, we've only talked about the underwater world of Jersey, but if you don't fancy getting wet, there's just as much to see on land – rock gardens of colourful flowers and meadows full of orchids. Whether you're above or below water, there's just loads to see in Jersey in the spring.

Portelet Bay on the southwest coast of Jersey

7 Culzean, Ayrshire

Getting there:

Culzean Castle and Country Park, Maybole, KA19 8LE. Located 6 kilometres west of Maybole, on the A719. Nearest train station: Maybole (6 kilometres).

Tel: The National Trust for Scotland – 0131 243 9300
Country Park Information – 01655 884400

Email: culzean@nts.org.uk

Opening times: Country Park is open year round. Castle and Garden April–October 10.30am–5pm (daily).

Charging policy: Entry charge ranges according to properties visited – see website.

Disabled access: Disabled parking at visitor centre and Deer Park. Wheelchair access to some parts of gardens and Country Park. Tapping rails on some paths. Induction loop in auditorium

Find out more

National Trust for Scotland
www.nts.org.uk/web/site/home/ visit/places/Property.asp?PropID= 10012&NavPage=10012&NavId=5111

Culzean Experience
www.culzeanexperience.org/

Visit Scotland
www.visitscotland.com/

The 260 hectare Culzean Castle and Country Park in Ayrshire is the most popular National Trust for Scotland property, attracting some 200,000 visitors every year. No wonder it's popular as there's something for everyone here, whether you're a keen ornithologist, a young naturalist wanting to learn more about our sea life or you just like to sit and feed the swans.

Culzean Castle was built by the Scottish architect Robert Adam at the end of the 18th century, and his grand castellated stately home on the clifftop is definitely worth a visit. But if you want to explore the park's wildlife, you can take your pick from a whole range of habitats. There's woodland, ponds, farmland, gardens, parkland, and even a rugged coastline – all of which support a variety of fauna and flora. Good populations of red squirrels and otters have been recorded here, along with 160 species of bird, 4 species of bat, 20 butterflies and well over 300 flowering plants.

We started our day in the woods. The 130 hectare mixed woodland at Culzean is the only significant wooded area on the Ayrshire coast, and 30 kilometres of pathways allow serious exploration. In spring, it's a great place to hear the dawn chorus. Culzean has always been renowned for its warbler population, and when the birds arrive from West and southern Africa to join the resident birds, the volume of song is not to be missed.

But you need to be up early, really early, to hear it at its best. In May, that's about 4.30am. When it was still quite dark, we heard goldcrest with its high-pitched seeping sound, song thrush with its rich and melodic song, and robin, a bird that sings most of the year. Its song is a really sweet, high warbling. There was wren, a little bird with a very big voice, and blackbird – its song has been described as mellow and fluty, even melancholy; some say it's the loveliest song of all.

Light is the key to setting all the birds off and, a little later, we heard the chaffinch. Its song is very loud and

Culzean Castle and Country Park

once it gets going it's difficult to hear anything else! There was also the chiffchaff, which has a very distinctive and very simple song: 'chiff, chaff, chiff, chaff' Next, and music to our ears, the sun stimulated the willow warbler to kick off. Its song is a cascade of notes descending down the scale. The willow warbler looks very similar to the chiffchaff - small, olive-coloured on top with pale underparts - so the difference in song is probably the best way of telling the two apart. In all, we heard 25 species - well worth getting up for.

The most dramatic habitat at Culzean is the five kilometres of cliffs, rocky shore and sandy bays. From the cliff walks you can see across the Firth of Clyde to the Isle of Arran, and paths lead down to the rocky, sheltered beach. Here at low tide with the castle looming up behind you, you can potter about for hours in your wellies in the seaweed-strewn rockpools.

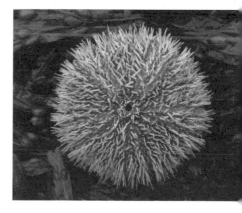

Sea urchin and seaweed

We found scale worms, which make a wave movement with their bodies to move, and brittle stars, which look a bit like starfish. Also spiny sea urchins, which have mouth parts with teeth in the middle of their bodies that they use to pull, tear and rip off algae from the rocks. There were lots of hermit crabs, the squatters of the sea world, who take over empty shells to shelter in, and a male pipe fish, which, when it comes to reproduction, does all the work. Like sea horses, the male carries the eggs in his pouch till they hatch.

There were also plenty of sea slugs, which are molluscs without shells, and very tasty to crabs and birds. When alarmed they shoot out a purple slime, which hides them as they disappear. The beach had a great diversity of creatures. Virtually every rock we turned over had a little gem below. Mind you, our hands did get very cold.

Opposite: Willow warbler in song

8 Calke Abbey, Derbyshire

Getting there:

Calke Abbey, Ticknall, DE73 7LE. Ticknall is between Swadlincote and Melbourne, 16 kilometres south of Derby on the A514. Access from M42/A42, exit 13 and A50 Derby South.

Tel: 01332 863822

Email: calkeabbey@nationaltrust.org.uk

Opening times: Garden mid-March–June and September–October 11am–5pm (Saturday– Wednesday); July–August 11am–5pm (daily). House mid-March–October (Saturday–Wednesday). Park until 8pm or dusk if earlier.

Charging policy: House and garden: Adults £6.80; children £3.40. Garden only: Adults £4.20; children £2.10. Family tickets available.

Disabled access: House - access to part of ground floor. Grounds - see map on website. Braille guide.

A serotine bat

Find out more

National Trust - Calke Abbey
http://www.nationaltrust.org.uk/
main/w-vh/w-visits/w-findaplace/
w-calkeabbey/

BBC Science and Nature - Serotine Bat
www.bbc.co.uk/nature/wildfacts/
factfiles/293.shtml

The baroque mansion of Calke Abbey

We were expecting bats to pour out of Derbyshire's Calke mansion at dusk like a scene from a Gothic *film noir*. Instead, there were only four of them. These four were pretty special, though; they were serotine bats, which are quite rare in the north, and are one of our largest British bats with a wingspan of up to 38 centimetres. They've got long, smoky-brown fur with pale bellies and large, black, triangular-shaped ears. They're easy to recognise in flight because they have a rather slow, erratic style, with sudden dips, swoops and glides.

The serotine bats only visit Calke for a few weeks a year in search of cockchafers (also called May bugs) – large grubs you might see in your garden that turn into big, fat, black beetles. To a bat that weighs little more than a 20 pence piece, one of these is a good meal.

The bats mate in August, but females can store sperm internally throughout the winter during hibernation. Around May, the females set up maternity colonies – 10–50 females gather together in a roost and each one will have, on average, one youngster in early July. At three weeks old the young make their first flight and by the time they're six weeks old, they can forage for themselves. Unfortunately, after filming these serotines on a bat walk, a hobby (a bird of prey) discovered them and ate the lot.

What really gripped our imaginations at Calke was the house itself – a baroque mansion, built 1701–04. It was owned by the Harpur Crewe family and every nook and cranny of the house is crammed with stuffed animals. However, conservationists no longer sanction this kind of approach and Calke is now a haven for living wildlife.

Fallow deer live in the grounds. Having died out following the last inter-glacial period, they were re-introduced by the Normans in the 11th century. Big estates like Calke kept them as ornamental animals in the same way as they might have had a hermit at the bottom of the garden. Spring is a great time to see the deer because it's the calving season. We visited in May and were incredibly lucky to find a female who was giving birth as we crept through the bracken towards her. Let's hope that, unlike the bats, our baby fawn survived.

9 Shapwick Heath, Somerset

Getting there:

One kilometre north of Shapwick village; access is from the A39 and B3151. Nearest car park is at the Peat Moors Centre. Nearest train station: Castle Cary (25 kilometres).

Tel: English Nature site manager – 01458 860120

Email: somerset@english-nature.org.uk

Opening times: Open daily.

Charging policy: Peat Moors Centre: Adults £2.95, Children, Concessions £2.45, Families £9.50.

Disabled access: Wheelchair access to hides, easy-access boardwalk.

A roe buck looking after his territory

Find out more

English Nature - Shapwick Heath Reserve
http://www.english-nature.org.uk/special/nnr/nnr_details.asp?NNR_ID=141

The British Deer Society
www.britishdeersociety.co.uk/PageL3.asp?PageName=Education&PageNameL2=Species&PageNameL3=Roe

Shapwick National Nature Reserve is a major wetland area consisting of 390 hectares of prime wildlife real estate. A former peat harvesting area, the site is now owned by Natural England who have transformed it into a water wilderness of open water, reedbed, wet grassland, fen, scrub and wet woodland.

Being part of such a large wetland, and with such a diversity of habitats, it is not surprising that an incredible variety of wildlife can be seen. This is particularly so in spring when roe deer begin to claim territories for the oncoming rut in summer, the air is filled with the staccato songs of reed and sedge warblers and the explosive call of the Cetti's warbler – everywhere you look, wildlife is gearing up for the breeding season.

Huge numbers of hobbies also arrive in spring, using the reserve to re-fuel before claiming territories elsewhere in the UK. The hobby was a rare breeding bird confined to southern heathlands 30 years ago, but recently the population has increased from just over a 100 pairs to anywhere between 500 and 900 pairs with breeding birds being encountered as far north as Northumberland. As the population of birds breeding in the UK rises, so do the numbers passing through Shapwick. As we counted the birds in the sky, we realised that from one spot we could see 15 different individuals.

The best time to look for roe deer on and around Shapwick is early in the morning. Unlike the red and fallow deer, the roe tends to be a solitary animal, retreating into the wet woodland at night and during most of the day and only coming out to feed in the wet grasslands before most people have risen from their beds. Late spring is an excellent time to look for the bucks as this is the time when their antlers are hard and fully grown, enabling them to establish and defend a territory. While filming a particularly handsome roe buck we were lucky to see him chase a young buck out of his territory right in front of us, and issue a series of short barks to show that he was in charge. This may be the UK's smallest native deer at only 65 centimetres at the shoulder, but he left us in no doubt that he was master of all he surveyed.

Shapwick National Nature Reserve

10 Isle of Skye, Scotland

Getting there:

Regular summer ferry from Mallaig to Armadale; runs less frequently in winter. Road bridge from Kyle of Lochalsh to Kyleakin. Buses run from the mainland to Portree.

Tel: Tourist Information Centre – 01471 822361

Opening times: Open daily.

Charging policy: Ferry charges apply.

Disabled access: See Access Panel website: www.access-panel.org.uk/search-result.php?location=all+locations&business_type=All+businesses&access_type=any

Find out more

Skye
www.skye.co.uk/

Visit Highlands – Skye
www.visithighlands.com/skye/

RSPB – Golden Eagle
www.rspb.org.uk/birds/guide/g/goldeneagle/index.asp

The Isle of Skye, situated off the west coast of mainland Scotland, is the largest and best known of the Inner Hebrides and, put simply, is an awesome place to watch wildlife, particularly if your quarry is eagles. Though it was driven to extinction just under a hundred years ago, dedicated conservation work has now seen the white-tailed eagle returning back to some of its old haunts, and nowhere is it more easily seen than on the Isle of Skye.

At almost two and a half metres, only the crane matches the wingspan of the white-tailed eagle in Britain. Its flight silhouette is massive, with broad, rectangular, deeply fingered wings, a protruding head and a short and, in adults, white wedged tail – this bird is the proverbial flying barn door! Unlike its cousin the golden eagle, the sea eagle is traditionally a coastal bird and territories can spread over 70 square kilometres, with nests usually located on cliff ledges or in the crowns of tall conifers close to the coastline.

Normally we would have very little chance of filming such a rare, elusive and well-protected bird, but we were even hoping to go one step further and feed one! For a few years now, a pair has nested on a crag overlooking the sea, just a small boat ride from the harbour at Portree, an attractive fishing town and the capital of Skye. How well the birds show each year depends on how successful their breeding attempt has been, because if they have not managed to rear any chicks then there are no hungry mouths to feed and the adults have no incentive to find as much food. If, however, they are successfully brooding chicks, the pressure increases to find more food to satisfy their offspring's voracious appetite. We therefore took it as a good omen when we heard the terrific news that the pair were currently rearing three chicks, an almost unprecedented event as it is most unusual for two chicks to survive in the dog-eat-dog world of eagle chicks, let alone three.

The reason why this pair were proving so successful at finding enough food to keep three chicks alive was down to a little help from a couple of enterprising fishermen. It had been noticed by a couple of the Portree fishing boats that hungry eagles would occasionally follow the boats in the manner of seagulls and take any scraps of fish on offer. Following this discovery, a small business has built up whereby birders are taken out of the harbour to see if the eagles can be persuaded to entertain the throng in return for a free lunch.

So it was with some excitement that we boarded the *Stardust* with skipper Dan Corrigall for the 15 minute journey around to where, hopefully, the birds would be perched high up on the crags. On our arrival at the designated spot, Dan told us to train our binoculars at a small distinctive point up on the rock and, lo and behold, sitting exactly where he was indicating, there was an adult sea eagle! The bird must have been at least 500 metres away and far too distant to film on a gently bobbing boat. But Dan had not performed his *pièce de résistance* yet, and to achieve this he pulled out a fish that he'd caught earlier that morning and proceeded to wave it in the air. Eagles, of course, have incredible visual acuity and have no problem picking out the glinting colour of a fish from half a kilometre.

We were treated to the great sight of a white-tailed eagle

The moment the fish was thrown into the water, the eagle took off and we watched in open-mouthed awe as it glided towards the boat. What can only be described as a flying plank came alongside us, folded its wing, spilling air along the way to reduce height, aligned itself with the fish and then finally shot its talons out before plucking the fish off the surface of the water! The bird flew so close to us that we were able to pick out its beautifully pale eye, enormous wedged bill and stunning white tail. As it flew off back to the eyrie, we simply whooped for joy in the full knowledge we had witnessed simply one of the most memorable moments of the series.

Loch Portree on the Isle of Skye

11 Crychan, Powys

Getting there:

Take the A483 northeast from Llandovery for 9 kilometres. At the Glan Bran public house, take road on your right for 5 kilometres.

Tel: Forestry Commission – 01550 720394

Email: llanymddyfri@forestry.gsi.gov.uk

Opening times: Open daily.

Charging policy: Not applicable.

Disabled access: Uneven and sometimes hilly terrain – check with Forestry Commission before visiting. There is no access specifically for disabled users in Crychan.

Find out more

Forestry Commission – Crychan Woods
www.forestry.gov.uk/website/wildwoods.nsf/LUWebDocsByKey/WalesPowysCrychan

Crychan Forest Association
www.crychanforest.org.uk/

Visit Wales
www.visitwales.co.uk/

Forestry Commission – Nightjar
www.forestry.gov.uk/forestry/Nightjar

The nightjar is a mercurial bird; to see one in the UK requires time, luck and dedication. It is one of the last migrants to arrive in late spring and is with us for just a few short months before heading back to sub-Saharan Africa for the rest of the year. It is an uncommon breeding bird in the UK, choosing to nest in remote places such as heath, moorland and young or recently felled forestry plantations.

There are few more suitable places that fit the nightjar's exacting specifications than the huge 4,000 hectare forest of Crychan. This massive mosaic of conifer plantation and open moorland is managed by Forestry Commission Wales and is located in Mid-Wales close to Llandovery.

Crychan is planted predominantly with conifer species such as Douglas fir, larch and Norway spruce, but there are large areas of broadleaf forest too. The topography within the forest is incredibly varied and ranges from numerous ridges and plateaus, affording excellent views across the moorland, to stream-laden valleys winding their way though the forest. While this combination of size and diversity makes Crychan a haven for an incredible array of flora and fauna, its rugged terrain and isolated nature have made it popular too as a rally-driving location and more recently with off-road mountain bikers.

It is, however, the forest edges and moorland that provide the ideal environment for the nightjar. During the day, the grey and brown mottled plumage of this cryptic bird makes it a master of camouflage, and when perched along a branch, instead of across it like other birds, it is almost impossible to see. However, nightjars are much more easily seen during the twilight hours of dawn and dusk when they begin feeding and displaying.

Nine times out of ten if you're in the right habitat at dusk in late spring, the nightjar is a bird that is almost always heard before it is seen, their presence usually being detected by the long drawn out 'churring' calls of the males, a sound guaranteed to make the hairs on your neck stand up! If you're very lucky, you may well see a male flying over the moor with long pointed wings and tail and distinctive white flashes as it displays by clapping its wings in an attempt to impress any unmated females.

The views of nightjar are often frustratingly short, however, and we were hoping to go one better by admiring a nightjar very close up! Tony Cross is an ornithology consultant with permission to trap nightjars for research work, and had placed a mist-net across a small part of

The open moorland of Crychan

the moor in an attempt to place radio-transmitters on the birds to track their movements. Accompanied with a tape recorder to play the nightjar call, designed to attract any nearby birds (a technique that is illegal unless you have a licence), we hid in the heather as dusk approached. Despite being treated to wonderful views of the nightjars as they flew all around us, the birds all seemed to have spotted the net and easily evaded its pockets. As dusk turned into night it looked as though we had failed to lure one into the nets. Undeterred, we closed the nets and retired back to the car for a break. After a few hours, interrupted only by the noise of the army on exercise in the woods, we re-opened the nets before dawn and were almost immediately rewarded with a female that flew into the net, attracted no doubt by a non-existent male 'churring' away from our tape recorder!

And what a stunning bird! Apart from the cryptic plumage, the most noticeable feature was the most enormous pair of eyes, an essential tool for any bird that hunts moths and other night-flying insects. It also has a huge gape and special stiff bristles either side of the bill, designed to effectively increase the size of the mouth to help catch prey. No sooner had we admired the bird, than Tony had attached a very light radio transmitter and the bird was released – a red letter bird on a long but rewarding night.

The nightjar – a master of camouflage

June

June is the month with the longest days and the most daylight, and the wildlife is making the most of it. The naturalist should also be out at all hours: there is so much to see in so little time!

A trip to the coast is an absolute must in June – the best sites being cliff-top headlands where you can witness one of the UK's greatest spectacles. Seabird cliffs are jam-packed with rows of guillemots and razorbills nesting on precipitous ledges, and fulmars and kittiwakes thrown into the mix. On the grassy banks, there may be burrow-nesting puffins, and the whole colony creates a glorious cacophony as individual birds try to make themselves heard above the crowd. On lower-lying coastal spots, tern colonies are also in full swing as they constantly ferry sand-eels back to their mates or young chicks.

June is also the month for orchids and the southern chalk downs have a fine array of rare and stunning species with wonderful names such as military, monkey, lady and lizard! Bats also are very much in evidence – pick out their silhouettes near hedgerows and woodland edges as dusk approaches.

1 Murlough, Northern Ireland

Getting there:

Located 45 minutes from Belfast. Follow signs for Murlough on the A24, just over 3 kilometres south of Dundrum. Ulsterbus no 20 between Belfast and Newcastle to Lazy BJ Caravan Park.

Tel: 028 4375 1467

Email: murlough@nationaltrust.org.uk

Opening times: Open March–May 10am–6pm (weekends, bank holidays), June–September 10am–6pm (daily).

Charging policy: Parking charges apply. Admission charged when facilities are open.

Disabled access: Access for visitors with disabilities.

Find out more

The National Trust in Northern Ireland
www.ntni.org.uk

The Northern Ireland Tourist Board
www.discovernorthernireland.com/Default.aspx

Captain's European Butterfly Guide
www.butterfly-guide.co.uk/species/fritillaries/ukl11.htm

When this part of the County Down coastline was being formed, it can't have been a pleasant place to spend the day. The dunes here are more than 5,000 years old and were topped up in the Middle Ages by sand that came in during a series of violent storms. All that medieval sandblasting can't have been fun. What we've got today, though, is a place that's an absolute cracker and one of the best nature reserves we've visited in Northern Ireland.

Firstly, the location is jaw-droppingly beautiful. Set in the shadow of the Mourne Mountains and Dundrum Bay, it'd be a great place to come even if there wasn't much wildlife. As a bucket and spade location, it's terrific. Thankfully, this is a place that's wildlife rich: from seals to birds of prey, from wading birds to a vast array of moths. As we walked across the beach, we even came across dozens upon dozens of sea potatoes, the brittle shell remains of sea urchins. It wasn't a bad start.

Head into the dunes and you're in a rare and internationally important habitat. This stretch of coastline contains about a fifth of all the dune heathland in the UK. There's something of interest here all year round – from waders and wildfowl in winter, to passing migrants in spring and autumn. In summer, there are two reasons to come. Firstly, this is one of the best spots in the UK to see the marsh fritillary butterfly. If you've never seen one before, then get yourself here pronto. Marsh frits are rich, colourful, Turkish rugs with wings. Remember those deep brown and coffee-coloured carpets that were popular in the 1970s? Well, these are the insect version of that. They're the most brightly patterned of all the fritillaries, and the Irish and Scottish races are an even brighter colour than their cousins in the rest of the UK. They are simply terrific to look at. Your chances of seeing them at Murlough are helped by the fact that marsh fritillaries are poor flyers. Catch them on a cool, overcast day and you'll be rewarded with close-up views, and, even if they do fly off, they won't go that far. This is one of the

reasons why they're not doing that well. Their poor flight and their reliance on a plant called devil's bit scabious on which their caterpillars feed, means they've disappeared from many parts of the UK. It's tough being one of these creatures; they're not that good at colonising new areas. Parts of the Murlough reserve are being managed just for them. Fingers crossed for their future success.

Another reason to head here is for the sheer wealth and variety of flowers in the dunes. Under the rain shadow cast by the Mourne Mountains, what you have are effectively desert-style conditions. This is the result of lime being washed out of the 6,000-year-old dunes and then new lime being added when the medieval storms brought more sand in. So what you get is a real mix of both acid- and lime-loving plants. Tolerating this harsh environment are lime-loving carline thistle and bee orchid rubbing shoulders with acid-loving flowering heather. It's a bit weird, but spectacular none the less.

What really grabbed our attention, though, were the areas of open ground dense with lichen. Now this is a substance you'd normally expect to find hanging from trees or clinging to tombstones, but at Murlough you can find it on the ground – a vast, springy carpet made entirely of this curious mixture of fungi and algae. It's one of our least understood and appreciated life forms. The reason that it's here is that it can tolerate the dry, hostile conditions – with the morning dew providing it with just enough moisture to survive. The lichens flourish here because no other plant can compete. Get a hand lens out and you'll see this stuff in all its majestic glory. Lichen can live for thousands of years and their structures make a cathedral seem like a simple design.

All in all, Murlough is a top spot. Take your bucket and spade by all means, but make sure you take your field guides as well. You won't regret it.

Murlough in the shadow of the Mourne mountains

The cinnabar moth

An elephant hawkmoth at Murlough

Opposite: The marsh fritillary butterfly

2 Skokholm Island, Wales

Getting there:

Dale Princess from Martins Haven, near Marloes to South Haven. Telephone Islands Booking Officer for information on day trips, which are subject to change due to weather.

Tel: Islands Booking Officer, Wildlife Trust West Wales – 01437 765462

Email: info@welshwildlife.org

Opening times: Summer: day visits (usually Mondays) organised by National Parks. Holiday breaks available.

Charging policy: All holidays are full board and include return boat fare.

Disabled access: The island has limited medical assistance beyond basic first aid, and a lack of medical supplies should your stay be prolonged due to bad weather.

Find out more

The Wildlife Trust of South and West Wales
www.welshwildlife.org

RSPB – Manx Shearwater
www.rspb.org.uk/birds/guide/m/manxshearwater/index.asp

RSPB – Storm Petrel
www.rspb.org.uk/birds/guide/s/stormpetrel/index.asp

Skokholm Island is a 100 hectare lump of red sandstone, which lies four kilometres off the Pembrokeshire coast at the southwest tip of Wales. Bought by The Wildlife Trust of South and West Wales in 2006, this island may be small, but it is packed to the gunnels with a whole array of seabirds during the summer months. With its neighbouring islands, Skomer and Grassholm, it forms one of the most important seabird breeding sites in the whole of the UK.

Skokholm is the ultimate getaway, catering for a maximum of 15 residential visitors a week who are looked after by the husband-and-wife wardening team. This multi-faceted pair spends from spring to autumn on the island working as ornithologists, cooks and tour reps all rolled into one!

As soon as we arrived at the harbour in South Haven, we were greeted by a large colony of puffins sitting outside their burrows on a grassy bank as they took in the morning air. The puffin must surely be one of the most instantly recognisable birds in the whole of the UK, resembling, as it does, a foot-high clown. Like most breeding seabirds, puffins nest in colonies, primarily because large numbers offer protection against the marauding gulls which constantly try to steal hard won sand-eels, or even worse kill and eat unwary chicks venturing too close to the burrow entrances. Wonderful though the puffins were, our prime quarry was a couple of Skokholm's other seabirds, the storm petrel and the Manx shearwater.

The storm petrel is one of those birds that you'll spend a whole lifetime without seeing unless you make it the subject of a special mission. About the size of, and superficially similar to, a house martin, this is a bird that, when not breeding at places such as Skokholm, spends its whole life way out at sea as far south as the western Atlantic off the coast of South Africa. The 'stormie' as it is known, is largely a sooty black colour with a vivid white band across its rump and a thick white stripe along the underside of its wing. Despite the fact that thousands of pairs are thought to breed in the old drystone walls that criss-cross the island, they are rarely seen during daylight, choosing the protection of the cover of darkness to come out for a feeding trip or to return to their burrows. The easiest way to find the location of the stormie burrows is to listen for its prolonged call, a constant churring sound that is interrupted at regular intervals by a 'hiccup', and which has been memorably described as sounding like a fairy being sick!

After brief views with a special infra-red camera to see the storm petrels fluttering up and down the wall as they prepared to go and feed for the night, we left them for a rendezvous with a bigger and much noisier nocturnal breeding seabird, the Manx shearwater. Skokholm has a population of around 46,000 pairs of 'manxies', which, together with the 102,000 pairs on the neighbouring Island of Skomer, are thought to make up almost half of the world population of this wonderful yet mysterious seabird. During daylight hours, when there was not a single manxie to be seen, it was astonishing to think that there were literally thousands of birds in burrows below our very feet. Like the storm petrel, the manxie only comes ashore to breed, and usually to offshore islands which are free of the dreaded brown rat, a ruthless alien invader that has decimated many a fine seabird island. Sticking to the burrow-free paths, we made our way to the lighthouse, the area with the highest concentration of burrows on the island. Like the storm petrel, the Manx shearwater is a nocturnal seabird that is usually heard before seen, and listening to the crowing, cooing, howling and screaming of the shearwaters as pairs located each other in the dark was a very eerie experience.

Everywhere we walked, we encountered manxies either waddling to their burrows, or the classic flickering black and white of these stiff-winged, long-distance travellers as they flew past us and out to their feeding grounds. And as we stood in the middle of the bedlam, we felt we had truly encountered the ultimate Skokholm experience!

The Manx shearwater, or manxie

A rare sight – a storm petrel, or 'stormie'

The lighthouse on Skokholm Island

3 Walney Island, Cumbria

Getting there:

From Barrow-in-Furness follow signs on the A590 for Walney Island. Cross Jubilee Bridge and turn left at traffic lights; after about 1 kilometre turn left down Carr Lane. Pass Biggar village and follow the road to the South End Caravan Site. Take the unmetalled road for a further kilometre until the reserve is reached.

Tel: 01539 816300

Email: mail@cumbriawildlifetrust.org.uk

Opening times: Open summer 10am–5pm, winter 10am–4pm; closed Mondays.

Charging policy: Adults £2, children 50p, free for Trust members.

Disabled access: Two nature trails and one hide have wheelchair access.

Find out more

Cumbria Wildlife Trust
http://www.wildlifetrust.org.uk/cumbria/Index.htm

South Walney Wildlife Reserve
http://www.wildlifetrust.org.uk/cumbria/Reserves/South%20Walney.htm

Naturalists often get carried away with rarities. The rarer the species, the more excited they get. We like our rarities too on *Nature's Calendar*. What we like best, though, are natural spectacles where one or two species flourish in one location: vast meadows blooming with orchids; a pond packed with great crested newts; or a nature reserve resplendent with the sight and sound of tens of thousands of seabirds.

Walney Island is just the place for one of these experiences. It's here you get one of the best, and closest, encounters with birds anywhere on the west coast of the UK. What they have at South Walney are gulls – lots and lots of gulls. The two main species are herring gulls – these are the kind that try and pinch your chips at the seaside – and the rarer and marginally smaller, lesser black-backed gull. There are about 14,000 breeding pairs of gulls here, and in summer it's the noisiest and most exhilarating spot to spend a day. The reason? Come in June or July when these birds are nesting and they defend their territories with gusto. That's why the staff at the Cumbria Wildlife Trust reserve office offer you a hardhat and a cane. If you have any sense, you'll accept their kind gesture. The stick will be useful to wave above you to prevent the gulls from getting too close; the hat to stop them pooing on your head. And believe us, these birds are pretty good at finding their human targets!

While you negotiate bomb alley, you'll get a feeling of being right in the thick of it with thousands of birds in the air at any one time. Below you, there are nests with clutches of eggs or squawking chicks. The noise is so loud that you'll feel you should have been offered earplugs as well. However, this is a brilliant spot and it's rare to get such a complete bird experience in one place – the sight, the sound and the smell, too.

These are two species of birds that some naturalists get a bit sniffy about. They're only gulls, they'll tell you. These, though, are underrated animals: get your bins or scope on them and you'll see the intense red ring around

their eyes and the bright red spot on the end of their bills. This red bill mark is what the chicks peck at to encourage the adults to regurgitate food. It's not a pretty sight, but it's fast food, gull style. The reason why the gull colony is here is partly because of the isolation and security that the reserve provides, but also there's the Irish Sea, Morecambe Bay and refuse tips just a few minutes' flying time away. There's plenty of food there for these gulls to exploit.

Take the journey to the northern end of Walney and you'll have a very different experience. The sound of the gulls is left behind and you're in a wonderful sand dune system that's been allowed to develop in its own unique way in the shadow of the western fringes of the Lake District. It's here you'll find the Walney geranium, a variety of cranesbill, with the most delicate pale pink petals. It really is a stunner. There are also plenty of the more common bloody cranesbill and it's a riot of pale pink and magenta where you get the two species side by side.

North Walney's claim to fame, though, is as a place to find one of our real amphibian rarities. This corner of the UK is a hotspot for the natterjack toad, a creature that has declined across the UK and remains under intense pressure. Come to Walney in spring and you'll be greeted by the night-time chorus of singing male toads. It's as if you've been taken to the Amazon. Come in summer, and you'll see the result of all that courtship, with the quickly evaporating slacks full of tiny natterjack toadlets. They may only be a fraction of the size of their mum and dad, but get down on your hands and knees and you'll see they share the same top quality paint job as their parents, with a distinctive yellow stripe down their backs. Remember, though, that this is a protected species and can't be disturbed or handled. Nevertheless, they're a wonder that should be marvelled at and cherished by us all.

Natterjack toads mating

Opposite: The black-backed gull

4 The Fleet Lagoon, Dorset

Getting there:

Located between Chesil Beach and the mainland of the Dorset shore, just west of Weymouth and the Isle of Portland. The Fleet Lagoon can be accessed by the A354 or the B3157.

Tel: Chesil Beach and Fleet Lagoon Nature Reserve – 01305 760579 Swannery – 01305 871858

Email: info@abbotsbury-tourism.co.uk

Opening times: Fleet Lagoon open year round. Trips on the *Fleet Observer* Easter-October. Chesil Beach Centre April-September 11am-6pm, October-March 11am-4pm. Swannery open summer 10am-5/6pm

Charging policy: Fleet Lagoon and Chesil Beach Centre not applicable. Swannery Adult £7.50, Children £4.50, Senior/Disabled £7. Family tickets and season tickets available.

Disabled access: Disabled access at the Swannery. No wheelchair access on the *Fleet Observer*.

Find out more

Abbotsbury tourism
www.abbotsbury-tourism.co.uk/

The Village of Abbotsbury Website
www.abbotsbury.co.uk/

The Fleet Observer
www.thefleetobserver.co.uk/

Not many people can say that they own a herd of swans, but one Dorset family have done precisely that since the period in which Henry VIII did his level best to get rid of the monasteries in the 16th century. More than 400 years later, the mute swans of Abbotsbury are a thriving local tourist attraction. You have to pay to see them, but what a sight – there are swans everywhere.

In early summer, the main attraction is the cygnets. You may be lucky enough to see eggs hatch right in front of your eyes; if not, you will certainly get some great close-up views of the fluffy white chicks. The adult swans on the nest are so used to people that they show no aggression beyond the occasional disgruntled hiss.

Abbotsbury is the only managed nesting colony of swans in the world and it boasts the world's only swan herd. As barrowloads of grain are dished out to the waiting swans, you can learn more about their history from the staff.

The swans at Abbotsbury were originally managed for meat by the Benedictine monks of the local monastery. They are no longer eaten, but their shed feathers are still a useful resource – among other things being turned into quills for calligraphers and providing the feathers which go to decorate the helmets of the Queen's Bodyguard: The Gentlemen at Arms.

In the height of summer there are feathers everywhere because this is when the swans moult and, as they do so, become flightless. At this time of year there are more swans at Abbotsbury than at any other time – not just because of the cygnets, but because the colony is joined by outsiders seeking safety in numbers as our heaviest flying bird becomes vulnerable. One clever trick of nature is that the females moult first. The males hang onto their feathers for an extra couple of weeks so that they can continue to defend their territories and their young.

The reason the swans are here at all is down to a very special body of water known as the Fleet lagoon, one of Britain's largest tidal lagoons. This 13 kilometre stretch of water is divided from the sea by an enormous bank of shingle known as Chesil Beach. The swannery is at the western end of the lagoon, while at the eastern end the lagoon meets the sea through a narrow entrance at Ferrybridge. The lagoon provides underwater meadows of eel grass, on which the swans love to graze – a single swan can consume about 4 kilos of plant food a day. But the eel grass isn't just food for the swans; it provides shelter for lots of other marine life and contains an important sea-bass nursery.

At the eastern end of the lagoon it's possible to take a trip aboard *The Fleet Observer*, a shallow, glass-bottomed boat, to learn a bit about the history of the coastline and to explore the bottom of the lagoon. Here you will find a quite extraordinary number of sea anemones, as well as scuttling crabs and the occasional startled fish. You may also spot little terns flying to and from their breeding colony on the Chesil Bank. This is one of our most-threatened terns, a summer visitor, and the colony is monitored by the RSPB to try to minimise disturbance.

If you've got time, take a walk along the Chesil Bank with the sea on one side and the lagoon on the other. Walking on shingle is great for the leg muscles! Chesil Beach is an extraordinary geological feature which is believed to have formed at the end of the ice age. Ten thousand years ago, when the ice began to melt, there would have been huge landslides caused by flooding and it's thought that the material from these landslides was washed along the coast from Devon to Dorset to form this impressive shingle bank. You can find out more at the visitor centre at Ferrybridge, which has impressive views of the Fleet and offers talks and guided walks.

The Chesil Bank has been partially breached by the sea in the past and is slowly moving inland, but for now, ten thousand years on, it is still doing an incredibly good job of protecting the lagoon and its rich wildlife, including the unique Abbotsbury swans.

The shingle bank of Chesil Beach

The mute swans of Abbotsbury swannery

5 How Hill, Norfolk

Getting there:

Major trunk roads to the Broads are the M11, A11, A12, A140 and A14 from London, the South East of England, ferry ports and the Channel Tunnel. How Hill is near Ludham, situated between Horning and Potter Heigham, along the River Ant.

Tel: Broads Authority – 01603 610734

Email: Enquiry form at www. broads-authority.gov.uk/contact.html

Opening times: Most broads and nature reserves are open daily.

Charging policy: Not applicable.

Disabled access: See Easier Access Leaflet at www.broads-authority. gov.uk/broads/live/visiting/access-for-all/Easier_Access_leaflet_05.pdf

Herringfleet Mill and the Broads at sunset

Find out more

Norfolk Nature Reserve – How Hill
www.norfolkcoast.co.uk/articles/ howhill.htm

Broads Authority
www.broads-authority.gov.uk

Swallowtail Central
www.swallowtailbutterfly.com/

The spectacular swallowtail butterfly

In early summer the Norfolk Broads is a place that literally hums with insects, most noticeably dragonflies patrolling the ditches and butterflies skimming past on their daily business. At this time of year, most 'insectphiles' usually head to the Broads with just one thing in mind, to see the UK's largest and most spectacular butterfly, the swallowtail. This butterfly is found nowhere else in the UK and at the right location, in the middle of June on a bright sunny day, a swallowtail sighting is virtually guaranteed.

How Hill is a little gem set in the heart of the Norfolk Broads on the banks of the River Ant. It is managed by the How Hill Trust and happens to be one of the best places to catch up with the swallowtails as they flit across fen and dyke in search of nectar, food and mates.

One of the best ways to catch up with this butterfly is to find its food plant. Milk parsley is a plant largely confined to the Norfolk Broads and always found along the dyke edges. The plant resembles cow parsley with its abundant white flower heads and leaves, similar to the fine feathery fronds you'd find on a carrot. A good way to see this plant, and navigate large tracts of this watery wilderness, is of course from a small boat. Unfortunately we weren't lucky enough to see any females actively egg-laying from our boat, but we did manage to find a couple of tiny, beautifully sculpted eggs that had already been laid.

Abandoning the boat, we headed back to the guided fen trail at How Hill to search for a clump of their nectar plants, such as meadow thistles, in the hope that the butterflies would stop to nectar there. A likely clump on the edge of the fen was duly located and scarcely had we waited ten minutes than a beautifully marked adult spiralled down from above and landed on one of the thistle heads. With its proboscis fully unfurled taking in the nectar, the swallowtail continued to pump its wings and in ten seconds, one flower drained, it fluttered to an adjacent flower. After an intense minute of working the thistles, the butterfly was off, up and away.

6 The Slad and Stroud Valleys, The Cotswolds

Getting there:

The M4 and M5 run through Stroud; coaches run from London Victoria. Nearest train stations: Stroud and Stonehouse.

Tel: Stroud Tourist Information – 01453 760960
Jim Fern (guided walks) – 01453 753104.

Email: tic@stroud.gov.uk

Opening times: Open daily.

Charging policy: Not applicable.

Disabled access: Stagecoach buses to explore the area are wheelchair friendly. Limited wheelchair access to Valleys – wet weather can create muddy terrain.

The picture postcard Cotswold valleys

Find out more

Official Stroud Tourism Website
www.visitthecotswolds.org.uk/walking.asp

Cotswold Walks and Guided Tours
www.cotswoldwalks.co.uk

Highways Agency – Adonis Blue
www.highways.gov.uk/aboutus/documents/gsld_feat_adonis_blue_btfly.pdf

The Slad and Stroud Valleys make up one of Britain's largest Areas of Outstanding Natural Beauty. This is Laurie Lee's *Cider with Rosie* country and it's home to a butterfly that was once extinct in this part of the world but now, thanks to some careful land management, is making an astonishing comeback. It's the Adonis blue.

We visited the Cotswolds in June and got up early to comb the hillsides. It's not actually that difficult to see Adonis blues because of their dazzling, iridescent colour – brighter than the bluest sky on a sunny day, which is of course the best time to see them. The rule of thumb is that if you're in any doubt about the colour, then it's NOT an Adonis blue, it's a common blue, which looks very similar but is just not as blue. As is often the case in the natural world, it's only the males that have such vibrant colour; females are a rather dowdy brown.

The sole food plant for the Adonis blue caterpillar is horseshoe vetch, which only grows in short-cropped grass. But the food plant isn't the only key to their survival. Adonis blue butterflies do rely on horseshoe vetch as the principal food for their offspring, but like other species of blue butterfly they have developed a bizarre relationship with ants. The caterpillars of the Adonis blue butterfly secrete a sugary solution which ants love; in return, the ants nurture and protect both caterpillar and chrysalis from predators. Now, while we knew this for a fact, we didn't think we had any chance of ever capturing it on film. But then we had one of those wild strokes of luck that just – forgive the pun – come out of the blue. Our wildlife cameraman disturbed a rock and spotted an Adonis blue chrysalis tucked into the base of the grass being lovingly attended to by ants. We could see the ants scurrying over and around it and could even see the bright blue of the wings beneath the fragile husk of the chrysalis. On reflection, it was like looking at the dull, grey, pebble shape of an uncut diamond, yet knowing it was about to break out into a multifaceted blaze of glory.

The stunning Adonis blue butterfly

7 Gilfach Farm, Powys

Getting there:

Gilfach is just off the A470,
11 kilometres from Llangurig and
3 kilometres from Rhayader. Follow the
brown Gilfach Nature Reserve signs.

Tel: Gilfach Nature Reserve – 01597
870301

Email: info@radnorshirewildlifetrust.
org.uk

Opening times: Visitor Centre April–
July 10am–5pm (Friday–Monday), July–
September 10am–4.30pm (daily).

Charging policy: Not applicable.

Disabled access: There is disabled
access to the Centre, toilets and on a
purpose-built trail.

Find out more

Radnorshire Wildlife Trust – Gilfach
Farm
**www.radnorshirewildlifetrust.org.
uk/gilfach.htm**

Gilfach Farm Nature Reserve
http://westwales.co.uk/gilfach.htm

Bird Guides – Pied Flycatcher
**www.birdguides.com/html/vidlib/
species/Ficedula_hypoleuca.htm**

You go to Gilfach Farm primarily for the birds – dippers, pied flycatchers and red kites are drawn to the valley where the rivers Marteg and Wye meet in the Cambrian Mountains of Mid-Wales. Gilfach is a traditional Welsh hill farm, which dates back to at least the 15th century. It's now owned by the Radnorshire Wildlife Trust, who have restored the ancient field boundaries: the stone walls, hedgerows and banks, together with a medieval longhouse – a traditional Welsh building used to house both people and animals, and now a visitor attraction in its own right. The 153 hectare farm is special not just because it connects its visitors to medieval times, but because it managed to escape most of the agricultural intensification of the late 20th century. It is now farmed organically.

There's a great range of habitats on the farm – from rocky upland river, where dippers bob and dive in the clear running water, to hedgerow-enclosed meadows rich in grassland plants and butterflies. It's this variety of habitats that provides so much to see. To help you explore it, there are well-signposted walks as well as a visitor centre and guided activities. From here you can go bird and badger watching, or take the children on insect hunts. A favourite find is the bloody-nosed beetle, an insect that gets its name from its habit of spewing out a foul, blood-like substance from its mouth when it feels threatened.

Among the most extraordinary features of the landscape are the anthill meadows, whose lumps and bumps could be hundreds of years old and which are regularly visited by green woodpeckers in search of an ant snack.

But it's the oak woodland that draws the most dapper bird on the farm – the pied flycatcher, a real Gilfach speciality. In summer, the male is jet black on top with white underparts, a white-edged tail, a big white patch across each wing and a white patch on his forehead just above his bill. In winter, when he returns to West Africa, he will become almost as brown and inconspicuous as the female – although he keeps the telltale white patch on his forehead throughout the year. As its name suggests, the pied flycatcher is an insect-eating bird and that's the main reason it loves oak trees. Oak trees support a wider variety of invertebrates than any other kind of tree in the UK – an estimated 500 different species. Pied flycatchers, of course, don't just catch flies; they'll happily feed on caterpillars, bees, beetles, woodlice and ants (and, in early autumn, berries). This readiness to adapt allows them to survive the cooler April days when they first arrive in the UK before many insects are on the wing. Pied flycatchers spend most of their time darting about the tree canopy, making them quite difficult to see. Early summer is your best opportunity – the birds have young in the nest and up to seven mouths to feed, so they're more active than usual flying to and from the holes or nest boxes in the tree where the female has constructed her nest.

Pied flycatchers are often found near fast-running streams, and that's almost certainly because where there's water you'll find plenty of winged insects. This, of course, is exactly where to find one of *Nature's Calendar's* favourite birds – the dipper. An easy way to tell if dippers are about is to look for droppings on the rocks in the middle of the water and then, if you sit quietly, you are practically guaranteed a sighting. This remarkable songbird is able to feed when completely submerged in fast-flowing water. It can swim underwater using its wings, and can even walk along the bottom with the wings held out to prevent it bobbing back up. Dippers hunt by sight under the water and have a transparent eyelid known as a nictitating membrane, which protects the eye when submerged, as well as a membrane above the nostrils which can be closed when the bird dives – the equivalent of us holding our noses underwater. Although not everyone on the *Nature's Calendar* team agrees, this bird has been crowned our King of Birds, and it turns out we're not alone in thinking it's special. According to the RSPB, in the High Atlas mountains of Morocco some Berber tribesmen hunt dippers because they think they have aphrodisiac properties. We prefer to watch them bobbing and curtseying on the rocks, and to contemplate the fact that, as yet, nobody knows why they do it.

Dippers bob and dive in the rivers

A pied flycatcher, a Gilfach speciality

8 Thorp Perrow, North Yorkshire

Getting there:

The arboretum is 6½ kilometres from Leeming Bar on the A1, just south of Bedale on the Bedale-Ripon road. Parking.

Tel: 01677 425323

Email: louise@thorpperrow.com

Opening times: Arboretum open year round dawn–dusk. Visitor facilities/falcons from mid–February to mid–November.

Charging policy: Adult £5.95, Senior citizen £4.60, Children (4–16) £3.10. Family, group, school and season ticket rates.

Disabled access: Electric wheelchair available. Facilities at tearoom and bird of prey centre.

Find out more

Thorp Perrow
www.thorpperrow.com

Bird of Prey Centre
www.falconrycentre.co.uk

Bumblebee pages
www.bumblebee.org/faq.htm

Thorp Perrow Arboretum holds one of Britain's finest private collections of trees and shrubs – 1,744 different species at the last count. In fact, you can take a veritable world tour of trees here by simply strolling around its 35 hectares of land. There are tree trails to follow, a nature trail and a children's trail, and even a wildflower area and a mini-beast station. It's all set in the beautiful, unspoiled countryside of the Yorkshire Dales, a stone's throw from the historic town of Bedale.

There's a huge range of shape and colour on offer at Thorp Perrow, but more interestingly there are masses of different textures of bark. Now, you may not be a tree-hugger, but you'll certainly find it hard to resist a bit of bark-touching here. You might even like to take your camera along for a few close-ups.

Though we saw giant trees such as sequoia or redwood at Thorp Perrow, we also encountered some smaller things of interest. On a single plant, we discovered five species of bumblebee – not surprising for an area brimming with so many nectar-producing shrubs and flowers – but what possessed us to try and handle an insect that buzzes and potentially stings? The knack? You just have to be able to tell males from females, because it's only the female bumblebees (or workers) that sting. It sounds simple but, in reality, telling them apart is tricky and you'll probably need a lot of experience in identification – so don't try this at home, folks! Once sexed, we were amazed at how soft and furry the males are. The one we stroked seemed quite unperturbed and just waved its legs about in minor protest. But this was no ordinary bumblebee. We were stroking a cuckoo bumblebee and, to the untrained eye, they look exactly like any other bumblebee, but there are subtle differences.

Bumblebees make a buzzing sound called 'booming', whereas the cuckoo bees' buzz is known as 'murmuring'.

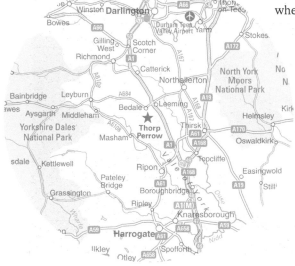

A bumblebee – but is it a male or a female?

They also exhibit quite different behaviour to your typical busy bee. The cuckoo bees we observed moved slowly and sluggishly, pausing for a long time on a single flower and not appearing to actively collect pollen as the other bees around them were frantically doing. The reason for this? The clue is in the name – the cuckoo bumblebee follows its avian namesake, as it has developed a similar sneaky trick. It hoodwinks other bumblebees into nurturing and feeding its offspring. This is why the cuckoo bee doesn't have to use up all its energy dashing around collecting pollen to feed its young.

A female cuckoo bumblebee will sneak into a bumblebee nest in early summer. At first she's attacked by the bumblebee workers, but eventually she's accepted by the colony as queen. She then kills the bumblebee queen and starts laying her eggs, which are cared for by the duped bumblebee workers in the host nest. The eggs hatch out in larvae and once they've become adult, they leave the nest and feed on nectar gathered from flowers. As Thorp Perrow has such a bumper crop of bees, it is therefore a great place to look for this wolf in sheep's clothing. Summer is the best time to see cuckoo bumblebees because the queens go into hibernation in the autumn and the males die before the onset of winter.

Bark of the English Oak

Bumblebees are not the only animals to see at Thorp Perrow, however. There are some lovely stretches of open water, which attract dragonflies and damselflies by day and Daubenton's bats by night. There's even a falconry which gives daily flying demonstrations and as a bonus there's a good café. So if you want a great day out seeing anything from giant redwoods to bumblebees, put Thorp Perrow on your list – go on, *bee* amazed!

Opposite: The cuckoo bumblebee has a softer buzz than the bumblebee

9 The Kent Downs

Getting there:

The Kent Downs are bounded on the north by the M2, the south by the M20 and the west by the M25. Nearest train stations: Chilham, Wye, Charing, Lenham and Hollingbourne.

Tel: 01303 815170

Email: mail@kentdowns.org.uk

Opening times: Downs open year round. Contact specific attractions for more information.

Charging policy: Not applicable. Contact specific attractions for more information.

Disabled access: Differs according to location. See websites for full information.

Find out more

Kent Downs AONB
www.kentdowns.org.uk

The Woodland Trust
www.woodland-trust.org.uk

Kent Wildlife Trust
www.kentwildlifetrust.org.uk

Orchid Habitats – Britain's Orchids
www.britainsorchids.fieldguide.co.uk/?P=habitats&SHC=1&PSD=1

There is something about orchids that appeals to naturalists more than any other group of flowers in the UK; their very name conjures up images of rare plants with exotic-looking blooms. While it's true that the vast majority of species of orchid do live an epiphytic lifestyle halfway up trees in locations such as the Andean cloud forests, we don't do so badly for them in the UK. With no fewer than 56 species of native wild orchid, pick a nice warm day in the right place in the middle of June and you should be able to see at least a dozen without any bother.

Orchids can generally be found in a huge diversity of sites, ranging from Scottish pinewoods to Norfolk fens, but the habitat generally considered to have the greatest variety of orchids and sheer number of spikes is that of the 'unimproved' and soil-poor chalk downs of southern England. Most of East Kent has this habitat in abundance and, when combined with the fact that this corner of the UK also has warm continental summers, it is no surprise to find a number of rare UK species at wonderful Kentish reserves such as Park Gate Down.

Our mission was to see how many species we could find in one day and, on entering the reserve, which consists of eight hectares of chalk grassland managed by the Kent Wildlife Trust, we realised we had started at the right place. The site simply had the most orchids we had ever seen in one place and wherever we looked there were huge clusters of orchid spikes. Apparently in good years there are over 10,000 spikes in the three meadows, and from where we were standing this looked like a woeful under-exaggeration! In certain places, it was almost impossible to walk for fear of stepping on the more abundant fragrant, pyramidal and common spotted orchids as we attempted to track down our first supremely rare orchid, the monkey.

It is found in only three sites in the whole of the UK, two of which are in Kent, so we approached a fine-looking monkey orchid specimen with due care and reverence, knowing we would not be welcomed back should a

Poppies around a field in the Kent Downs

stray camera case be carelessly placed on top of one of these supremely rare flowers. On hands and knees is the best way to appreciate an orchid of this star quality and, on closer inspection, the individual flowers that make up the flower spike did have more than a passing resemblance to a spider monkey, with the hood forming the head and the long, curvy lobes of the lip the slender arms and legs of this tropical primate. Park Gate Down had another rarity up its sleeve, though, and scarcely 50 metres away was a single-flowering lady orchid. Despite this specimen having gone slightly over, the sepals and petals which formed the lady's dark bonnet and the lip representing her crinoline ballgown were still very discernible! After a couple of hours, we had totted up eight species and were off to our next site, Queendown Warren.

Queendown Warren is another site managed by the Kent Wildlife Trust and, although similar in habitat to Park Gate Down, a slightly differing microclimate meant this site had a different suite of orchids. Here we were able to see three more species of orchid not seen that day, including the famous bee orchid, white helleborine and, another Kent speciality, the man orchid with, you've guessed it, man-like flowers – complete with two narrow 'arms' and two narrow 'legs'!

Having now seen eleven species of orchid, our last site was the Royal St George's Golf Club at Sandwich. This famous golf course has been the site of 13 major Open championships, the last being held in 2003, but chances are slight that Tiger Woods would have realised he was walking right past one of the most famous orchid sites in the UK!

Look closely in the rough near the beach and sure enough you are likely to encounter the flowering spikes of one of our tallest and most bizarre orchids, the lizard. With a strange smell of billy goat, and flowers that do bear a fanciful resemblance to lizards, this is an orchid that is once seen, never forgotten. One day and twelve orchids; Kent truly is an orchid twitcher's paradise!

The spectacular lady orchid

Opposite: Close-up view of the Bee orchid

10 The Golden Valley, Herefordshire

Getting there:

Accessible from the B4348 on the eastern edge of the area. Bus route 39 serves the area on Sundays and Bank Holiday Mondays. Nearest train and coach stations: Hereford and Abergavenny.

Tel: 01497 831496

Email: info@golden-valley.co.uk

Opening times: Open daily. Contact specific attractions for more information.

Charging policy: Not applicable. Contact specific attractions for more information.

Disabled access: Varies according to location. See websites for more information.

Find out more

The Golden Valley Experience
www.golden-valley.co.uk

Environment Agency - River Dore Water Vole project
www.environment-agency.gov.uk/ subjects/recreation/345720/ 974815/974854/976981/1344099/ ?version=1&lang=_e

River Monnow Project
www.monnow.org.uk

The Golden Valley in Herefordshire has a diverse literary heritage. It was the inspiration for C S Lewis' *Chronicles of Narnia* and you can see why – razor-sharp hills, secret valleys and rolling pasture are all part of this hidden gem that's off the usual tourist trail. The valley is also home to a fictional character, Ratty, in Kenneth Grahame's *The Wind in the Willows*, who is not actually a rat but a water vole. The rivers Dore and Monnow running through the Golden Valley used to be prime water vole habitats, but the species has declined dramatically throughout the country. When we visited the Golden Valley in June, we were privileged to see the first release of water voles back into the Monnow.

You can tell a water vole from a brown rat because they are smaller with a more rounded body, tiny, half-hidden round ears, a blunt muzzle, bright orange teeth due to the build up of iron, and a shorter, lighter-haired tail. It's a shame that they're disappearing because this is one of Britain's most ancient British mammals; fossils have been found in the Thames Valley and Norfolk dating back to the Pleistocene era. They live on river banks and use their large incisors to burrow into the sides of streams to create a system of tunnels and chambers. The entrance is usually just below the surface of the water to help protect them from their natural predators – weasels, stoats, foxes and herons.

As you'd expect, water voles are very good swimmers. They're mainly vegetarian, eating around 227 plant species, but will also take insects, molluscs and occasionally dead fish. Each female has a territory of about 70 metres along the edge of the river bank, and during the breeding season between March and September she will produce up to four litters, each with three to nine young. The reason these mammals are profligate is because natural predation levels can reduce the population of youngsters by up to 70 per cent. Males patrol larger territories, about 170 metres in length, which encompass several female territories. Even if you don't see the animals themselves, you might see their latrines which are used to mark out the edge of the territories and which will be full of torpedo-shaped droppings.

Derek Gow, a water vole expert, has bred water voles for over a decade and has honed his technique until he has been able to release hundreds of them – 500 at the last count – back into this stretch of the River Monnow, starting when we visited in summer 2006. The voles have a 'soft release': they're put in a wire cage by the river bank that they can get in and out of. When they feel confident enough, they'll set up territories of their own.

But simply releasing the voles is not enough. The worst offenders, as far as these creatures are concerned, are the North American mink that have escaped from mink farms and can hoover up water voles as if they were mere canapés at a cocktail party. Various schemes are in place to try and catch the mink and a tracking device has been developed to pinpoint where they live. A floating raft containing soft clay is just too tempting for the inquisitive mink, who will check it out and leave their telltale footprints behind.

A lot of work has been done to try and restore the River Monnow to its former beauty. Over the past five years, more than 60 kilometres of the river bank have been restored, including coppicing and fencing off the side of the river so that cattle don't erode and damage the water's edge. Now the river is once more home to enough brown trout for fishing to recommence, and our own native crayfish is also making a comeback. The River Monnow is lovely and holds the added attraction of water voles, but the surrounding hills are great for rambling around. And don't forget a final stop at the delightful town of Hay-on-Wye, where there are more secondhand bookshops than anywhere else in the country. A lovely spot to pick up a natural history guidebook, as well as a clutch of novels: *Wind in the Willows*, anyone?

A water vole feeding in the reeds

The inspirational Golden Valley in summer

July

While July is one of the warmest months, it is also a 'crossroads'. Many songbirds fall quiet as they raise broods and feed newly fledged young, and wildfowl and seabirds begin to reach the end of their breeding season. However, it is well worth watching out for newly fledged birds of prey in July as they learn their aerial ropes. An abundance of juvenile birds will also test your identification skills!

Many flowers reach their peak in July and a super-abundance of insects facilitates pollination. In agricultural areas, field margins are at their best; while poppies are easy to locate, you may have to travel to see corn marigolds and cornflowers. Heathlands are dominated by the purples of the heathers and, should you wish to find some reptiles, get there early as they are at their most obvious and immobile as they catch the morning's first rays.

Where there are small insects, there will also be large predatory ones: July is a superb month for dragonflies, especially at wetland sites. They spend their short life mostly on the wing as they patrol for females or lunch.

1 Blakeney Point, Norfolk

Getting there:

Blakeney is off the A149 Cromer-Hunstanton road. Walk from Cley Beach, 5 kilometres, or ferry from Morston Quay, just west of Blakeney on coast road. Nearest train station: Sheringham.

Tel: 01263 740241

Email: blakeneypoint@nationaltrust.org.uk

Opening times: Open daily. Restricted access to some areas April–July.

Charging policy: Parking £2.50. Small charge for group/school guided tours.

Disabled access: Partly accessible. Access can be difficult because of undulating terrain, intermittent tides and a shingle ridge.

Find out more

National Trust
www.nationaltrust.org.uk/main/w-vh/w-visits/w-findaplace/w-blakeneypoint/

UK Safari – Puss Moths
www.uksafari.com/pussmoths.htm

Seal Trips
www.beansboattrips.co.uk

Blakeney Point is a long sand and shingle spit; it's one of the largest expanses of this type of coastal habitat in Europe. You can walk to the point from Cley Beach, which is about 3 miles away, or you can catch the ferry from Blakeney or Morston. In July, when we travelled out to the spit, the samphire, or glasswort, was really lush.

The main reason for our trip was to see the seals. Blakeney Point is one of the key sites for common seals to haul themselves out of the sea for a bit of a rest after a few days' fishing. They do seem to like to gather in big numbers at these haul-out sites – at Blakeney, you can sometimes see as many as 600 seals gathered on the shore. They'll travel up to 50 kilometres from where they've been feeding to get there, and usually remain faithful to a particular beach spot. June and July is a good time to see the common seals because this is soon after they've had their pups so there'll be plenty of cute little babies to look at. The youngest will be about four weeks old, brought here by their mothers after they've been weaned.

Intermingled with the common seals are grey seals. The key to telling them apart is that the commons look like maritime labradors, with their round faces and snub muzzles. The greys have longer faces and regal Roman noses. The Latin name for the grey seal means 'hook-nosed little sea pig', but they're definitely not that ugly! The greys are much larger animals, weighing up to 250 kilos – that's twice as heavy as the commons. They breed in autumn, so won't have pups at this time of the year, but when they do the pups will be bright white, unlike the common seals whose pups have the same sandy-coloured fur as their parents.

Cheek by jowl with the seals is a rather more raucous colony of terns – little, Sandwich, common and the odd Arctic. As they nest right on the pebbles, the young are camouflaged to look like small, fluffy stones.

Both common and grey seals haul up at Blakeney Point

The spit is owned by the National Trust and has a number of rare plants – we counted four different species of the purple, papery flowers of sea lavender. Apparently there are nearly 30 species and sub-species of this gorgeous little plant. Along with the samphire, there's sea purslane, sea kale and sea beet, all of which are edible, though we stuck to sandwiches.

Alongside the shingle are giant sand dunes which are old and fragile – some are a few hundred years old. There's also an odd little enclosure containing willows and poplars and it was here that we saw something quite extraordinary. These short trees, planted as a biology experiment years ago, have become home to a colony of puss moths. At first you can't see a single caterpillar but, once you get your eye in, you realise that the trees are literally covered with the beasts at this time of year. They're very large, bright green, hairy caterpillars with a chocolate-brown or purple saddle trimmed with white, and a pink ring around their 'face'. At the other end they have two tails and, when they're agitated, they shoot flagella (which look like bright pink streamers) out of the ends! Around this time of year the caterpillars start pupating. We didn't realise that we would get to see this unusual behaviour, let alone be able to film it. When they're ready to pupate, the caterpillars turn a vivid burgundy and head down from the tree to the roots, where they bury themselves in the ground and create a tough cocoon for themselves. Inside the cocoon they will turn into equally striking adults – pale grey with black and peach markings, and almost as furry as a small cat!

A puss moth caterpillar

Opposite: The hatched-out puss moth

2 The Bass Rock, Scotland

Getting there:

Daily boat trips around Bass Rock from North Berwick harbour depending on weather and tides. There are annual landings on Bass Rock – telephone Seabird Centre for details. The Scottish Seabird Centre and North Berwick are signposted from the A1. Nearest train station: North Berwick

Tel: Scottish Seabird Centre – 01620 890 202

Email: Enquiry form on www.seabird.org

Opening times: Scottish Seabird Centre open daily (exc Christmas Day).

Charging policy: Scottish Seabird Centre: Adults £6.95, Concessions £4.50, family, group and membership rates available.

Disabled access: The Centre has full disabled access and parking.

Find out more

History of Bass Rock
**www.north-berwick.co.uk/
bassRock.asp**

Scottish Seabird Centre
www.seabird.org

Aquatrek Boat Charters
www.aquatrek.co.uk

There are certain places in Britain where at the right time of year you can witness a thrilling wildlife spectacle – the sight and sound of thousands of animals all together at the same time. There are other places where you can get so close to the wildlife you're eyeball to eyeball. On the Bass Rock in the summer you can do both, for this is the site of the largest single rock gannet colony in the world – 100,000 birds.

The Bass Rock is a distinctive Scottish landmark situated in the Firth of Forth, just four kilometres from the shore. Like the other islands in the Firth, the Bass was formed over three hundred million years ago and is the remains of a volcano, a hard plug of solidified lava.

The Bass Rock has played an important role in human history. It was a religious retreat during early Christianity, it's been a fortress and a prison, and it held a strategic position during many wars between Scotland and England. Today it's uninhabited by humans and that's just as well, because virtually every inch of the island is now taken over by gannets.

In fact, gannets have always been the true owner-occupiers of the Bass. The first records of them on the island date from the 15th century, but they have probably nested here for many thousands of years.

Each year they begin to arrive on the Bass from January onwards, returning from the coast of north and west Africa. As you approach by boat from the town of North Berwick, you're mesmerised by the carpet of white, and in the air above the rock by the halo of white dots as thousands of birds hover, riding the wind. Climbing the steps from the jetty, you're immediately hit by the noise, then by the smell, and then by the white spectacle of thousands upon thousands of birds packed closely together. Once you could walk along a

Gannets are the owner-occupiers of the rock

path around the island but not anymore as everywhere is covered by nesting birds. This really is a seabird city. Not just a place where birds are thrown together in a chaotic mass, but an organised metropolis with accepted behaviour and rules.

The birds tend to return to the same nest site each year, arriving as early as possible to secure their place. Gannets usually pair for life and here they reunite, bonding with displays of bill-fencing, which will continue all the time they're together on the rock until the end of October. Each pair keeps to itself unless another bird invades their territory. Then they will fight ferociously to defend it. Mostly, though, fighting isn't necessary as the nests are evenly spaced, just out of reach of the neighbour's bill.

Both male and female birds take it in turns to incubate the single egg, and then feed the chick. When one adult is planning to fly off to forage at sea, it lets the other know by sky-pointing – repeatedly pointing its bill up towards the sky. At sea they flap and then glide low over the water, sometimes travelling hundreds of miles to fish. They feed by flying high and circling to spot shoals of fish, before plunging into the sea at high speeds, bill first, with wings folded.

On the rock, as long as you don't disturb them by entering their tiny territory, you can sit remarkably close and take great pictures. The gannet is a supremely handsome bird – large and bright white with black wing tips, a yellowish-orange-coloured head and striking round blue eyes.

You can spend many hours watching these birds in the business of raising their young and communing with each other. But, eventually, the time comes to leave them to the island that is their own.

Opposite: The distinctive Bass Rock in the Firth of Forth

3 The Treshnish Isles and Staffa, Scotland

Getting there:

Boats from Oban to both Treshnish and Staffa. Various companies provide sightseeing tours.

Tel: Hebridean Trust – 01865 311468

Email: info@hebrideantrust.org

Opening times: Dependent on operation of ferry (April-August).

Charging policy: Not applicable. Ferry and tour costs vary.

Disabled access: No wheelchair access on the island. Contact ferry company before booking.

Find out more

The Hebridean Trust
www.hebrideantrust.org

Oban Tourist Information
www.oban.org.uk

Gordon Grant Tours
www.fingals-cave-staffa.co.uk/ treshnish.asp

Wildlife Hebrides – Puffin
www.wildlifehebrides.com/topten/ puffin/

When we received our itinerary for a trip to the Treshnish Isles in the Southern Hebrides for a few days of 'puffin therapy', we were left feeling a bit mystified. Did we need puffin therapy, and why? Well, as it turned out, we did need some and, what's more, we highly recommend it.

The Treshnish Isles are a small group of uninhabited islands roughly five kilometres west of the Isle of Mull, to which they owe their existence. They have been likened to a fleet of battleships cruising through the Hebrides in line astern, and are much less well known than the neighbouring Isle of Staffa. They're hard to find on a map, but that's nothing to the feeling of remoteness we felt as we stepped off the plane on the nearby Isle of Tiree and onto a runway surrounded by meadows of wildflowers, known locally as 'machair', a word for rich seaside grassland. Overhead, the sky was a bright bowl of blue, which did not surprise us because Tiree is one of the sunniest places in Britain. However, the weather is known to be changeable in the Hebrides, and change it did – throwing a bewildering four seasons of weather at us in the two days we were there.

For those of you who think you're not familiar with this remote region, you may change your mind when you learn that Staffa is home to one of the most well-known, but least visited, caves in the UK. Fingal's Cave is so famous it even has its own overture (also known as *The Hebrides*), written by Mendelssohn. It has to be on everyone's tick-list of must-see places to visit, which is a whole lot easier now than when it was being formed, because Staffa and the Treshnish Islands are the true daughters of Mull, the remains of hot lava-flows that were spewed out of Mull volcano sixty million years ago.

There's only one way to see Staffa and the Treshnish Isles properly and that's by boat. Though most boats leave from Mull or Oban, we set off from Tiree in beautiful, sunny weather and, after a journey of a couple of hours, the flat tabletop shape of Staffa came into view on the horizon. As we got closer, finally, there it was – the great, square,

black, gaping maw of Fingal's Cave — made even more dramatic by cliffs of near-vertical hexagonal columns of basalt lava. If you're lucky enough to visit in favourable weather, as we did, it's actually possible to land and walk around the base of the cliffs on an old Victorian pathway right into the cave itself. The cave stretches a massive 69 metres back into the rock and is 20 metres high, making it quite simply a spectacular, natural cathedral. We were all blown away.

Anyway, back to the wildlife. We re-embarked and set off across the waves to the Isle of Lunga, the largest of the group of islands that make up the Treshnish Isles. It was time for our puffin therapy. So what, exactly, is puffin therapy? Well, quite simply, it's a chance to become so totally engrossed in the comings and goings of this most delightful of seabirds that all the cares and worries of everyday life just slip away. From our vantage point on a sunny, grass-covered cliff, we could practically touch them as they flew in and perched on the rocks beside us, with beaks stuffed full of sand-eels. They looked at us quizzically, heads on one side, before waddling off into their burrows to feed their young. Moments later they shot out of their burrows, like arrows, straight out to sea for another fishing trip. So engrossed were we in this unique therapy that we failed to notice a rapidly approaching sea-fret and rainstorm being borne in on a stiff wind. Wham, suddenly we were being battered by horizontal rain. So much for the 'therapy'.

Fingal's Cave on the Isle of Staffa

The distinctive sight of a puffin on a cliff top

Opposite: Puffin therapy – on the wing

4 Lundy Island

Getting there:

The *MS Oldenburg* from both Bideford and Ilfracombe. Bideford is accessed by the A39 and the A386; for Ilfracombe take junction 27 off the M5 onto the A361, bypass Tiverton and stay on the road through Barnstaple to Ilfracombe.

Tel: Lundy shore office – 01271 863636

Email: info@lundyisland.co.uk

Opening times: Boat trips March–November

Charging policy: Day and longer period tickets available; prices vary.

Disabled access: No facilities for the disabled. Some shops have ramp access, and some of the grounds have level areas.

Find out more

National Trust
www.nationaltrust.org.uk/main/ w-vh/w-visits/w-findaplace/ w-lundy/

Lundy Island
www.lundyisland.co.uk

Lundy Seabird Recovery Project
www.english-nature.org.uk/ News/story.asp?ID=457

Lundy is a lump of granite roughly five kilometres long by one kilometre wide that rises over 120 metres out of the sea at the point where the Bristol Channel meets the Atlantic Ocean. The island lies 18 kilometres off the coast of North Devon and is orientated lengthways in a north–south direction, meaning that the west side bears the full brunt of the prevailing south-westerly winds, while the east side is much more sheltered. These different levels of exposure lead to pronounced differences in the wildlife that inhabits each side.

The marine life around the island is so rich that Lundy is England's only Marine Nature Reserve. The creation of a 'No Fishing Zone' on the east of the island has meant that lobsters, crabs and fish now flourish there. The calm waters on this side are also a wonderful place to get very close to some of Lundy's resident grey seals, which use the sheltered east side as a feeding and resting area before the frenetic breeding season begins in the autumn.

The film crew was hoping to go one better than the typical view of grey seals bobbing about in the water or basking on the rocks. If you want to see grey seals at their most graceful, you need to enter their world, a place where they are the total masters of their own environment. In other words, we had to get into the water with them! Under the assistance of skipper Clive Pearson, who is regularly enlisted to enable visitors to achieve the ultimate seal experience, we located a still patch of water on the sheltered east side and donned our wetsuits, flippers, masks and snorkels ready for action. The presence of our boat, while we kitted up, had already garnered the attention of half a dozen seals who curiously eyed us up as we slipped into the water.

Now the seal, it has to be said, is often a touch clumsy out of water, but it is a very different matter when they are actually in it. While we floated on top of the water looking down, the seals treated us to the most wonderful underwater display as they looped the loop, swam past us upside down and generally played around us. Although they

Lundy cliffs from the cliff top

were shy of coming face to face, we would often turn round to find a seal floating right behind us, only to shoot away like a slimline torpedo as soon as we changed direction. On one or two occasions, we even looked down to find one nibbling our flippers! Eventually the cold water defeated us and we retired back to the boat for a mug of steaming tea and some dry clothes, as we prepared for dry land and a trip over to look at Lundy's famous summer seabird colonies on the windy western cliff ledges.

Marching over to the west of the island, we were hoping for a glimpse of a symbolic seabird. The island derives its name from the Norse for 'puffin', dating back to the times when this comical but charismatic seabird used to be abundant on the island. Even in 1939, there were thought to be over 3,500 pairs of puffins on Lundy, but due to colonisation of the island by black rats, which are thought to have swum ashore from the numerous shipwrecks around the island, numbers have sharply declined as the booming rat population preyed on the hapless seabird. After alarm that the puffin was about to disappear, with the population down to only a few pairs, immediate action was taken to remove the rats and the puffins have recently shown signs of coming back from the brink.

As we admired the ranks of guillemots and razorbills lined up like milk bottles along impossible ledges, and the white-stained cliffs marking the kittiwakes' nests, on the grassy bank above the auk colonies we found a single puffin coming out of a burrow. Let's hope the future is brighter for this wonderful seabird now that Lundy has been declared a rat-free island.

Razorbills lined up like milk bottles

Opposite: Graceful grey seal underwater

5 Teifi Marshes, West Wales

Getting there:

Take the A484 or the A487 to Cardigan, follow the signs towards Cilgerran. On entering the village a left turn gives access to the Teifi Marshes Reserve along the old railway line.

Tel: Welsh Wildlife Centre – 01239 621212

Email: info@ysgolnatur.co.uk

Opening times: Open daily.

Charging policy: Not applicable. Parking £3.

Disabled access: Many footpaths are suitable for disabled and assisted wheelchair access.

Find out more

The Welsh Wildlife Centre
www.welshwildlife.org

Visit Cardigan, West Wales
www.visitcardigan.com

BBC Southwest Wales – Nature
www.bbc.co.uk/wales/southwest/nature/features/pages/buffalo.shtml

Nature's Calendar is all about getting out into the countryside at exactly the right time of year to see for yourself some of the amazing wildlife on offer, often when it's putting on a real seasonal spectacle. So when we recommend West Wales and then say that it's a brilliant place for water buffalo, you might think that we've gone made and ended up somewhere in Asia. In fact, it's thanks to the water buffalo that the Teifi Marshes reserve at Cilgerran is alive with birds, from waders to warblers, and is also home to an impressive number of mammals including water voles, sika deer and otters.

Managing the reserve at Teifi Marshes is all about trying to keep the grasses at bay to let the wetland plants and creatures flourish. The trouble with grazing this sort of land with cows and sheep is that they can be fussy eaters – given the choice, these animals won't go into wet or rough areas – whereas water buffalo will happily graze everything, even when submerged up to their necks in water, and on land they also help break up scrub with their horns. The water buffalo at Teifi belong to a local farmer who turns them out on the reserve from April to October and their placid temperaments make them a real favourite with the visitors.

Without the water buffalo, the area around Teifi Marshes would become dense and overgrown, blocking out the light and preventing growth of the specialist plants. Grazing means it remains an open habitat of mainly fen and swamp and with these conditions come some of our most hard-pressed wildlife, pushed out of much of the countryside by land drainage and agriculture.

Visiting Teifi Marshes couldn't be easier. You can walk there from the centre of Cardigan or park by the award-winning visitor centre – a tall, glass building which makes a real design statement in the landscape and offers some great views of the marshes. From here, there's a circular walk around the marshes called the Otter Trail which takes about an hour and a half. There are six hides on the route and the names of many of them will give you a clue as to what you're most likely to see. But don't count on it. Our cameraman spent the day in the 'Kingfisher' hide without once seeing a flash of turquoise. But that's the good thing about Teifi; you can come here again and again and always see something new, even if it's not what you went looking for. Oh, and when we say Otter trail, they are there – but not when we were. That said, there are plenty of sightings – usually in the evenings or early morning – so it's well worth looking out for signs of worried waterfowl. This is a place that buzzes with dragonflies – 17 different species have been counted here – and echoes with the call of the curlew, one of summer's most evocative sounds. But because Teifi Marshes is about reedbeds, why not take the opportunity to look out for some of its smaller specialist summer visitors like reed warblers and sedge warblers? These little brown birds are more often heard than seen. The sedge warbler, with its creamy-white eyestripe, has a song which is the more highly rated of the two. It's a series of sweet, clear warbles, buzzes and trills, while the song of the reed warbler is a more repetitive and less musical chattering. Worldwide there are 400 different kinds of warbler, many of them woodland birds. Most of them are rather brown and drab and, as with the sedge and reed warblers, it's often the song that helps tell them apart.

Reedbeds are important, but the reserve offers other habitats that are worth exploring. There are two woodland walks, one of them alongside the River Teifi, and these offer the opportunity to spot redstarts and pied flycatchers. To sum up, the Teifi Marshes are a great place to spend time in summer, but try to get there either in the early morning or late afternoon. Midday in summer is a quiet time for birds, so you could be disappointed.

The reedbeds of Teifi marshes

Golden-ringed dragonfly

The unlikely sight of water buffalo in the UK, at Teifi Marshes

6 Bookham Commons, Surrey

Getting there:

The Surrey North Downs are easily accessible from the A3, M25, and A24. Nearest train station: Bookham

Tel: 01372 453401

Email: enquiries@thenationaltrust.org.uk

Opening times: Open daily.

Charging policy: Some small charges for events.

Disabled access: Some disabled access, telephone before visiting.

The elusive Purple Emperor butterfly

Find out more

National Trust
www.nationaltrust.org.uk/main/w-global/w-localtoyou/w-south_east/w-south_east-countryside/w-south_east-places-north_downs/w-south_east-places-north_downs-bookham_commons.htm

BBC Science and Nature – Purple Emperor Butterfly
www.bbc.co.uk/nature/wildfacts/factfiles/405.shtml

Bookham Commons – the remnants of the wildwood of southern England

There is one butterfly that is considered the Holy Grail of British butterflies. It's undoubtedly one of the most charismatic, its wings have a fabulous purple sheen, and the males conduct ferocious aerial battles. It's also very difficult to see: firstly you need to go to the right wood, and secondly you need to know where to look once you're there.

We concentrated our search on Bookham Commons, nestling on the Surrey North Downs, an area consisting of oak woodland, ponds and meadows. Some say Bookham is one of the few remnants of the wildwood that once covered the whole of the south of England, and, in 1923, in the face of possible development, the whole area was bought by the residents to save the oak woodlands. It was later given to the National Trust.

The elusive butterfly in question is the purple emperor, and the difficulty with seeing it is that it spnds most of its time high up in the treetops, feeding on aphid honeydew and tree sap. The best time of year to see the purple emperor is throughout July and into August, and the task of tracking them down is made easier by the fact that they have a favourite tree. The males tend to congregate round a master oak tree, to which they'll return year after year, fighting off any incomers to their territory. The tree is usually on the highest ground because the butterflies gather at the highest point in the wood to establish territories. There are few greater thrills than standing beneath a master oak tree and watching male purple emperors soaring and wheeling above the canopy.

Their display is most spectacular when they're defending their bit of tree from other males. If a rival flies too close, the male will take off and a great battle will ensue. The two will spiral round and round each other until one gives in and flies off.

If you are desperate for a closer look that doesn't involve crooking your neck, early in July – just a week or so after emerging – the males will come down from the treetops in search of salts to build up their strength during mating. The Victorians, who were avid butterfly collectors, developed lots of tricks for attracting them to the ground – luring them with squashed fruit, mashed up fish and, even, urine. We can't vouch for any of these methods, but it has been known for males to swoop down to investigate a mirror flickering in the sunshine. Whatever technique you adopt, it's got to be worth a try!

7 Castle Eden Dene, County Durham

Getting there:

Easily accessed by the A19 and A1086; clearly signposted from Peterlee town centre.

Tel: English Nature – 0191 5860004/ 5182403

Email: Online enquiry form at www.durham.gov.uk

Opening times: Footpaths open daily.

Charging policy: Not applicable.

Disabled access: Steep paths and uneven surface (call for advice on the most accessible paths). Some walks/ events specially organised – call for information.

The northern brown argus butterfly

Find out more

English Nature
www.english-nature.org.uk/about/ teams/team_photo/CastleEden Dene042.pdf

Durham County Council
www.durham.gov.uk

Butterfly Conservation
www.butterfly-conservation.org/ species/bdata/butterfly.php?code= nor

Castle Eden Dene National Nature Reserve

Marking the entire southern boundary of the English town of Peterlee, itself sandwiched between the big industrial cities of Middlesbrough and Sunderland, lies the green lung that is the Castle Eden Dene National Nature Reserve. This steep-sided ravine was formed by the post-glacial melt-water from the last ice age. It is the largest area of semi-natural woodland in the northeast of England, and a surviving reminder of the wildwood that once covered large areas of Britain.

Starting at Gunner's Pool Bridge, we planned to walk the entire length of the Dene, from the top to where the valley finally tumbles into the North Sea. Standing on the bridge, precipitously straddling the gorge, we were struck by the sheer walls of the ravine, cloaked in hart's tongue fern. Descending into the gorge we were surrounded by ancient trees such as yew, and sturdy English oaks, as well as the odd dead elm tree.

Spring is often considered to be the best time to see woodland flora, but our mission was to see a number of less obvious woodland plants and insects that peak in summer.

Enchanter's nightshade is a delicate member of the willowherb family used by the Anglo-Saxons to protect them against spells cast by elves. The flowers are indeed enchanting – to us, the individual tiny blossoms looked like butterflies suspended on pins. Flowering alongside were the simple five-petalled yellow flowers of wood avens, another plant with supposed magical powers.

As we walked along the valley, we came across hogweed growing where light had penetrated the canopy. Although humans find the smell unpleasant, it was obvious that the insect world begged to differ. The frothy white flower heads had become a beacon for a whole range of summer insects, including hoverflies, bumblebees and a species of soldier beetle with the hilarious nickname, the 'hogweed bonking beetle'. This predatory little red and black beetle is invariably found on the flowers in a state of near constant copulation – and guess what they were doing when we found them?

As we reached the Dene mouth and emerged into the light, we were greeted by a summer riot of colour in the meadows – the purples of bloody cranesbill and common knapweed, the pinks of restharrow and betony and the yellows of bird's foot trefoil and common rockrose. But there was one final treat in store for us – a glimpse of the rare northern brown argus butterfly, a real northern specialist.

8 Thorne Moors, South Yorkshire

It was not how we imagined birdwatching would be. For a start it was dusk, a crescent-shaped moon glimmering through the pines, and we were standing around in the open – neither hidden nor camouflaged – waving hankies like demented Morris dancers. We'd come to see an unusual and elusive bird, the nightjar. As its name suggests, it's a crepuscular creature, coming out at dusk. It has a raptor-like quality to its appearance, yet it's actually related to the swift family. We heard the males calling before we saw them – and what a call! It sounds like the noise an old-fashioned modem makes when it's trying to connect to the internet – though how people described it before dial-up is hard to imagine. How they make the sound is also an enigma – but they can sing 2,500 of these mechanical notes a minute. Nightjars used to be called goat-suckers because of the legend that they sucked the udders of goats and turned their milk dry. Their other old country name is rather gentler: fern-owl, which, as nature writer Richard Mabey says: '... conjures the bracken-dominated hillsides and woodland breaks it once frequented'.

In July, when we visited, the males were guarding territories. They are cryptically coloured with mottled plumage, but they each have a little patch of white on their chest, hence the white hankies. The white acts as a super-stimulus, sending the males into an incandescent rage at the interloper. And it worked! One circled around us; the flight is incredible, aerially dramatic and yet jerky. Another of their tricks is to hover, wings outstretched like an avian angel. Sadly we didn't see this – but you might be luckier.

Thorne Moors in South Yorkshire is a good spot to see these birds. It has always been a stronghold, despite declining numbers in the UK, and now it's being managed specifically for nightjars. The wardens have been clearing much of the scrub, so there are open patches of heather interspersed with stands of birch and pine – just the kind of mosaic habitat they like. It's good to try and see them in spring and early summer

before they head back to Africa in August and September. More importantly, from your point of view, the wardens also run nightjar walks. And there is indeed something pretty special about being on a moor at night, the sky bright with stars, while a bird spins around your head rattling like a high-tech fax!

Thorne Moors and its twin Hatfield Moors are the largest remaining lowland raised peat mires in Britain. Their 1,900 hectares are home to specialised plants, including bog rosemary, bog myrtle, bladderwort and marsh cinquefoil, as well as up to 200 species of bird, and very localised species such as the large heath butterfly. One of the most special animals you might see is an adder. Like all reptiles, adders are cold-blooded, so they need to bask to warm themselves up. In the summer months, you need to be up early to catch them sunning themselves by the side of the path before they slide off into the undergrowth. They're easily recognisable with their distinctive black zigzag pattern, but the colour of the rest of their scales can vary with females tending to be reddish or brown, and males a more contrasting white or yellow. Adders hibernate from the beginning of October and will emerge in spring when they mate. Courtship can be protracted – but hopefully ends up with the female giving birth to live babies. Our only venomous snake and a protected species, adders could be a threat if disturbed, so it's best to leave them be and to stop your dog from checking them out with its nose!

The lowland raised peat mire of Thorne Moor

The southern hawker dragonfly

Opposite: A female basking adder

9 The National Botanic Garden of Wales, Carmarthenshire

Getting there:

Situated ten minutes from the M4 and ¼ kilometre from the A48 in Carmarthenshire. From the A48, take the B4310 and follow brown tourist information signs to the Garden. Nearest train station: Carmarthen

Tel: 01558 668768

Email: info@gardenofwales.org.uk

Opening times: Open daily (exc Christmas Day): April-October 10am-6pm; November-March 10am-4pm.

Charging policy: Adults £5, OAP £3, Children free.

Disabled access: Garden accessible to all visitors. Motor powered and manual wheelchairs available. Regular shuttle buggy service between gatehouse and garden.

Find out more

National Botanic Garden of Wales
www.gardenofwales.org.uk

Great British Gardens
www.greatbritishgardens.co.uk

Natural History Museum – British Native Plants
www.nhm.ac.uk/fff/checklist_british_plants.html

Designed by Norman Foster and Partners, the Great Glasshouse at The National Botanic Garden of Wales is one of the largest single span glasshouses in the world. It's an unexpected sight, just a few minutes' drive from the M4, nestled in the Carmarthenshire hills and overlooked by the remains of Roman forts and medieval castles. The history of the Botanic Garden stretches back 400 years. The land originally formed part of the Middleton estate, but during the 1700s the family were forced to sell it to pay off their debts. It was later bought by William Paxton who began its transformation into a water park. He also instigated the Double Walled Garden, which has its own microclimate, and which you can still visit today.

Summer is one of the best times to come because so many flowers are in bloom, both in the walled gardens and in the glasshouse. The plants in the glasshouse are divided according to continents so you can stroll through the African veldt, past the quiver tree (whose hollow trunks the Koi san tribe used to hold their arrows) and round a corner into 'Australia', dense with burgundy kangaroo paws and eucalyptus-smelling protea. Amazingly, British wildlife thrives here too. There's a colony of house sparrows nesting in the wall around the waterfall, as well as a few robins and blue tits actively defending their territories. The staff have even seen some of the birds drinking nectar like their antipodean cousins.

The idea is that the glasshouse acts like a floral ark, filled with rare plants from around the world. One example is McCutcheon's Grevillea: five years ago, there were only ten of these small Western Australian shrubs left in the wild, all growing together in one small patch. One of these plants was micropropagated at King's Park Botanic Gardens in Perth, Western Australia, and sent to The National Botanic Garden of Wales in 1999. It flowered for the

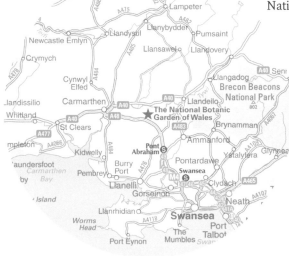

first time in 2003 and senior horticulturalist, Jess Gould, then managed to get it to produce seeds.

As well as exotics, the Botanic Garden is helping to preserve some of our most endangered and rarest native flora. For instance, the Snowdonian hawkweed was thought until recently to be extinct, but when a specimen of this raggedy, dandelion-like plant was discovered growing on rocks around a waterfall in the Brecon Beacons, the Botanic Gardens decided to collect the seed and try to propagate it. They've also had success with rare trees, including Ley's whitebeam. This native looks a bit like a rowan and is related to the wild service-tree. The berries are edible when they've been 'bletted' by frost. There are only 16 Ley's whitebeam found in two Welsh locations, so the gardens are doing everything they can to try and save it.

The walled gardens are equally interesting, botanically. Instead of skipping across continents in seconds, here you stroll through millions of years of evolution in minutes. The gardens are planted to show how flowering plants evolved, based on the latest DNA and microscopic research. Here, you travel from primitive water lilies at the centre of the garden to the latest cultivars by the outer walls, through 150 million years of botanical history. If you visit in June or July, you'll be assailed by a heady wall of scent and a riot of colour from myriad kinds of day lily.

There's plenty of wildlife, too. The mosaic of lakes, streams, marshes, semi-natural woodlands, meadows and formal gardens are a great habitat for over 100 types of butterfly and moth, more than 56 species of bird, over 180 types of lichen, 92 species of moss and 26 types of snail! It's also a good place to spot reptiles, such as the grass snake (Britain's largest reptile), because of all the ponds and the piles of compost and chippings. If you've got time, check out the beehives – the bees live in a corner of the walled garden and pollinate all the plants, regardless of where they originally hailed from. If you're really lucky, you may even be able to buy a pot of their exquisite, exotic-tasting honey.

The Great Glasshouse of the National Botanic Garden of Wales

Galeopsis segetum – one of the rare plant species

Opposite: Lampranthus

August

August is almost synonymous with summer holidays and with the Great British public trying to make the most of our short summer. August is also the time that wildlife is busily trying to complete all their breeding cycles before the nights begin to draw in again.

Heading to the coast is the most obvious choice for holidaymakers and naturalists alike and sea-watching can be very rewarding. Rocky promontories in the west of the UK are particularly good, and patience can be rewarded by views of harbour porpoise, bottlenose dolphins and, if you are in the right place at the right time, basking sharks. Down on the beaches, rockpooling can be a great experience, providing you check out the tide times beforehand!

August is also the time when large flocks of wading birds such as turnstone and sanderling, which have spent the summer breeding in the Arctic tundra, arrive on our beaches and rocky coastlines. Some of these birds will spend the rest of the year here, while others will pass through on the way to beaches in southern Africa or even further afield.

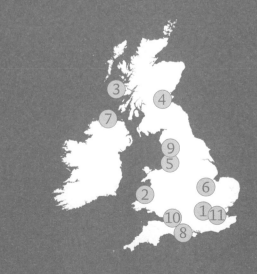

1 Bushy Park, London

Getting there:

Hampton Court Gate is just off Hampton Court Road and Teddington Gate is off Sandy Lane. Nearest train stations: Teddington/Hampton Wick/Hampton Court (5–10 minute walk to Sandy Lane Gates).

Tel: Bushy Park Office – 020 8979 1586

Email: bushy@royalparks.gsi.gov.uk

Opening times: Open daily. Pedestrians: 5am–10.30pm; vehicles 6.30am–dusk (7pm in winter). September– November, park opens 8am.

Charging policy: Not applicable.

Disabled access: Disabled access available, disabled car park and toilets on site.

Find out more

Royal Parks
www.royalparks.gov.uk/parks/bushy_park/

Deer-UK
www.deer-uk.com/red_deer.htm

Birds of Britain - Green Woodpecker
www.birdsofbritain.co.uk/bird-guide/green-woodpecker.htm

The Royal Parks of London are top spots for watching wildlife – not least because the traffic and sheer numbers of visitors make the animals and birds far more accustomed to human company. Bushy Park near Hampton Court is London's second biggest Royal Park, and it's a place where you can take a stroll alongside our largest land mammal, the red deer. It's an extraordinary experience seeing red deer walking majestically past tourists, London policemen and television cameras just ten kilometres from the city centre.

Much of what you see at Bushy Park today is thanks to Henry VIII, who was given Hampton Court Palace by Cardinal Wolsey in 1529. The King also took over ownership of three parks, which together make up Bushy Park as we know it today. Being, like many of his ancestors, a keen huntsman, Henry VIII turned the area into a deer hunting ground and today you can still see the remnants of the original Tudor walls that enclosed the park.

Walking with some of the three hundred or so red deer is a privilege, and one that shouldn't be abused. It is probably safest done during the summer, when the animals are largely in single sex groups, rather than during the autumn rutting season, when the stags turn their minds to breeding and can get a little aggressive.

In summer, red deer are at their most red. By July, the males' antlers are fully grown, but still covered in a layer of skin known as velvet. By late summer, the blood supply to the velvet is stopped and it begins to peel off; the antlers also become desensitised as the nerves die in preparation for the battles ahead. Summer is one of the best times to compare the antlers and count how many points they have. A young stag's first antlers are normally small spikes and, at this stage, he is known as a 'knobber'. Stags over two years old begin to grow branching antlers and more points or 'tines' are usually added each time a new set of antlers is grown. If a large red deer develops six tines on each antler, totalling twelve, then the stag is known as a 'royal'.

One of the most atmospheric sights we came

across was red deer cooling themselves off in the river – but did you know that, without another of our best known kings, the river wouldn't have been there at all? Historically, Hampton Court suffered from a lack of water. This problem was solved by King Charles I, who commissioned a 19 kilometre artificial river during the 1630s. It was built entirely by hand at a cost of over £4,000, a terrific sum of money in its day, and it has evolved into a fantastic wildlife resource and a great place to relax in summer.

The Royal Parks have over the years been influenced by many famous hands and become design classics. Take the magnificent avenue of horse chestnut trees which lead right up to the palace gates. These were designed by our most famous architect, Sir Christopher Wren, and they are a natural wonder in their own right, along with some magnificent historic lime trees.

Bushy Park is also a wonderful oasis for birds, including some colourful and distinctly non-native parakeets, descendants of escaped aviary birds and now well established breeding birds in many parts of southeast England. The park is also a hotspot for woodpeckers – all three native species can be found here, but it's the green woodpecker you're most likely to see. In the summer, the youngsters are around – gawky-looking, speckled green birds with their distinctive red caps – as they demand ants from their parents. A green woodpecker can eat about 2,000 ants a day and will return time and again to their favourite ant hill to feed – so find the ants and you might be rewarded with a sight of this exotic-looking yet native bird.

The red deer of Bushy Park

Green woodpecker feeding their young

Opposite: The magnificent horse chestnut tree avenue

2 Cardigan Bay, West Wales

Getting there:

Cardigan Bay Marine Wildlife Centre, New Quay, can be accessed by the A486 or the B4342 from the A487. The A484 also runs through the area. Once in New Quay, follow the signs to the Centre.

Tel: 01545 560032

Email: info@cbmwc.rog.uk

Opening times: Marine Centre open daily Easter-late summer. Cardigan Bay open daily.

Charging policy: Not applicable.

Disabled access: Some access available for wheelchair users. Telephone before visiting.

Find out more

Cardigan Bay Marine Wildlife Centre
http://www.cbmwc.org

Visit Cardigan
http://www.visitcardigan.com/

BBC Mid Wales Wildlife - Bottlenose Dolphins
www.bbc.co.uk/wales/mid/sites/wildlife/pages/dolphins.shtml

Trying to see dolphins and porpoises around the UK's coastal waters can be a frustrating experience at the best of times, with many hours put in for comparatively scant reward. If you are one of those people who is desperate to see dolphins close at hand without wanting to mount a full-blown Atlantic Ocean or North Sea expedition, then our advice would be to get yourself down to the picturesque seaside town of New Quay on the shores of Cardigan Bay in West Wales. If you don't get to see dolphins here, then chances are you won't see them anywhere!

The whole of Cardigan Bay is considered an outstanding marine environment. There can be excellent views of seabirds and grey seals in the summer months but, without doubt, the wildlife star attraction is the resident population of bottlenose dolphins, one of only two known colonies in all the UK's coastal waters. The summer is definitely the best time to take a gentle boat trip out into the bay to try and get close up and personal with these enigmatic creatures.

The Cardigan Bay Marine Wildlife Centre is an education and research centre dedicated to raising awareness of the marine environment. The research work of the team focuses on studying the population of bottlenose dolphins in the bay, which are thought to number up to 130 individuals, with small groups recorded virtually every day in the bay just off New Quay.

The Wildlife Centre is able to take interested parties along on their research trips, which gives wildlife enthusiasts a chance to see the dolphins at close hand and also assist with their study work on the dolphins. Tools of the trade for research co-ordinator Steve Hartley consist of a pair of binoculars to locate the dolphins in the first place, a camera with a 300mm lens to photograph their dorsal fins and a notebook to write down numbers seen and details of any interesting behaviour. The shape and markings from scarring on dorsal fins of bottlenose dolphins can be as individual as a human fingerprint. When Steve and his team photograph a particular dorsal fin, they can compare it to a large photographic database of known bottlenose dolphins in the bay, and hopefully draw some conclusions about what they are up to.

Clambering aboard the boat, the conditions were perfect as we set a course for one of Steve's research areas in the middle of the bay. We had only just arrived at the designated area, and had been on the water for less than 15 minutes, when a cry was heard from one of the researchers on look-out: 'Dolphins ahead!' Keeping the boat on a steady line and letting the dolphins come to us - rather than chasing them - is an important code of conduct for any of the dolphin watching boats, and come they did as we watched four hooked fins cut through the water in our direction.

As the three adults and one juvenile came to investigate the boat, they were at times only a metre or two away and they took it in turns to bow ride, giving us the most marvellous views. Adult males can reach well over three metres in length and weigh up to 500 kilos. As they cut through the water, their two-tone coloured bodies and very pronounced beak, which gives the bottlenose its name, were immediately obvious. While Steve and his team snapped photo after photo of the dorsal fins we were left to admire them. The bottlenose is one of the species most often kept in oceanariums because they are considered to be one of the most intelligent, curious and energetic dolphins. As they started to leap clear of the water alongside the boat, we were tempted to add 'show-off' to that list of attribtutes – and, boy, did they put on a good show!

Bottlenose dolphin

Dinas Island and the cliffs facing Cardigan Bay

3 Isle of Coll, Scotland

Getting there:

Sailings from Oban daily in summer, three times per week in winter.

Tel: RSPB Warden – 01879 230301

Email: Enquiry form at www.collbirds. co.uk/index.php?option=com_ contact&Itemid=3

Opening times: Island open year round, visiting times are dependent on ferry timetable and weather.

Charging policy: No charge to land on island, accommodation and ferry charges apply.

Disabled access: Assistance is available at both ports for disabled people, as well as on board. Disabled access available around Coll, some natural features (e.g. beaches) have limited access.

Find out more

Visit Coll
www.visitcoll.co.uk

Wildlife Scotland – Corncrake
http://wildlife.visitscotland.com/ species/birds/wading-ground- nesting-birds/Corncrake

Caledonian MacBrayne Ferry
www.calmac.co.uk/

W e'd been promised – no, virtually guaranteed – basking sharks off the Isle of Coll in the Hebrides. Apparently 30 of these enormous fish had been spotted the week before, circling round the island as they hoovered up plankton with their giant mouths agape. Impressive animals, they are the second largest fish in the world, growing up to eleven metres long and weighing over four tonnes. They trap plankton in their gill rakers (long, comb-like structures on the gills) and can filter up to 2,000 cubic metres of sea water per hour! Unfortunately, no one had spoken to the sharks about our visit and, while it looked as if we might end up spending a lot of time in the local pub, fortunately this tiny island, only 20 kilometres long, did contain some other wildlife that was quietly spectacular in its own way.

Once, the British countryside echoed with the peculiar call of the corncrake, a throaty rasp that's a little bit like strumming on the teeth of a comb with your credit card. The bird's Latin name, *Crex crex*, reflects the sound of the call, which males can repeat up to 20,000 times in a night! Corncrakes migrate to Africa in late summer, so our visit in August was a great opportunity to see this year's youngsters before they left home. What is surprising about corncrakes is that the young have grey eyes but, when they come back from their sojourn abroad, their eyes will have turned red, indicating that they are now old enough to breed.

The bird has declined in numbers and is now highly endangered. The reason has a lot to do with the mechanisation of agriculture. Because corncrakes nest on the ground and spend a lot of time skulking through long grass, they are often shredded by hay-making tractors. By the late 1980s ornithologists realised that the corncrake had been lost from much of Britain and it was clinging on in places like Coll, the Orkneys and the Hebrides. As a result, the RSPB has been trialling ways of helping the corncrakes on Coll. The organisation has encouraged farmers to allow some fields to be kept for hay, keeping animals out at certain times, planting corridors of long grass between fields, and mowing from the inside of the field towards the edge to allow the birds to escape. The next stage of the recovery plan is currently under way: corncrakes are being bred at the Zoological Society of London's Whipsnade Wild Animal Park and have been released at Nene Washes Nature Reserve in Cambridgeshire. Fifty-five birds were released in 2003 – the goal is to release one hundred young birds a year over the next three years.

Coll has another special feature: the machair, pronounced 'mach err'. It's one of the rarest habitat types in Europe and can be defined as a type of sand dune pasture sweeping from the beach to where the sand encroaches onto peat further inland. Machair sand has a high shell content, sometimes 80 or 90 per cent, and is found only in the northwest of Britain and Ireland. William MacGillivray, a leading Scottish naturalist, described the machair in 1830: '... the fragments of the shells of molluscs, are rolled by the waves towards the shore, where they are further broken down ... The wind then blows them beyond the watermark, where, in the presence of time, hillocks are formed.' The machair land on Coll is home to many rare flowers, such as Irish lady's tresses, a type of orchid named after the fashion, apparently, for Irish ladies to braid their hair, as well as other flower species like harebell and yellow rattle. It also provides a suitable habitat not just for the corncrake, but also for twite, dunlin, redshank, ringed plover and lapwing. Although we were disappointed not to see sharks, you may be luckier, and there is also the delight of the Coll half-marathon to tempt you, not to mention the island's only pub.

The endangered corncrake

An example of the machair

4 Loch Leven, Kinross

Getting there:

Once on the slip road east of junction 5 of the M90, take a left turn and then a right turn onto the B9097 and drive for approximately 3 kilometres. The reserve is signposted. Nearest train station: Fort William.

Tel: Vane Farm Visitor Centre – 01577 862355

Email: vanefarm@rspb.org.uk

Opening times: Visitor Centre 10am–5pm daily; trails and hides open 24 hours a day (exc Christmas Day, Boxing Day, New Year's Day and 2 January).

Charging policy: Visitor Centre: Adults £3, children 50p, concessions £2, family £6, RSPB and Wildlife Explorer members free.

Disabled access: Wheelchair access available at Nature Centre.

Find out more

RSPB – Vane Farm
**www.rspb.org.uk/reserves/guide/
v/vanefarm/index.asp**

Loch Leven Castle
**www.kinrosshouse.com/
lochleven_touristinfo.html**

Perthshire
**www.perthshire.co.uk/index.asp?
lm=50**

The calm, beautiful waters of Loch Leven in Kinross, Scotland, are less than a one-hour drive from the bustling city of Edinburgh. We went there in August for a lesson in all-year-round birdwatching, and also managed to commit the biggest gaff of the series by mistakenly identifying a glider as an osprey – OK, it was a long way off, and maybe we got the scale slightly wrong!

Loch Leven, where Mary, Queen of Scots was imprisoned in on Castle Island in the 16th century, is surrounded by beautiful rolling hills. It's also a place where you get two wildlife experiences for the price of one: there's an RSPB reserve, Vane Farm, on the southern side of the Loch, but Loch Leven is also a National Nature Reserve itself. In fact, it has international importance because of the vast numbers of duck and waders that visit every year. The habitat is attractive to ducks and waders not only because of its size – it covers an impressive 13 square kilometres of ground – but principally because it's shallow, having an average depth of only four metres, and is packed full of invertebrates, which makes it perfect for dabbling ducks and waders, which you'll find here in their thousands.

When it comes to birds, most people fall into one of two categories – they're either birdspotters or birdwatchers. 'Spotters' can identify birds, but know very little about their habits. Bird 'watchers', on the other hand, know pretty much all there is to know about a particular bird's behaviour throughout the year. Our trip to Loch Leven proved one thing: that, even if you're meant to be an expert on the subject, it's easy to mess up identification if you're not familiar with your subjects – in this case, ducks and their change of plumage throughout the year.

There are plenty of ducks to study at Loch Leven and one you shouldn't have any problems finding is the tufted duck because several hundreds of pairs breed here every year.

Tufties are smallish, plump diving ducks. They dive for about 20 seconds to depths of two to three metres, and the great thing is that males and females are really easy to tell apart, or so we thought. The male has striking black and white plumage, with a long drooping crest, and bright yellow eyes – think dinner suit, tuxedo; the 'James Bond' of the bird world. The female, on the other hand, is Miss Moneypenny – flat-heeled brogues, dull brown tweed suit and unobtrusive. But that all changes in summer.

What you might not be aware of is that after the breeding season ducks, especially, go into 'eclipse' plumage. That is, they discard or 'moult' their old feathers and replace them with new ones. They need to do this in order to improve their flight performance and maintain their waterproofing. Moulting literally makes them sitting ducks, because for a short period they can no longer fly. At this time of year, male tufties look almost the same as females; they just have slightly paler grey flanks. Eclipse plumage is much duller than normal plumage for a very good reason – if you're a duck that can't fly you need to keep hidden from predators.

Tufties, however, weren't the only birds we had trouble identifying at Loch Leven. One of the hurdles you're up against when you're out filming is that through the camera you can only see black and white – apparently it's a technical thing, but not exactly helpful when you're asking the cameraman to focus on the osprey in the 'patch of blue sky above the red and white chimney'! And when he did finally focus on the small approaching spec on the horizon, it turned out to be a glider, which is more than a little bit embarrassing for a birder!

Castle Island and Loch Leven

Tufted duck in flight

Opposite: Osprey on the lookout

5 Martin Mere, Lancashire

Getting there:

Situated off the A59. Follow signposts from the M61, M58 and M6. Nearest train station: Burscough (approx 1 kilometre)

Tel: 01704 895181

Email: info.martinmere@wwt.org.uk

Opening times: Open daily 9.30am–5.30pm (5pm November–February). Closed Christmas Day.

Charging policy: Adult £6, Child £3.80, Concession £4.80. Family and group tickets also available.

Disabled access: Excellent access throughout the centre including the hides and toilet facilities. Braille trail, talks and tactile exhibits can be organised. Reduced rates apply for helpers.

Find out more

Wildfowl and Wetlands Trust
www.wwt.org.uk/visit/martinmere/

British Dragonfly Society
www.dragonflysoc.org.uk/

BBC Science and Nature
www.bbc.co.uk/nature/wildfacts/factfiles/286.shtml

Martin Mere is one of the largest lakes in the northwest of England. It was created during the last ice age when glaciers hollowed out a huge bowl in the landscape just north of Liverpool. Today it's managed by the Wildfowl and Wetlands Trust and is a haven for wildlife, though it hasn't always been. Three hundred years ago most of the lake was drained and harvested for valuable reserves of peat. It only flooded in winter and, for the most part, was given over to agriculture. In 1972, the Wildfowl and Wetlands Trust reclaimed the land for wildlife. Huge areas of land are now flooded all year round and there are 202 hectares of beautiful wetland to explore. If you visit in August, as we did, you're guaranteed multiple encounters with all things flying.

It was a beautiful warm summer's day when we visited and the air was full of the scent of flowers and the sight of zooming dragonflies. The problem was they moved so fast on the wing that no sooner had we spotted them than they had gone. So, we decided to resort to cunning tactics to get a better view – we went dragonfly fishing. Knowing a little bit about a creature's behaviour can often help you get a better view. Lots of dragonfly species like to hunt from a 'perch', a favourite twig such as a piece of reed hanging over the water, which gives them a good view over their territory. So we planted a twig in a patch of mud at the side of the water and settled down to wait. Wouldn't it be great if theory worked in practice?

Our first visitor was a blue damselfly, which scorned our perch and settled on the mud near our feet! Damselflies are the smaller cousins of dragonflies, but it's not just size that tells them apart. Both have four large wings and large eyes, but damselflies rest with their wings together along their bodies. Dragonflies, on the other hand, rest with their wings outstretched. We watched several vivid emerald-green Southern Hawker dragonflies patrolling the stretch of water and noticed that they're incredibly fast flyers – the maximum speeds of the largest species are thought to be 25–30 miles per hour.

We sat patiently a little longer – as you sometimes have to do when filming wildlife – and suddenly two large emperor dragonflies arrived, flying in formation, a male and a female. We watched in fascination as a smaller female flew low over the water, curved her abdomen down until it was touching the surface, then straightened up, flew on and repeated the movement; the male hovered nearby seeming almost to escort her. It was only after a few moments that we realised what she was doing. She was laying eggs and the male was keeping guard over her. They repeated this performance several times before flying off over the reeds.

It's not only insects that you'll get to see at Martin Mere. There are plenty of hides around the reserve from which you can observe the wildfowl and, in addition, the trust organises walks four times a year out onto the wild part of the reserve. We set off in the early evening sun on a bat and barn owl walk. Having spent most of the day watching insects, we could readily appreciate that we would see bats aplenty, but barn owls might not be birds you would always associate with wetlands. Apparently quite a few barn owls fly onto the reserve to hunt, because the land around the lakes and pools is managed to provide habitat for small rodents, the barn owl's prey. We hadn't been out long before we were treated to our first view of a ghostly pale bird flying low over the fields. Barn owls sometimes seem rather eerie, appearing so suddenly and silently. As the sun dropped over the horizon and the sky turned a brilliant orange, bat detectors were switched on and tuned in. Since we were so close to the water, most of us had tuned to the frequency for Daubenton's bats, which hunt over water, and we were not disappointed. As the light faded, the bat detectors started to crackle and we could see the bats flitting about over the water. It was the end of a perfect long summer's day at Martin Mere, made particularly satisfying because all the wildlife turned up for once and performed beautifully – which doesn't always happen.

Daubenton's bat, which hunts over water

A beautiful blue damselfly

Martin Mere, created during the last ice age

6 Rockingham Forest, Northamptonshire

Getting there:

Drill Hall House, Benefield Road, Oundle, Peterborough PE8 4EY. Located between the towns of Kettering and Peterborough; from the A1 take the A43, which runs through the area. Nearest train station: Stamford (10 kilometres)

Tel: 01832 274278

Email: info@rftrust.org.uk

Opening times: Open daily.

Charging policy: Parking charges apply (usually £2 per day within the forest).

Disabled access: Easy access for wheelchair users.

Red Kite on a carcass

Find out more

Rockingham Forest Trust
www.rockingham-forest-trust.org.uk/

Forestry Commission
www.forestry.gov.uk

RSPB - Red Kite
www.rspb.org.uk/birds/guide/r/redkite/index.asp

The red kite has a wingspan of almost two metres

Birds of prey are no great respecters of boundaries. As we were driving to Fineshade Wood in Rockingham Forest to see red kites, several flew overhead. Magnificent birds, they became extinct in England and Scotland and it's only recently that a successful re-introduction has taken place. Rockingham Forest, an area of nearly 500 square kilometres of woodland stretching from Oxford to Peterborough, is the latest site for their re-introduction.

Red kites are scavengers. Once they were so common – more common even than the carrion crow – that in Tudor times flocks would gather to snatch scraps from the streets of London. But this beautiful bird was persecuted by gamekeepers and, by the end of the 19th century, the species had been lost completely from England. In order to restore the red kite to the countryside, conservationists began a re-introduction programme in 1989. Kites were introduced to the Chilterns between 1995 and 1998, having mainly been sourced from stock in Spain, where this bird is still common. In 2005 alone, 42 chicks fledged from 20 nests at Rockingham and throughout England there are now thought to be over 200 breeding pairs.

Easy to identify, red kites are rusty red with a wingspan of almost two metres. Their beaks are hooked and incredibly sharp – the right tool for tearing up carrion – and their call is a high-pitched mewing, not easily forgotten. The birds pair for life and each spring raise two to three chicks.

What's brilliant about Rockingham Forest is that not only are you likely to see them flying around, you are virtually guaranteed a rather closer view of them from a webcam set up by Natural England. In the visitors' centre in Fineshade Wood you can watch them feeding their nestlings, or you can log on from the comfort of your own home.

Kites construct rather messy nests out of sticks, but will line the nest with all manner of things including washing pinched from the line, as Shakespeare noted in *The Winter's Tale*: '… when the kite builds, look to lesser linen'. Recently, ornithologists have discovered a lottery ticket, ladies' underwear and lots of teddies in their nests, many mauled almost beyond recognition!

7 The Giant's Causeway, Northern Ireland

Getting there:

Directly by road, either on foot or using the seasonal Ulsterbus from Coleraine or Londonderry, or a longer walk to the Shepherd's Steps and back via the Giants Causeway (3 kilometres).

Tel: 028 20731855

Email: info@giantscausewaycentre.com

Opening times: March–October 10am –5pm, November–February 10am–4.30pm. Closed Christmas.

Charging policy: Not applicable. Charges apply for guided tours.

Disabled access: Wheelchair access. Ulsterbuses accessible.

The 'fashionable' black guillemot

Find out more

The Giant's Causeway
www.giantscausewayofficialguide. com.

Discover Northern Ireland
www.discovernorthernireland.com /product.aspx?ProductID=8206

National Trust – Giant's Causeway
www.nationaltrust.org.uk/main/ w-vh/w-visits/w-findaplace/ w-giantscauseway/

Basalt columns of the Giant's Causeway

This spot is covered with a very familiar mammal – humans – and no wonder! Half a million of us make the trip each year to see one of the most famous piles of rocks anywhere in the world, but what most of us miss out on is the wealth of wildlife right under our noses.

Just a hundred metres from the causeway is one of the best rockpooling locations on the North Antrim coast. What you'll find here is a huge collection of creatures from pipe fish (cousins of the sea horse) to deep purple-coloured beadlet anemones, plus all the usual suspects: shore crabs, blennies and prawns. The creature we found most fascinating was a cushion star, which has five stubby arms, rather than the longer legs of a normal starfish. It comes in a range of colours, from olive green and brown to orange, and some have all three colours at once. Unlike their longer-legged cousins, these starfish aren't predators; they're scavengers. They feed on decaying plant life and animals by pushing their stomach out through their mouths and secreting enzymes that digest the food. What makes these creatures really strange, though, is that they start out as males and turn into females after about four years. They lay about a thousand eggs in May and these hatch into tiny, stubby cushion stars.

This part of the North Antrim coast is good for birds, too. In the time we were there we spotted heron, fulmar, curlew, oystercatcher, cormorant, starling, wheatear and rock pipit. Not bad. The one bird that stood out from the rest, though, was a seabird that makes most birders go weak at the knees, a bird that's straight out of a 1960's fashion magazine. If Mary Quant had ever designed a bird, she'd have come up with the black guillemot. With its black body and white wing patches, its bright red legs and the crimson gape of its mouth, it's a design classic.

Guillemots are members of the auk family – like puffins – but you won't find them in the same numbers. Black guillemots prefer to hang around in ones or twos on rocky headlands. We saw half a dozen in the space of 20 minutes – we were in seventh heaven.

8 Studland, Dorset

Getting there:

Studland is reached by the B3531 from Corfe Castle, from Poole via the Sandbanks ferry or is walkable from Swanage. Nearest train stations: Branksome or Parkstone (both 5½ kilometres).

Tel: 01929 450259

Email: studlandbeach@nationaltrust.org.uk

Opening times: Open daily.

Charging policy: Ring Estate Office for information on boat launching, horse permits and beach hut hire. Parking charges vary.

Disabled access: Wheelchairs and pushchairs suitable for beach use are available for loan.

Find out more

National Trust
www.nationaltrust.org.uk/main/
w-vh/w-visits/w-findaplace/
w-studlandbeachandnaturereserve/
w-studland-gettingthere.htm

Isle of Purbeck - Studland
www.isleofpurbeck.com/studland.html

British Reptile Conservation
www.onewildworld.co.uk/
reptiles/conservation.htm

Most people go to Studland in Dorset for the beaches. With over five kilometres of glorious sand, it's a top tourist attraction. You can drive onto the ferry at Poole and, within 5 minutes, you're in a world of sun, sand and outstanding scenery that includes the picture postcard chalk rock formation, Harry's Rock. A word of warning, though. If you're visiting in the school holidays, you'll almost certainly have to queue for the ferry and some people prefer to chance the longer route by road, taking in Corfe Castle on the way.

What many visitors to Studland may not realise is that while they're lounging on the beach or taking pictures of Old Harry, they're right on the doorstep of one of the most exciting wildlife reserves in the UK. This is reptile country – a very rare heathland habitat where you can go on a big six safari with the chance of spotting all of our native snakes and lizards. These include the rarest of them all, the smooth snake, and its favourite snack the sand lizard – wonderful creatures that are found in just a handful of locations in southern England. In addition to these two varieties, you can also find adders, grass snakes, common lizards and the legless lizard, the slow-worm. One way to confirm that a slow worm isn't a snake is to check for eyelids when it blinks – lizards have eyelids, but snakes don't. To be a reptile spotter, though, you do have to be at the right place on the heath at the right time of day and local knowledge or expert assistance helps enormously.

However, there is much more to look at than just reptiles in this picturesque purple landscape. Walk along any of the white sandy paths that cut across the heathland behind the beach and you will come across some of the best adapted killing machines on the planet. Welcome to the world of insects, among the fiercest and most extraordinary predators on earth.

Now the great thing about watching insects is that they seem completely unperturbed by the presence of human spectators – which isn't something you can say about most wildlife. From the moment you arrive in the car park, you've got a great chance of seeing some pretty violent heathland action being played out right in front of your eyes.

Take the bee-killer wasp, appropriately also known as the bee-wolf because it hunts like a wolf. It's not the sort of wasp most of us dread meeting on the beach or at a summer picnic – the sort that dives into your fizzy orange or makes a nuisance of itself around the children's ice-creams – this is a solitary wasp that is after just one sort of prey, honey bees. It usually catches

The glorious beaches at Studland

them as they gather pollen from the heather, but it can also take them in flight and, when it does, it paralyses them and then picks them up to transport back to its sandy burrow, dug alongside one of the paths. The sight of a bee-wolf carrying a bee sometimes bigger than itself in its undercarriage is compulsive viewing. The wasp doesn't kill the bee, however, it buries it in a state of suspended animation in one of its sandy underground chambers as live meat for its larvae. It's one of the big differences between bees and wasps – bees feed their larvae on honey; wasps feed theirs on meat. By keeping the honey bee alive, the bee-wolf ensures it won't rot before the eggs hatch out. When the bee-wolf has finished filling her underground chamber with paralysed bees and has laid her eggs, she will carefully fill the entrance with sand so that other insects can't steal the food she's set aside for her youngsters, or lay their own eggs on the fresh meat.

The bee-killer wasp

All over the heathland you'll find other wasps engaged in similar predatory behaviour – some specialise in capturing heathland caterpillars for their larvae, manhandling them like rolls of carpet into their burrows, and carefully weighing up small stones to ensure they're just the right size to block the entrance – and it's all played out beneath your feet and often quite unnoticed. It's without doubt one of the greatest shows on earth.

9 Whitbarrow, Cumbria

Getting there:

From the A590 follow signposts through Witherslack and 2 kilometres beyond. At Witherslack Hall turn right and onto rough track for parking. Follow footpath across field and up Scar to Reserve.

Tel: 01539 816300

Email: mail@cumbriawildlifetrust.org.uk

Opening times: Open daily.

Charging policy: Not applicable.

Disabled access: Footpath is steep and can be slippery. Some access at Reserve, telephone before travelling.

Find out more

Whitbarrow National Nature Reserve
http://www.wildlifetrust.org.uk/cumbria/Reserves/Whitbarrow%20NNR.htm

English Nature – special sites
www.english-nature.org.uk/special/nnr/nnr_details.asp?NNR_ID=205

BBC Gardening – Hardy Ferns
www.bbc.co.uk/gardening/plants/plantprofile_ferns.shtml

For a few of us, rocks are like wonderful, glossy, colour travel brochures to some of the most exotic places on the planet. Not only do they allow you to travel through space, they let you travel through time as well. That takes some beating, but it's just what we did when we travelled to Whitbarrow in the Lake District.

Whitbarrow is a large, whale-shaped hill about six kilometres southwest of Kendal. Its lower slopes are covered in trees, but on the top is a wonderful limestone pavement, and it is from the rock that the hill takes its name – Whitbarrow means 'white hill'. This is home to some really specialist plants and butterflies. Limestone rock is made up of the remains of thousands of fossilised sea creatures that were once swimming around in a sub-tropical sea – picture coral reefs and the Bahamas in your head! The limestone at Whitbarrow was laid down over 350 million years ago when Britain was down near the equator – see, space and time travel! Now, limestone looks like pretty hard rock, but it's really susceptible to being dissolved away by rainwater, which is slightly acidic. Rainwater attacks the joints in the limestone, gradually deepening them until a pavement of blocks or clints are formed, surrounded by deep cracks or grikes. This all sounds a bit mechanical, but the end product is the most spectacular landscape feature – a limestone pavement.

If you're really keen on rocks, you may well spend your time here with your nose glued to the ground looking for fossils – and there are loads to find at Whitbarrow. But that doesn't necessarily mean you'll miss out on the nature all around you because, here at Whitbarrow, there is vegetation in every crack and crevice, including plenty of ferns. Like the rocks that they're attached to, ferns are an ancient tribe and are among some of the most primitive plants on earth. Nevertheless, despite such a simple structure, they have an amazingly complex lifecycle, which leads you to wonder how they have ever survived at all, let alone for so long.

Ferns are flowerless plants and reproduce by means of spores rather than seeds. The spores are kept in tiny sacks on the undersides of the leaves, which you can often see when you turn the leaves over. If you're not certain you can see them, place a frond upside down on a piece of paper, cover it with a weight and leave it for a couple of days. When you come back, you'll find that the spores have been released as a fine, usually black or brown-coloured, powder onto the paper. They show up like coloured dust tracing the outline of the fern. Now this is where it gets complicated. The spores are released in autumn and are dispersed by the wind. Landing in a crevice, each spore grows into a tiny green disk, which has both male and female organs. The ferns then essentially have sex with themselves. Sperm are produced and these travel in a film of rainwater to the female organs where they fertilise the eggs, and, hey presto, a new plant grows! It just goes to show how something you thought was dull can actually turn out to be fascinating on closer acquaintance. Clearly a bit of water is needed to help the ferns reproduce and for that reason they are more common on the western side of Britain, which gets more than its fair share of rain. Many specialised ferns do particularly well on the limestone pavement at Whitbarrow because the grikes have their own damp microclimate.

Hartstongue fern

At first glance, ferns all look the same – green and frondy. But look more closely and you'll see some subtle differences. We spotted several different types on one small area of pavement: one called rustyback – turn the leaves over and you'll see a giveaway rusty-orange colour underneath; another one called limestone fern, which has a distinctive black stem; and hartstongue fern, which is easy to identify because it has long, thin, tongue-like leaves.

If ferns don't really do it for you and if you visit in August, as we did, you'll find the hillside covered in scented flowers and shrubs: there's the rare, dark red helleborine, wild strawberries and juniper bushes. All this plant life attracts masses of butterflies, including the common blue, specialities such as northern brown argus and the rare high brown fritillary. So whether fossils, ferns or fritillaries are your bag, there's plenty to discover on Whitbarrow!

Rustyback fern

Rock outcrop and Whitbarrow Reserve

10 Cheddar Gorge, Somerset

Getting there:

Take the A371 between Weston-super-Mare and Wells; then follow the M5 to junction 22. Follow brown tourist signs up the A38 to Cheddar.

Tel: 01934 742343

Email: caves@cheddarcaves.co.uk

Opening times: Open daily: July-August 10am-5.30pm, September-June 10.30am-5pm. Closed Christmas Eve and Christmas Day.

Charging policy: See www.cheddarcaves.co.uk/tickets.htm

Disabled access: Audio guides specifically for blind and partially sighted people. Wheelchair access to some public areas.

Find out more

Cheddar Caves and Gorge
www.cheddarcaves.co.uk

Cheddar Village
www.cheddarvillage.co.uk

About Britain
www.aboutbritain.com/Cheddar CavesandGorge.htm

The Mammal Society - The Dormouse
www.abdn.ac.uk/mammal/dormouse.shtml

When the word 'cheddar' is mentioned, strangely enough most people think about lunch rather than specialist wildlife eking out a living in some of the most wild and rugged scenery in the southwest of England. But Cheddar is famous for much more than its cheese. The Cheddar Gorge is the largest gorge in Britain and the site of Britain's oldest complete human skeleton, the 9,000-year-old Cheddar man.

The gorge itself consists of carboniferous limestone on top of red sandstone and the near vertical sides indicate that the gorge was river-formed during successive ice ages. Standing on top of the gorge some 113 metres above the road gives the most wonderful views over the whole of the Somerset Levels to the south. However, should you be on top of the gorge in early summer, it's worth a glance down at the plants growing on the edges of the cliffs as here you might find a stellar rarity by the name of Cheddar pink. This beautiful little flower, with its pink-fringed petals and frosted leaves, exists nowhere else in the UK apart from the clifftops of the gorge and it represented a very good start to our filming trip, which would end deep in the bowels of the gorge.

Further still down into the gorge, we met up with Michael Woods, an expert mammologist, keen to take us into the gorge's ancient oak-hazel woods to look for dormice. In times gone by, the common dormouse was a familiar animal to country folk, yet today it is a creature rarely encountered. However, it is still possible to see this shy and nocturnal animal (if you are with someone who has a licence) because the dormice have a terrible fondness for man-made nest-boxes, making them much easier to find when carrying out survey work. Surrounded by hazel, surely the favourite food plant of the dormouse, we waded in to check the boxes and in no time Michael had encountered a solitary female cosily wrapped up inside a nest-box full of honeysuckle bark, dried leaves and moss.

Dormice are simply the most delightful of our small mammals and easily distinguished from all other mice and voles by their fluffy tail, orange-yellow fur, big black eyes and chubby build. This is an animal that virtually never ventures onto the forest floor, but lives a bush and treetop lifestyle finding everything it needs to survive above the ground. The dormouse was gently placed back in its box, as we had an appointment with a colony of bats in the caves at the bottom of the gorge.

Gough's Cave is the largest known cave in the valley bottom at Cheddar, and consists of up to a kilometre of

magnificent caverns which have been carved out by ancient underground rivers that still actively flow beneath the cave. The cave was rediscovered by Richard Gough in 1890, and one or two of its nooks and crannies are perfect roosting spots for lesser horseshoe bats.

With the help of bat expert Roger Martindale, we were able to squeeze into one tiny cave that was home to over 15 lesser horseshoes. Suspended from the ceiling, these bats, which are slightly smaller than a man's thumb, were completely enshrouded in their own wings, which were themselves covered in tiny water droplets. Being curious bats, as soon as we entered the cave our bat detector was able to pick up their echolocation as they sized us up. What a wonderful sound they made too, the best approximation we could come up with was a cross between The Clangers and Morse code!

The lesser horseshoe bat, it has to be said, is not our most attractive bat – they have a strange horseshoe nose-leaf used for directing their ultra high-pitched sounds – but they are certainly one of the most engaging. As they twizzled around, pivoting on their feet clamped to the rock above, our red spotlights made them dazzle like tiny disco glitterballs!

The dormouse and its favourite food

The rare Cheddar pink

Cheddar Gorge and the Somerset Levels

11 London Wetland Centre

Getting there:

Situated less than 1 kilometre from the South Circular (A205) at Roehampton and the A4 at Hammersmith. Nearest tube and bus station: Hammersmith.

Tel: 020 8409 4400

Email: info.london@wwt.org.uk

Opening times: End March–October 9.30am–6pm (last admission 5pm); November–March 9.30am–5pm (last admission 4pm). Closed Christmas Day. Late May–late September late Thursday opening.

Charging policy: Adult £7.25, Concessions £6, Child £4.50, group and family prices available.

Disabled access: Level access and hard-surfaced paths, low-level viewing windows and level access to ground floor hides. Fixed loops in admissions area and in audio visual theatre.

Find out more

London Wetlands Centre
**www.wwt.org.uk/visit/
wetlandcentre/**

RSPB - Gadwall
**www.rspb.org.uk/birds/guide/g/
gadwall/index.asp**

An oasis of calm is certainly not what you would expect to find in the heart of a capital city only a tube ride away from the centre, but this is what greeted us as we arrived at the London Wetland Centre in Barnes, southwest London. Take the tube and then hop on the number 283 bus – you can't miss it, it's clearly labelled the 'duck bus' – and it will take you to wildfowl heaven.

The London Wetland Centre has a captive breeding programme, and on entering the centre you can become acquainted with some of the rarest and most endangered species of wildfowl on the planet. We have two favourites. The first is the 'Ne Ne', a bird with feet specially adapted to walk on volcanoes. It heralds from Hawaii and, until a re-introduction programme, it was the world's most threatened species of goose. The second is the laysan teal from Laysan Island, also right up there at the top of the 'almost didn't make it' list. In 1930, there was only one female left, and the entire species survived because her one clutch of eggs hatched out – talk about a close shave.

The Wetland Centre isn't just about exotic foreigners, however. The reserve, which is built around the remains of four redundant Victorian reservoirs and covers an area of 40 hectares, also holds resident breeding populations of European birds, such as gadwall and shoveler ducks, both of which are present in significant numbers.

Gadwall are about the size of a mallard, and the inexperienced birder might be forgiven for dismissing the female gadwall as a female mallard. A good way to identify them is to look for their overall grey-brown colour and a characteristic white flash or speculum on the trailing edge of the wing. Also, when the female gadwall is 'up tails all' dabbling for water plants, snails and worms, the underside is a noticeably much paler buff colour than that of the female mallard. The UK currently has a breeding population of 790 pairs of gadwall, but

in winter this number can swell to more than 17,000 birds who arrive on their migration from mainland Europe.

But the London Wetland Centre isn't just about birds. The wetland habitats and surrounding grasslands abound with reptiles and insects. Keep your eyes peeled for common lizards and slow worms, which although they look like snakes are actually legless lizards. There's also a recently released population of grass snakes – but if they see you coming first, you're unlikely to see them. Look out for them swimming sinuously through the water in search of their favourite prey of frogs and newts. In summer, you'll certainly hear, but also probably see, grasshoppers and crickets in the grass and we spotted a wonderful black and yellow striped wasp spider enthroned in the middle of its web. Don't be afraid to take a closer look. The web is a masterpiece of construction work, with the spider crouched in the centre, surrounded by zigzag gantries of webbing. No one really knows why it builds its web like this – it could be to deter predators, but equally, because it radiates ultra-violet light, it could be to attract insect prey such as grasshoppers. Forgive the pun; it's a mystery waiting to be unravelled!

The London Wetland Centre is the perfect place not only to bird watch, but also to unwind, especially if you have fractious kids who are sick of sightseeing. The centre runs all sorts of kids' activities, from children's night-time safaris, to bat walks and pond dipping; there are fantastic hides, loads of volunteers to help you identify things and a super café – what more could you want?

The wasp spider and its amazing web

Opposite: A male mallard at the centre

September

The first month of autumn is a time of change as the shrubs and trees, which were covered with flowers in summer, become laden with nuts, berries and seeds. August is also the best month for going on fungal forays.

Families of migratory birds preparing for a flight south cash in on this autumn abundance, as do mammals keen to put on weight or bury stashes of nuts for the oncoming winter. Badgers and foxes can adapt their diet to take advantage of the abundance of fruit such as blackberries, and hazelnuts are in demand with the mammal community as dormice, wood mice and bank voles compete with grey squirrels to get their paws on this protein-rich autumnal food.

Grasshoppers and crickets are still busily reeling away throughout September and often into the first October frosts. But, with most of the mass insect emergences passed, lack of food and shortening days probably trigger the departure of insectivorous birds like swallows and house martins. They often spend a few sociable days perched on telegraph wires surveying the scene before the long journey to sub-Saharan Africa.

1 Stiperstones, Shropshire

Getting there:

Signposted roads lead up from the A488, with a choice of car parks. Long Mynd and Stiperstones Shuttle operates Saturday, Sunday and Bank Holiday Monday, April-October.

Tel: 01743 284280

Email: enquiries@ shropshirewildlifetrust.org.uk

Opening times: 10am-4.30pm (Monday-Saturday).

Charging policy: Not applicable. A charge applies for pre-booked tours.

Disabled access: An 'all-access' path is wide, level and wheelchair friendly.

Find out more

Shropshire Wildlife Trust
www.shropshirewildlifetrust.org. uk/nr_26.html

BBC – Red Grouse
www.rspb.org.uk/birds/guide/r/ redgrouse/index.asp

Shropshire Hills Shuttles
www.shropshirehillsshuttles.co.uk/ routes.html#price

There are some places in Britain where the very bones of our island nation stick up through the earth and, oh boy, do they have a story to tell. We unravelled a remarkable tale as we investigated a 500-million-year-old beach now resting at a height of 425 metres in the heart of Shropshire. We were sent to do the 'Stiperstones Stomp' for our autumn programme on wilderness walks, and it turned out to be a geological and culinary treat! In fact, we probably consumed as many calories at the end as we burnt off doing the eight kilometre walk from the reserve car park to Habberley.

Most people are attracted to the Stiperstones ridge because it forms such a prominent feature in the landscape, and the reason for this is that it is made of a particularly hard and mature sandstone called quartz. This is a very tough mineral and one that will survive the process of weathering longer than any other minerals that we commonly find in sand, like mica and calcite (which comes from shells). Also the grains are rounded. These two clues tell us that the sandstone at Stiperstones was probably laid down on a beach, where time and tide would have winnowed away any softer grains and rounded up the surviving quartz grains. But there's another giveaway here to prove that this area was once a beach – along the Stiperstones walk there are layers of lovely, rounded beach pebbles still visible.

If you're a rock enthusiast, you may find it hard to drag yourself away from the rocks to look at the nature when the surrounding landscape looks virtually empty. But don't be deceived, it's not! If you visit in September and start your walk early in the morning, you are virtually guaranteed great views of one of our largest game birds – the red grouse. The red grouse is a bird of heather moorland and, in fact, a good supply of healthy, young heather is crucial to these birds' survival, because that's what the red grouse principally feed on, although they will eat seeds, berries and insects too. Our first view was a pretty typical one. We were idly scanning the heather with binoculars when we spotted two beady

The Stiperstones quartz ridge

eyes surrounded by a bright white eye ring and topped by a vivid red wattle staring intently back at us. We had been clocked by a male! The red grouse is fiercely territorial and, if another grouse gets too close to its territory, the occupant will explode up out of the heather making a clattering call that sounds as if it's shouting 'go-back, go-back!' at the intruder. If you can recover from the shock quickly enough, you might get a glimpse of one of its best features, its legs – it looks like it's wearing a little pair of feathery white trousers.

Despite its name, the male red grouse is mostly an attractive chestnut colour, in contrast to the black colour of the male black grouse. However, even without this convenient colourcoding, you're unlikely to get them mixed up, because the black grouse tends to be more restricted to moorland edges, usually close to conifer plantations. In addition to the red grouse, there's a healthy population of ravens nesting in the woods round about Stiperstones and they regularly fly up to the ridge to hunt for carrion. You're also likely to see both buzzard and kestrel scanning for prey over the heathery slopes. Although heather is the dominant plant at Stiperstones, many other species also eke out an existence, and late summer to early autumn is a great time to see and taste all kinds of autumn berries. There are bright red cowberries, black crowberries and a purple-berried plant many people know as bilberry, or by its Scottish name blaeberry, but which in Shropshire is known as 'winberry'. The locals are very proud of their winberries, and collect them in great numbers to turn them into a delicious winberry pie. We recommend you do as we did and treat yourself to a slice in The Bog Visitor Centre when you get to the end of your walk. Be prepared to come away with a purple tongue and lips, however, because winberries easily stain and, as a result, were once collected on a vast scale for use in the dyeing industry.

Bilberries, or winberries, as they are known locally

Opposite: The bright red cowberry

2 Slapton Ley, Devon

Getting there:

Slapton Ley is accessed by minor roads from the A379. Car parks on the shingle bar and within the reserve. Nearest train stations: Totnes and Plymouth.

Tel: Reserve – 01548 580685
Field Centre – 01548 580466

Email: reserve.sl@field-studies-council.org

Opening times: Open daily.

Charging policy: Not applicable.

Disabled access: Wheelchair access to information centre and hides.

Find out more

English Nature
http://www.englishnature.org.uk/special/nnr/nnr_details.asp?nnr_name=Slapton+Ley&C=0&Habitat=0&natural_area=&local_team=0&spotlight_reserve=0&X=&NNR_ID=142

Slapton National Nature Reserve
http://www.slnnr.org.uk/links/slaptonley.html

Field Centre
http://www.field-studies-council.org/slaptonley/

Slapton Ley National Nature Reserve is the site of the largest natural freshwater lake in southwest England, which is protected from the salty sea by a narrow strip of land called the Slapton Sands Shingle Ridge. Totalling 211 hectares, the site is much more than just a floating harbour for ducks, however. It comprises a diverse range of wetland habitats, including marshland, extensive areas of reedbeds and wet woodland.

The whole of the reserve is administered by the Field Studies Council (FSC) who, along with Natural England, manage the area as an 'outdoor laboratory' and a base for educational courses and research. Research work has been carried out on the site more or less continuously since 1959, and it is thought that more is known about the ecology of this one site than of any of the other National Nature Reserves in the UK.

If the whole area were to be viewed from the air, it would be the lagoon that dominates the site, and it is effectively divided down the middle at Slapton Bridge. Above Slapton Bridge, the lagoon is called Higher Ley and consists almost entirely of reedbed with encroaching willow-scrub and very little standing water. Below the bridge, the Lower Ley part of the lagoon consists of open water fringed by reeds. The various habitats at Slapton Ley make the reserve worth visiting at any time of the year, as there is always something to see. However, should you only be able to make one visit, then late autumn is definitely the time to choose as this is when the reserve hosts two superb and contrasting spectacles.

Starlings and pied wagtails are species that we frequently see in the summer in small family groups, pairs or singletons, but after the breeding season, both species of bird tend to stay in the UK and gang together with their respective kin to spend the winter at large communal roosts. Certainly in the case of starlings, and to a lesser extent with pied wagtails, the UK population is boosted for all or part of the winter by Continental birds from Scandinavia, Germany, Poland and even as far away as Russia.

Although both species do still roost in cities, probably the largest concentration of natural roost sites is generally found in and around reedbeds. Here the water below the reeds helps to keep the air relatively warm and a constant temperature, while the watery habitat ensures the birds are safe from ground predators. Finding a good and warm reedbed can often be difficult for individual birds, so it makes sense for them to share reedbeds with others. Birds are statistically safer in a crowd when avian predators like sparrowhawks are around and, incredibly, the roost also acts as an information exchange, with birds that are having difficulty in finding food being able to follow other birds that are in better condition the following morning.

Standing on the Slapton Bridge with dusk approaching, it is possible to see two spectacles for the price of one. The only problem we encountered was working out which way to look, as the wagtails roost in the reedbed of Higher Ley, while the starlings usually choose the reedbed near Ireland Bay in Lower Ley.

The first sign that the wagtails were arriving was a small flock building up on the beach side of the shingle ridge. As the flock became larger, small rafts of pied wagtails would flitter up and fly over the A379 road with their characteristic bounding flight, before pitching down into the reedbed. In all, we counted in excess of 600 birds, but this was no more than an estimate as it became difficult to count them with the distraction of the starling display over our shoulder away to the south!

Starling roosts are just one of the UK's natural history events that, in our biased opinion, rival that of wildebeest crossing the Masai Mara. From an initial 'flag' of starlings, numbers built quickly and impressively to a figure that we estimated to be at least 75,000 birds. Before they dropped into the reeds, the flock put on a show – it swarmed, swirled, twirled and morphed into a multitude of different shapes, and no sooner had the show begun than the birds had melted away into the reeds, leaving us wanting more, which is exactly how it should be.

Pied wagtails spend the winter in the UK

The amazing blue of a swallow drinking

Slapton Ley freshwater lake and the village of Torcross

3 Kenwood Estate, North London

Getting there:

Hampstead Lane, NW3. Nearest train station: Hampstead Heath (2 kilometres); nearest tube stations: Archway or Golders Green then bus 210, or Highgate (1 kilometre).

Tel: 020 8348 1286

Email: customers@english-heritage.org.uk

Opening times: Open daily: April–October 11am–5pm, November–March 11am– 4pm. Closed 24–26 December and 1 January.

Charging policy: Not applicable.

Disabled access: Free parking and mobility vehicle from the car park to the House and restaurant.

Find out more

Kenwood House – English Heritage Site
www.english-heritage.org.uk/server.php?show=conProperty.106

RSPB – Ring-necked Parakeet
www.rspb.org.uk/birds/guide/r/ringneckedparakeet/index.asp

BBC Science and Nature – Grey Squirrel
www.bbc.co.uk/nature/wildfacts/factfiles/190.shtml

Every year thousands of visitors flock to the Kenwood Estate, run by English Heritage, to enjoy open-air concerts and plays in the beautiful landscaped grounds, or to wander around the neo-classical Kenwood House and admire paintings by Rembrandt, Vermeer, Turner, Reynolds and Gainsborough.

But the Kenwood Estate, with its meadows, woodland, grassland and lakes, is also a good place to see wildlife, and the great thing about the animals is that they're so used to people it won't just be the masterpieces with which you'll be able to get up close and personal.

For instance, there's a healthy population of rabbits who find the underlying sandy soil perfect for their labyrinth of rabbit warrens and, as they graze contentedly on the abundant grass, they tend to ignore the visitors. We tested this and got, incredibly, to within a metre of one before it scampered off.

One of the best times to enjoy the wildlife here is in the autumn, when the birds and mammals are busy gathering, eating and burying the plentiful food on offer.

A good place to start your search is the Duelling Ground in the woodland. This small clearing was where 18th-century gentlemen would settle their disputes with pistols. No such drama now, but we caught up with the normally secretive jay, the most colourful member of the crow family. In autumn, jays are famous for collecting and burying acorns and they've been known to stash away up to 5,000 of these little food parcels in a season.

Grey squirrels were just as busy doing the same thing. There's a large population in Kenwood thriving in the predominantly broadleaved woodland of the estate. The greys have probably been here since the early 20th century, about the same time

that the shy, retiring red squirrel was last seen on Hampstead Heath.

Greys can be seen feeding not just on acorns, but on anything organic. This includes pillaging the contents of Kenwood's bins. One bold creature was seen dragging along a baguette twice its size. On our visit, we even saw a cheeky individual digging up an acorn that a jay had just buried, and scurrying off to bury it elsewhere.

Another resident at Kenwood is the ring-necked parakeet, whose numbers have tripled in the last three years. Parakeets originate from the Indian subcontinent, but, since escaping from aviaries in the UK, they've now colonised large parts of southeast England. It is thought that the English population now numbers around 5,900. Parakeets are characterised by their bright green plumage, rosy beaks, and a black and pink ring encircling the necks of adult birds. They have pointed wings, a long tail and very steady, direct flight. Often, though, it's their noisy, raucous call that attracts your attention.

In autumn, you can watch them through your binoculars in the beech trees feasting on the food. They hang upside down inching their way to the very ends of branches, where they remove the beech mast in order to extricate the nutritious nut. Inside is a nut which a whole range of birds feeds on – from chaffinches to pigeons. The parakeet manipulates the mast, using its feet like hands, and then prises it open using its beak and tongue.

No prizes for guessing who else was up the tree doing exactly the same thing – a grey squirrel.

The neo-classical Kenwood House in north London

Grey squirrels spend the autumn storing food for the winter months

Opposite: The ring-necked parakeet

4 Wallington, Northumberland

Getting there:

Take the B6343 from Morpeth (19 kilometres) or the A696 from Belsay (9½ kilometres), then take the B6342 to Cambo.

Tel: 01670 773600

Email: wallington@nationaltrust.org.uk

Opening times: Grounds dawn-dusk (exc Christmas day). For times for walled garden and house, see website.

Charging policy: House, garden and grounds: adult £8, child £4, family £20, groups £6.80.

Disabled access: Wheelchairs available for loan, access to some public areas.

Native white-clawed crayfish

Find out more

National Trust
www.nationaltrust.org.uk/main/
w-vh/w-visits/w-findaplace/
w-wallington/

UK Safari - Crayfish
www.uksafari.com/crayfish.htm

Waterscape - River Wansbeck
www.waterscape.com/
River_Wansbeck

The south front of the fine William and Mary house at Wallington

Dating back to 1688, Wallington is one of the finest houses and estates in northeast England. While many people come to view the house or wander around the gardens, few visitors realise the estate provides a sanctuary for two native species very much under threat from aggressive trans-Atlantic invaders, the red squirrel and the crayfish.

Autumn is a busy time for red squirrels and every single one we saw was either burying peanuts from the feeders or acorns from the surrounding oaks, or eating in an attempt to put on weight in preparation for the oncoming winter. The red squirrel is one of the UK mammals that doesn't hibernate, but toughs it out during the cold weather. In summer, red squirrels are a bright chestnut colour but, as winter approaches, their coats turn a brownish hue, making them look much darker and closer in appearance to the dreaded greys. However, reds still have their wonderfully distinctive ear tufts at all times of the year, making them easy to differentiate even in poor light.

The Wallington Estate has many areas to explore, including a stretch of the Wansbeck river, which meanders for two kilometres through the southern part of the estate. Not only is the river very picturesque, but it is also one of the most important sites in the UK for the rare and native white-clawed crayfish. Elsewhere in the UK, crayfish populations have crashed dramatically as our native species has simply been unable to compete with another aggressive American invader, the signal crayfish, which is a passive carrier for a crayfish plague, a disease that has decimated our native species.

Wansbeck River is fortunately a 'signal free zone' at present, and the section of river which passes through the estate is particularly well suited to the native species with long stretches of the riverbed covered with large stones, providing them with a perfect refuge from predators. Let's hope that it remains that way.

5 Peatlands Park, Northern Ireland

Getting there:

Peatlands Park is located at Junction 13 off the M1.

Tel: 028 38851102

Email: peat.info@doeni.gov.uk

Opening times: Open daily 9am–9pm Easter Sunday–September; 9am–5pm October–Easter Saturday.

Charging policy: Not applicable.

Disabled access: Full access for wheelchairs.

The sundew has developed alternative ways of feeding itself

Find out more

Peatlands – Places to Visit
http://www.peatlandsni.gov.uk/places/index.htm

Peatlands Park
http://www.ehsni.gov.uk/places/parks/peatlands.shtml

Discover Northern Ireland
http://www.discovernorthernireland.com/product.aspx?ProductID=2847

It was the pine cone that really blew us away. It looked a bit tatty – missing a few scales – but then Professor Valerie Hall, from Queen's University, Belfast, revealed that this cone had been preserved in the peat for 8,000 years. A pine cone that was formed 6,000 years before Jesus was a twinkle in his dad's eye – and it still opens and closes in response to the weather.

Peatlands Park is a little slice of moorland on the border of the counties of Armagh and Tyrone. We visited in September, when the peat bog was awash with gorgeous autumnal hues. You can see where the peat used to be cut and dried for turf to burn, and take a train, which was once used to ferry the turf out of the bog, round part of the park. In places the bog is absolutely pristine and the peat twelve metres thick. As you can imagine, this kind of environment supports a rather unusual ecosystem, from dense, damp mats of sphagnum moss to church-incense-scented myrtle bushes. There are even cranberries festooning the bog grass.

Because there are so few nutrients in a peat bog, many plants have evolved alternative ways of feeding themselves. The sundew is a carnivorous plant that catches flies with its sticky, red tentacles; the flies then asphyxiate in the sweet mucilage the plant releases. The plant is highly developed and even able to move its tentacles to bring its prey into contact with as many of these stalks as possible. Some of these plants can live for 50 years and have become so adapted to their lifestyle they no longer have an enzyme to help them absorb nitrates from the soil.

Even more unusually for Ireland, the bog garden is filled with pitcher plants. A native of North America, the brilliant-green, vase-like pitchers are full of a cocktail of enzymes that digest hapless insects that fall into the trap. The mouth of the pitcher is covered with backward pointing hairs to prevent food from crawling out.

With limited oxygen available for plant growth and low-nitrate levels, the bog is certainly a hostile environment – and yet it is these very qualities that allow things such as Valerie's pine cone to have been preserved in the peat.

Peatlands, the moorland in autumn

6 Glen Tanar, Aberdeenshire

Getting there:

Glen Tanar Estate, Brooks House, AB34 5EU. Leave A90, follow signs for Stonehaven, then for A957 to Banchory. At Crathes take A93; in Aboyne turn left at the green, left at T-junction. Follow signs to Glen Tanar along B976, turn left at Tower of Ess into Estate.

Tel: 01339 886451

Email: office@glentanar.co.uk

Opening times: April–September 10am–5pm (Wednesday–Monday); October–March 10am–5pm (Thursday–Monday).

Charging policy: Small parking charge.

Disabled access: Ranger Service can help less able visitors on request. Contact Ranger Service for guided events for disabled groups.

Find out more

Glen Tanar
www.glentanar.co.uk/

Visit a Forest in Scotland
www.forest-education.org/ visitaforest/sites/ab/estates/oo1.htm

Visit Deeside
www.visitdeeside.org.uk/about_the_ area/places_to_visit/glen_tanar.htm

Glen Tanar is one of those locations that's straight out of a tourist brochure. Snow-capped peaks, crystal-clear mountain streams and pine forest as far as the eye can see. With over 100,000 hectares, there's almost too much to take in. But, worry not, because this spot provided us with one of our best wildlife experiences in the whole of Scotland. What we were looking for were creatures that are real specialists of this kind of terrain: capercaillie, Scottish crossbill and salmon. Capercaillie are a bit tough to see. These large, turkey-sized members of the grouse family should stand out like sore thumbs, but in fact they're really secretive creatures of the forest. Most of the time, you'd have more chance of seeing Lord Lucan riding Shergar than you would of finding one of these animals. Not only are they hard to spot, there aren't that many of them either. In spring, at places such as the RSPB reserve at Loch Garten, you might get a glimpse of a male capercaillie at one of their mating sites known as 'leks'. Otherwise, it's a bit like looking for a needle in the proverbial haystack.

We boosted our chances of seeing capercaillie by visiting the Glen Tanar estate when they did their annual count of these birds. Numbers of capercaillie are low and falling, so getting an accurate picture of how they're faring year on year is really important. At Glen Tanar the birds are flushed from the forest by a team of beaters. Lying in wait are counters, who then record the numbers and the sex of any birds they see.

Not wanting to yomp through knee-high heather with the beaters, we wisely spent our time with the counters; we've got to admit it was the easy shift, but it was pretty exciting nevertheless. We could hear the beaters in the distance and then a quick call of 'over' as the first capercaillie, a female, flew out of the forest and past us. The view was fleeting, but well worth it. It was followed by three more birds, including one that took an age to clear out of view. There were three more drives through the forest and by the end of the day 20 birds had been spotted.

The reason that the capercaillie are here at all is because this estate still has remnants of the Caledonian pine forest and lots of its principal tree, the Scots pine. Despite its size, the capercaillie is vulnerable. They need large interconnected areas of mature Scots pine in which to live, with ground cover of blaeberry (or bilberry south of the border), heather and other plants to provide the adults and their chicks with food. Once upon a time, this kind of habitat would have covered much of the Highlands but now only a tiny fraction remains. Glen Tanar is one of the last strongholds for this endangered bird. Ironically they've already become extinct once – only to be re-introduced in the mid-19th century –

and some believe they're prime candidates for extinction again. Their future success hangs by a thread.

The other specialist of the pine forest is the Scottish crossbill. This thick-set finch with its distinctive crossed bill is only found in one country in the world – Scotland. They are at the heart of a raging debate within the bird fraternity as to whether they merit the distinction of being a full species, and it's only recently that their endemic UK status has been confirmed. You can see crossbills in other parts of the UK, however, so how do you know whether you're looking at a Scottish species or not? Well, to the naked eye, they look pretty much the same, so it's really down to location. If you're in the Caledonian pine forest, you can be reasonably confident that it's a Scottish crossbill. If you're in a pine forest in England, it's just a common crossbill.

Male capercaillie lekking

Scottish crossbills like to feed on the cones of Scots pine and other conifers in the forest, and their bills are highly adapted at nipping the outer case of the cone to reveal the tasty seed underneath. You'll get flocks flitting around the forest all the time, but they tend not to stay still for long. Our tip would be to stake out a particular patch of forest and see what turns up. If crossbill aren't being compliant, you may well get views of siskin, another pine forest specialist. If there are trees with berries on nearby – such as rowan – you might get good views of bullfinch too. All in all, a veritable feast of finch.

Our closest encounter with the wildlife at Glen Tanar was coming face to face with a stranded salmon in the river that runs through the estate. The River Dee is nearby and this is top salmon country. In autumn, fish return here to spawn and work their way up to their 'redds' in the shadow of Mount Keen. Well, that's the theory, but here we were looking at one fish that wasn't going to make it that far.

Scottish crossbill – on a pine tree

We'd just unpacked the camera gear to get shots of a waterfall when we noticed a male fish gasping for air, having misjudged its leap and landed in a tiny pool of water with barely enough water to cover its gills. After a bit of manhandling, we managed to move the salmon into a position where it could find its way back into the water. Some may feel we interfered, that we should have let nature take its course. Our view was that this was one creature that deserved a break.

A salmon makes its way back upriver

7 Devereux Wootton Farm, Herefordshire

Getting there:

Devereux Wootton Farm, Norton Canon, Hereford, HR4 8QN. Exit the A480 near Norton Canon on to the B4230. The farm is signposted on the left.

Tel: 01544 318247

Email: patrick@wrixon.co.uk

Opening times: Open all year, telephone to arrange a visit.

Charging policy: Not applicable.

Disabled access: Disabled access is limited at Devereux Farm, telephone with their exact requirements and they will try to accommodate you.

Find out more

Defra
http://cwr.defra.gov.uk/Default.aspx?Module=CountryWalkDetails&Site=5281

Birds of Britain - Kestrel
www.birdsofbritain.co.uk/bird-guide/kestrel.htm

UK Biodiversity Action Plan - Hedgerows
www.ukbap.org.uk/UKPlans.aspx?ID=7

Looking over the landscape of this part of Herefordshire, not far from the Welsh border, you're immediately struck by the peace and beauty of the place. On the distant horizon is Hay Bluff, one of the highest points of the Black Mountains and, in between mile upon mile of rich farmland, grassland dotted with sheep, hedgerows, ploughed fields, orchards and woodland.

The 200-hectare Devereux Wootton Farm is about 16 kilometres from Hereford and is a mixed farm with arable land, sheep and orchards. Opened as a showcase to demonstrate how wildlife and farming can be integrated, the farm has eight kilometres of public paths and bridleways, and autumn is a great time to sample some of these rarely trodden byways.

While we walked, it was noticeable how much of what we saw has been specially planted to provide habitat and food for the wildlife. The farm is a mosaic of small plots covered by tall scrubby vegetation, long grass margins on the edges of fields, and new hedgerows planted in an attempt to redress the disastrous loss of these wonderful wildlife corridors over the last 50 years.

The scrubby plots brought rewarding birding views very quickly, as they contain a mix of seed, such as sunflower and millet, that birds love. Flocks of hundreds of greenfinches flew in and out of the fields, plundering the plants for their seeds, before flying off again to seek the sanctuary of the hedges. Their twittering song is distinctive, and the flash of yellow and green make these finches truly colourful. You might see chaffinch and, if you're lucky, goldfinch too.

As finches are one of its favourite prey, you might also glimpse a sparrowhawk flying out of nowhere fast and low to catch a finch unawares with its powerful claws. This specialised hunting machine has recovered following a population crash in the 1960s.

It's worth taking a break in the field margins. These are sown with a mixture of grass species and are allowed to grow high, providing great cover for small mammals. You'll have to be patient and sit quietly, but you may be

A kestrel looks for its next meal in the hedgerow

lucky enough to see some of the small inhabitants that live here, including field vole, bank vole, wood mouse, yellow-necked mouse and the common shrew.

Mice have larger ears and eyes, and pointed noses compared to the blunt snouts of voles. The biggest is the yellow-necked mouse. They have limited distribution, and the Welsh borders is one of the best places to find them. They're chunkier than the wood mouse, with a pale yellow collar across their throats. When caught in traps, they're feisty little creatures inclined to bite whoever tries to hold them!

These field margins are also great places to try and spot birds of prey hoping to take advantage of all this mammal food – such as kestrels, for instance, which we often see hovering along the edges of motorways. They choose roadside verges because their main food, voles and mice, thrive in the undisturbed grassland. To kestrels, therefore, the 30 kilometres of field margins at Devereux Wootton were like a series of motorway cafés.

Another bird of prey to look out for is the buzzard. After being persecuted in the past, they're reappearing everywhere, and are now the commonest of all our raptors – especially here. This borderland area between Wales and England, known as the Welsh Marches, has one of the densest populations of buzzard, but even so it's still a thrill to see them riding the thermals without a wing flap – poetry in motion.

Before you leave, do check out the hedgerows. There are tall, dense ancient ones growing alongside others planted just a few years ago, and they're all covered in berries – such as sloes, hawthorns and rosehips. Great food for birds, but also for humans if you dig out those old recipe books.

You might see a greenfinch in the hedgerow – maybe on a hawthorn bush

Opposite: The yellow-necked mouse

8 Isle of Anglesey, North Wales

Getting there:

The motorway network and the A55 and the A5 offer access to and right across the island.

Tel: Anglesey Tourism Association (ATA) – 0845 074 0587

Email: info@visitanglesey.com

Opening times: Open daily.

Charging policy: Not applicable.

Disabled access: Disabled access available around Anglesey but varies. Contact Anglesey Tourism Association.

Find out more

Tourism information
www.visitanglesey.com/

Anglesey, Wales
www.anglesey-history.co.uk/

Conchological Society of Great Britain and Ireland
www.conchsoc.org/

BBC Northwest Wales – Penrhos
www.bbc.co.uk/wales/northwest/
outdoors/placestogo/reserves/
penrhos.shtml

The Isle of Anglesey is situated just a stone's throw from mainland Wales and boasts over 200 kilometres of coastline. Like many islands, variety is the key here and Anglesey has got pretty much everything, from rocky and sandy beaches with shells, to dramatic sea cliffs with fabulous rock formations, not to mention a massive range of inland habitats and a wealth of wildlife.

Of course, it would be impossible to show you everything Anglesey has to offer in just one visit, so we chose to focus on Penrhos Nature Reserve in the north of the island and one of our favourite pastimes – shell collecting.

There are over 650 shells common to British beaches, and most of us will have picked up one or another of them at some time. Kids love them, and there's probably not a parent among you who has not got back home from holiday to find their kids' pockets stuffed full of shells and sand, or a neat row of them on the bathroom sink, and the basin full of sand!

The great thing about collecting shells is that it's politically correct. Shells are simply the discarded hard parts of marine molluscs – the soft-bodied creature that created the shell is long since dead and gone by the time you pick them up off the beach.

Shells are built up in three layers, a hard outer 'horny' layer for protection, a chalky one beneath, then a glossy inner one, which can be iridescent and is sometimes used for jewellery. Shells come in two basic types: bivalves, which is when two shells are joined together by a hinge, and univalves – a single shell. Bivalves are things like cockles and mussels, while univalves are often conical in shape like limpets, or turret shaped like winkles and whelks.

A shell is designed to grow with its occupant. Look closely and you'll see that a limpet has growth rings on it almost like the rings that make up the trunk of a tree; whelks increase in size by adding an extra 'whorl' or twist. Shells have a wonderful variety of shape and form, but that's not all there is to love about them; they also have fabulously

descriptive names: pelican's foot shell, tusk shell and tower shell – go on, take a guess at what they look like!

One of our favourite shells is the cowry. You commonly see beautiful big specimens of these in gift shops, but most of these have been imported from abroad. It is possible to find them on British beaches, however, and, although they're not that common, they are easily overlooked, making finding them a great challenge. In our case it became fiercely competitive. Cowries are a single shell or univalve, usually about the size of a pea or smaller. The rounded shell is curled over so that both sides meet in a straight line on the flatter underside, and they are ridged from front to stern. There are two types on British beaches – pale, pinkish white ones (Arctic cowries) and darker, brownish ones with black spots (European cowries) – and if you take on the cowry challenge, you'll need a good selection of each kind to have any chance of winning!

It's hard to do justice to a place like Anglesey in a programme such as *Nature's Calendar*, but suffice to say that shells are not the only thing to find on the island – there are wonderful rocky beaches with rockpools to explore at any time of the year, in summer the cliffs in the west are home to thousands of nesting seabirds and, if you fancy a winter getaway, visit Newborough Warren, a coniferous forest built on a massive dune system in the southwest of the island, and get a great view of hundreds of ravens coming into roost.

South Stacks sea cliffs, Isle of Anglesey

Common mussels are bivalve shells

Opposite: A European cowry – a univalve

9 Galloway Forest Park, Scotland

Getting there:

From the south take the A75 to Newton Stewart signposted to Stranraer; from Glasgow take A77 to Girvan then A714 to Newton Stewart, or A77 to Ayr then A713 to New Galloway.

Tel: District Office – 01671 402420

Email: galloway@forestry.gsi.gov.uk

Opening times: Telephone District Office for visitor centre times.

Charging policy: Parking charges apply.

Disabled access: Easy access for disabled. There is an All Abilities trail suitable for people in wheelchairs.

Find out more

Forestry Commission
www.forestry.gov.uk/galloway-forestpark

RSPB – Red Kite
www.rspb.org.uk/birds/guide/r/redkite/index.asp

Wildlife Scotland – Red Deer
http://wildlife.visitscotland.com/species/land-animals/Red-Deer

Galloway Forest Park is huge – nearly 500 square kilometres of mountain, forest, lochs and rivers. It's the biggest forest park in the UK, and the scenery is so rugged and dramatic it's known as 'the Highlands of the Lowlands'.

It's also home to all sorts of wildlife – golden eagle, hen harrier, four species of owl, red squirrel, and the elusive otter and pine marten – and it's criss-crossed by quiet roads, tracks and paths for you to explore.

But where to start in such a vast park? And what animals to look for? Well, the highest peak in the area is the Merrick, at 843 metres above sea level, and from here you can get fantastic views of the scenery all around. But climbing it is a bit strenuous, and there are no guarantees that you'll see that golden eagle. Better, perhaps, to concentrate on two species of wildlife that are very accessible, but also magnificent – red deer and red kite.

Autumn is a great time to see red deer, and into early October is the rut, when the males compete with each other for access to females to mate with. To see two stags clashing – with their antlers locked together, pushing back and forth until one gives in leaving the victor triumphant – is one of the most exciting wildlife spectacles you can ever witness.

The red deer is our largest land mammal, and you can see them all over the Forest Park. But if you want to make it easy on yourself, head for the Red Deer viewpoint near Clatteringshaws visitor centre. This 80-hectare deer range has regular guided tours with the chance to feed the deer, which are very used to people.

When we visited, the rut was already under way. You can smell a mature stag, and watch and hear him roar. His sole purpose is to gather together as many females as he can. If he's a young stag, he'll have to challenge the dominant male, and this may lead to a clashing of antlers. We saw one stag standing proudly on a rocky precipice looking just like the Monarch of the Glen. Every now and then he would walk around his group of females, smelling them to assess if any of the hinds were in season, and making sure they knew who was boss.

The Forestry Commission Scotland, who manage the park, run an annual red deer rutting event, which almost guarantees fighting stags. They remove the dominant stag a few days earlier and keep him in a smaller enclosure. On the event day they release him. By then he's so pent up with frustration, he's bound to take on any other male that tries to move in on his females. If this is a bit too stage-managed for your taste, then put aside some time to watch the herd. If you visit around the first two weeks in October, your timing should be spot on.

Just outside the park is a guaranteed wildlife spectacle: the feeding of the red kites. After centuries of persecution, when red kites were almost wiped out, there have been a number of successful re-introduction programmes throughout the UK, including in Galloway. There's a red kite trail alongside Loch Ken, where you should manage to spot this beautiful bird riding the thermals. To distinguish it from another bird of prey like a buzzard, look for its distinctive forked tail.

These animals are mostly scavengers, and will take meat that's put out for them. This is what farmer Ann Johnstone does at 2pm every day at Bellymack Hill Farm near Laurieston. As soon as the meat is down, red kites, along with the odd buzzard, start circling. It takes a while for them to take the food but, once one starts, they all do. They'll continue to feed on and off for a few hours – swooping out of the air, twisting their tails like rudders and plucking the meat off the ground – but every now and again there's a frenzy. If the sight of up to 30 red kites swooping and diving doesn't make you gasp, nothing will!

Male red deer rutting

A red kite swoops down for food

The 'Highlands of the Lowlands' – Galloway Forest Park

10 Dalby Forest, North Yorkshire

Getting there:

Take the A170 Helmsley to Scarborough road to Thornton le Dale and follow brown tourist signs.

Tel: Visitor Centre – 01751 460295

Email: nym@forestry.gov.uk

Opening times: Open daily Easter–October

Charging policy: Foot, cycle and horse access free; at peak times cars £5, minibuses £7.50; coaches (by appointment only) £25.

Disabled access: Disabled access to site and visitor centre

Find out more

Forestry Commission
www.forestry.gov.uk/dalbyforest

Dalby Forest
www.touristnetuk.com/NE/ forest-enterprise/

Wildlife Trust – Small Mammals
www.wildlifetrust.org.uk/dorset/ faqs/small%20Mammals%20FAQ. doc

Dalby Forest, near Pickering, contains over twenty million trees. As you can imagine, therefore, the forest is massive: it covers an area equivalent to roughly 3,500 football pitches, so it did seem a bit unfair when we were sent there in autumn to search out our smallest mammals. Talk about looking for needles in a haystack! We clearly needed some help and fortunately members of the Forestry Commission, who manage the woodland, were more than willing to give us a hand. Very early in the morning, they helped us to set small mammal traps in and at the edge of an area of the forest that had been clear-felled, a perfect habitat for mice and voles, which need low-growing cover to tunnel through and to protect them from their many winged predators. Two hours later we went back and struck lucky! We had caught several woodmice and two short-tailed voles. It seemed like a good opportunity to compare their different features.

Woodmice have a sharp pointed face, huge ears like radar dishes, enormous eyes and tails that are longer than their bodies. In contrast, short-tailed voles have a much blunter face, smaller eyes, minute ears and a characteristic short tail from which they take their name. It seems likely that these differences are due to lifestyle. Woodmice are nocturnal, and to escape predators such as owls they need particularly good hearing and sight, but also a rather acrobatic approach to life – and there's no doubt a long tail helps with balance. Short-tailed voles, on the other hand, spend far more time hidden away in the grass burrowing little tunnels through the cover. If you think about it, big ears could be a serious disadvantage in such conditions – constantly getting snagged on bits of bramble.

Now, during the course of filming *Nature's Calendar*, we've been asked to do more than a few weird things – and, hey, we're always willing to oblige in the name of nature. But being asked to blow on small mammals' genitalia seemed above and beyond the call of duty! Apparently, however, this rather bizarre practice is crucial to identifying males from females, which is important when monitoring small mammal populations. And it's a technique that doesn't just

work with the small scurrying kind; it works with the small flying kind too.

We had barely mastered our 'blowing technique' before we were called upon to help sex bats. The Forestry Commission has put up a couple of hundred bat boxes on a few of their many millions of trees. Our visit to Dalby Forest took place in October and we were fortunate enough to join the rangers on their last check-up of the year before the bats vanished off to their winter hibernation sites. A number of bats were roosting up for the day in the boxes, and our new-found skills were called into action. We found seven or eight pipistrelle bats, all but one of which were female. All bat species are protected in the UK and you need a special licence to handle them, so we were only called upon for our fur-ruffling abilities.

Bats are the only mammals that can fly and, as such, can exploit a source of food – flying insects – that their land-bound relatives cannot. In winter, however, food on the wing is scarce so they must go into hibernation, which involves entering a state of torpor much deeper than their daily roosting behaviour. To avoid using any unnecessary energy, the hibernation site must be dark with a pretty constant temperature – caves, trees and roof spaces are favourite sites.

A number of species of bat roost and hibernate upside down because their limbs, which are so well adapted for flying, cannot support their weight in a standing or sitting position. British bats mate in autumn, but the females of some species can store viable sperm until the following spring and then use it to fertilise their eggs. The young are usually born singly and drop into a pouch made by the female curling over her tail. The young bat will cling onto the mother's teat for about a fortnight, after which time she will hang the juvenile up in a safe place by its feet and go off in search of food. Wouldn't it be nice if we could do the same with our offspring!

Dalby Forest – the home of literally millions of trees

Pipistrelle bat and young

....

Opposite: Short-tailed field vole

October

October is a time of huge change: the leaves turn wonderful autumnal hues but, for grey seals, and red and fallow deer, this is when the breeding season takes off in style. The summer migrants have well and truly left and the huge numbers of winter thrushes, waders and wildfowl that spend winter in the UK are imminent. Small mammals stash food for the lean times ahead or concentrate on putting on weight before they hibernate.

One unmissable spectacle very early in October is rutting red deer. The antlered stags spend the month with sex on their mind, often driving themselves to the point of exhaustion to ensure they get it. Seeing the males bellowing and strutting around as they control their harems is a magnificent sight. On beaches of the Northern and Western Isles bull seals are also fighting for mating rights.

Tawny owls are particularly vocal in October as they assert their territorial rights over patches of wood and suburban parks. And don't forget to just enjoy the colours as the chlorophyll fades from the deciduous trees for another year.

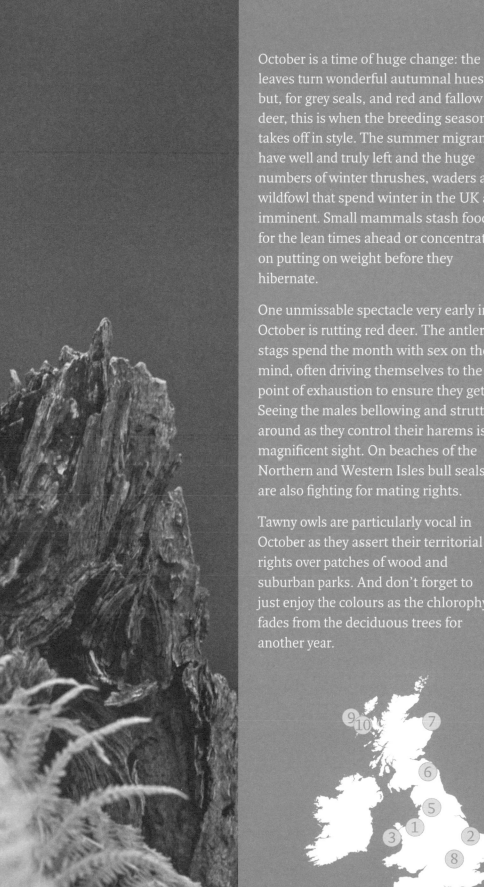

1 The Dee Estuary

Getting there:

Access from Talacre, which is signed off the A548, 3 kilometres east of Prestatyn. Buses run daily from Flint or Prestatyn.

Tel: 01244 537440

Email: deenaturalists@btinternet.com

Opening times: Open daily.

Charging policy: Not applicable.

Disabled access: Some access available, telephone for advice.

Find out more

Bird Watcher's Diary
www.deeestuary.co.uk/highbirdo6.
htm

Deeside Naturalists' Society
www.deeestuary.co.uk/dns/index.
htm

RSPB - Black-tailed Godwit
www.rspb.org.uk/birds/guide/b/
blacktailedgodwit/index.asp

Bird Guides - Dunlin
www.birdguides.com/thml/vidlib/
species/Calidris_alpina.htm

The Dee Estuary is one of the most important estuaries in the UK and Europe for its populations of waders and wildfowl, which swell to astonishing numbers during the winter. During the autumn, the Dee is like an avian international crossroads where birds that have bred throughout the northern hemisphere spend time restocking their reserves before either moving further south, or deciding whether this will be their home for the next six months.

The estuary itself is actually funnel-shaped and lies between the Wirral peninsula in northwest England and Flintshire in northeast Wales. The whole site consists of an enormous slice of inter-tidal sand and mudflats with large areas of saltmarsh. There are a number of areas from which you can view the birds but, as ever when visiting a site like this, it's absolutely crucial you check the tide before setting out – get it wrong and you will see either next to nothing or just specks on the horizon; get it right, however, and the birds will come flocking.

Without doubt one of the premier spots for watching the birds on the estuary is at the Connah's Quay reserve, a site owned by Powergen and managed by the Deeside Naturalists' Society. This superb site, situated close to where the River Dee discharges into the estuary and with the Power station as a backdrop, gives an excellent viewpoint over the whole of the estuary as the birds are pushed up onto the reserve preceding a high tide.

Although small numbers of oystercatcher, redshank, curlew, dunlin and lapwing can be seen at low tide in the drainage channels from the West Hide, the best time is an hour and a half before high tide when numbers build and the birds get closer and closer. As we stood with binoculars and scopes at hand, and with the water steadily rising, it certainly felt like a gathering storm as the numbers of birds slowly rose, pushed off their feeding grounds further up towards the mouth of the estuary at Hilbre Island, Salisbury Bank and Thurstaston.

Feeding in the channel next to the hide, we had wonderful views of at least six spotted redshank alongside its much more common cousin, the redshank. Superficially, in winter plumage these two species of redshank look very similar, but the much more unusual 'spotshank', as it is known, is paler and more elegant than the redshank. Spotshanks are double-passage migrants, meaning that birds seen in the spring are on their way north to breeding grounds in Scandinavia, Northern Russia and Siberia but, in the autumn, they'll be using the Dee as a refuelling pit stop before travelling to winter anywhere from West Africa, through

India to Vietnam. The spotshanks have a unique way of feeding for a wader and, as they waded up to their bellies and up-ended like a duck, we knew we were being treated to some top behaviour.

The Dee is now considered an area of international importance for wintering numbers of black-tailed godwit. As the rising tide pushed whole rafts of these birds towards us and across onto Oakenholt Marsh in front of the distinctive Flint Castle, we attempted to count a huge flock of this Icelandic breeding wader as they were nudged across the ever-decreasing mudflat. Approximately 3,000 was the final tally we came up with, which could have easily represented a quarter of all the UK's wintering black-tailed godwit population!

In front of Flint Castle, we saw huge numbers of the diminutive dunlin as they scoured the marsh looking for any morsel of food recently uncovered by the tide, until, in a flash, every single bird took flight. A peregrine was picked up diving at the dunlin – one dive, another dive, and a third dive – and as the peregrine flew off back over the castle, we noticed it had indeed made a capture. As we stood with our mouths open, we realised it was moments like that that we all go birdwatching for.

A flock of oystercatchers in the estuary

The diminutive dunlin

The Dee Estuary

2 Snettisham, Norfolk

Getting there:

From the A149 Snettisham and Dersingham bypass, take Beach Road for about 1 kilometre. The reserve is signposted on the left.

Tel: 01485 542689

Email: snettisham@rspb.org.uk

Opening times: Open daily.

Charging policy: Not applicable.

Disabled access: Two hides are accessible for disabled visitors. Visitors with limited mobility may drive to the first hide – contact the warden to obtain a permit. Disabled viewing points are also available.

Find out more

RSPB
www.rspb.org.uk/reserves/guide/s/snettisham/about.asp

Snettisham Park
www.snettishampark.co.uk/

Norfolk Ornithologists' Association
www.birdguides.com/html/clubs/EAnglia/norfolk1.htm

We are so lucky in Britain – we live on an island in the epicentre of a busy migration route. In autumn, hundreds of thousands of birds are on the move, some going south for a warmer winter, others coming here from the even colder Arctic, and many also passing through.

One of the best places to see migration in action is in northwest Norfolk. We started before dawn on Snettisham beach. A full moon ensured ethereal views, but more importantly created a large high tide. We were looking forward to one of the UK's most impressive wildlife spectacles – thousands of waders flying over our heads.

The ultimate swarming wader has to be knot. They arrive from Arctic Canada in early autumn to feed in the Wash, but on the highest tides they are pushed off the mudflats and forced to roost on the lagoons behind the beach at the Snettisham RSPB reserve.

Initially, the only birds we could see were groups of oystercatchers and curlew flying past. Then we caught sight of the first cloud of knot – a mass of about a thousand birds, morphing into globular shapes like a living lava lamp. The noise of thousands of beating wings a few metres over our heads was spellbinding.

As the tide reached its peak, more flocks flew across, an awesome spectacle in both scale and beauty. On arrival at the reserve, the knot usually land on the shingle banks of the lagoon. Leaving the beach, we walked round to the reserve and settled in a hide overlooking the lagoons and the recently arrived knot. As ever, when confronted by a huge population of birds, the number one question was 'How many?' On the ground, the birds were so tightly packed that the best method was to try and estimate what made up a thousand birds and then try to calculate the 'thousand blocks' in the flock. The best count – which was scarcely more than a guess – was around 80,000. At random moments, the birds would become flustered and a giant living wave rippled across the flock, giving the impression that the bank was seconds away from sliding into the lagoon. Then a lone oystercatcher walked through the flock, for no apparent reason other than mischief, forcing the smaller knot to move out of its way and leaving a hole in its wake.

Suddenly the entire flock took off without any warning, wheeled to the right, split into two groups, merged back together then, as one giant cloud, drifted towards our hide, turning the sky into a flickering mass of grey and black. The only noise was the wind whipping past 160,000 wings.

Though a display as grand as this is not guaranteed, check the tide times when you plan your trip to avoid disappointment.

After breakfast, we stopped off at the Norfolk Bird Observatory Reserve in Holme – a great place for passing migrants. That week they'd seen starlings, greenfinches, goldcrests and wrens, many of which will have been winter immigrants from the Continent. Don't think that the birds on your feeders are all resident in the UK!

Migration is such an unpredictable but short-lived time, and we were keen to capitalise on every chance. Therefore, we couldn't resist the short bus ride to the RSPB reserve at Titchwell Marsh. Titchwell is one of the premier bird reserves in the UK, where a phenomenal array of birds can be seen throughout the calendar year. In addition, the reserve, due to its coastal location, has unearthed quite a few unusual and surprising birds over the years. Autumn, particularly, is a time to expect the unexpected, but we were still flabbergasted to find an exhausted little auk sitting at the foot of the dunes on the beach. This most maritime of birds, which may have bred anywhere from western Greenland to Arctic Russia, had obviously been blown away from its normal wintering grounds in the North Sea.

While we were revelling in a bird that we only normally see as a dot in the telescope, way out to sea, the warden gently picked it up and took it down to the water. With luck it would get its bearings and join its kin further north. Isn't migration exciting?

A hide at Snettisham RSPB reserve

Large knot flock roosting at Snettisham

3 The Lleyn Peninsula, North Wales

Getting there:

The A497 and A499 run through the area and the B4417 provides further access around the local area. Tourist Information Centre is opposite the train station and next to the harbour in Pwllheli town centre.

Tel: Tourist information centre – 01758 613000

Email: Pwllheli.tic@gwynedd.gov.uk

Opening times: Open daily.

Charging policy: Not applicable.

Disabled access: Disabled access at various locations, telephone Tourist information centre for advice.

Find out more

Pwllheli Information page
www.pwllheli.org.uk/info.html

Lleyn Peninsula
www.llyn.info/

The Lleyn Peninsula Website
www.llyn-wales.co.uk/

Bardsey Island
www.bardsey.org/english/bardsey/welcome.asp?pid=1

Bardsey Island lies about three kilometres off the tip of the Lleyn Peninsula in North Wales. This diminutive island has long been known as a top spot for watching migration in action, as birds following the coastline to and from their breeding grounds in spring and autumn often use it as a place to rest before continuing their onward journey.

Unfortunately, we didn't get the chance to sample the avian delights waiting on Bardsey because the strong prevailing winds meant that a landing would have been simply too difficult, so Plan B had to be put into action!

To prove that visible migration is not just confined to islands, and can be seen in many locations, we decided to see what passing migrants we would be able to spot around the Lleyn Peninsula, itself a landmass that extends for nearly 50 kilometres out into the Irish Sea. The best places to start looking are generally coastal locations such as points, where a rocky promontory can be found jutting out into the sea. After a quick inspection of the map, we settled on Porth Ysgaden on the north side of the peninsula.

On our arrival at the site, it was immediately obvious that a number of birds were clearly navigating along the coastline, with the promontory at Ysgaden representing the closest point to these passing birds. While we set up our equipment and telescopes, seabirds, such as gannets and razorbills, that had already left their breeding grounds, could be seen moving in a southwesterly direction following the peninsula. The most exciting thing about birdwatching during migration times is that literally anything can turn up so, in addition to the occasional sandwich tern and red-throated diver powering past us, imagine our surprise when a flock of around a hundred golden plover was picked up, moving along the coast! The golden plover is an upland specialist that spends the breeding season on blanket bogs, heather moorland and upland grasslands. However, in autumn, golden plover move down to low-lying agricultural areas and the

Bardsey Island from the Lleyn Peninsula

coast to spend the winter. With the nearest breeding population being in the upland areas of Snowdonia, it was obvious that we were watching a species that migrates by altitude rather than principally by latitude. Flocks of golden plover in their winter plumage are a joy to behold – whitish pale on their underside and a mostly golden colour on their upperparts – and as we watched them against a blue sky backdrop, they constantly seemed to flicker gold and white as they twisted and turned in a tight flock over the sea.

On the south of the peninsula, the muddy harbour in the town of Pwllheli is well known as a place to look for migrant birds, but we did not expect to find so many migrating insects! Surely the best plant to examine for the year's last flush of insects is ivy, as autumn is the time when the plant produces its greenish-yellow, nectar-rich flowers. Even so, we were still surprised to find two species of migratory butterfly and a migratory moth on one patch of ivy covering the harbour wall!

Most painted ladies seen in the UK originate mainly from spring breeding grounds around the deserts of North Africa and Arabia, where butterflies then teem northwards across the Continent reaching the UK in most years. Close to the painted lady, a red admiral could be seen feeding away, another species that may well have arrived at the Lleyn following a Mediterranean upbringing.

The final immigrant insect to have made the trip to North Wales was a silver Y, so called because of the distinctive 'Y' pattern on its forewing. As the adults and caterpillars are unable to survive the UK's winter, this moth, or its parents earlier in the year, must have made the trip over from the Continent.

It was obvious that not just Bardsey but the whole of the Lleyn Peninsula is a very good place for an autumn pit stop!

Painted Lady butterfly

....

Opposite: Upland specialist golden plover in its summer plumage

4 Isles of Scilly

Getting there:

Scillonian III operates a summer service from Penzance to St Mary's. There are also daily inter-island launches between April and October.

Tel: Tourist Information Centre – 01720 422536

Email: tic@scilly.gov.uk

Opening times: Open daily.

Charging policy: Ferry and accommodation charges apply.

Disabled access: The islands are largely wheelchair accessible. Transport by helicopter from Penzance and by ferry is wheelchair friendly.

Find out more

Isle of Scilly Holiday and Tourism Guide
www.simplyscilly.co.uk/home/ index.html?_area=home&_areaid= 170841

BBC Hands on Nature
www.bbc.co.uk/handsonnature/ islands/scilly_access.shtml

Isles of Scilly Steamship Company
www.islesofscilly-travel.co.uk

While it might be true to say that everyone has a secret obsession, just occasionally you meet up with a bunch of people who are so completely addicted to something that you start to think you might be missing out. This is what happened when we went to the Isles of Scilly and met up with some 'twitchers'. What was more surprising is how quickly we also became hooked.

A twitcher is someone who will go to sometimes extraordinary lengths to see rare birds. Twitching itself is all about 'ticking' birds off a list: the British Bird List, to be precise, which currently stands at around 570 species. Most twitchers start by ticking off the common British native birds of which there are about 300. After that, it's a matter of increasing your list by locating rare visitors and migrants from abroad. Now, if you want to do that then visit the Isles of Scilly in October. We did and it's twitching heaven.

The Isles of Scilly are located some 40 kilometres off the southwest coast of Cornwall. There are over a hundred small, low-lying islands, all warmed by the waters of the Gulf Stream, with a practically sub-tropical climate. This position typically makes them the first port of call for exhausted and very rare migrant birds swept off course by the weather.

We had barely stepped off the plane onto the Island of St Mary when we received our first call from a bunch of jovial and enthusiastic twitchers whom we had arranged to meet. A very rare migrant bird had just arrived that morning and we needed to get over there quickly. A mad scramble for camera equipment ensued and we were whisked away to the site.

Well, who would believe it? About 250 twitchers armed with binoculars, scopes and cameras with huge lenses were huddled together on the path, all looking up a tree! We struggled into the melee, surrounded by numerous voices murmuring: 'see that dead branch hanging down? It's about a foot to the left near the fir cone ...' We must have been blessed with remarkable luck, because we spotted it almost immediately, and got what we later learned were 'crippling views' of ... a small brown bird! Welcome to the world of twitching. It's not size, colour or being flamboyant that count – its rarity – and we were looking at a *very rare* small brown bird. It was a red-eyed vireo, which is, in fact, not rare at all in its own country – North America. But this little bird had been swept off its migration route to Mexico across the Atlantic and ended up here, on the Scillies.

Isles of Scilly

St Zennor
Pendeen
St Just
Penzance
Sennen
Land's End
Mou
A3071
A30

Isles of Scilly
Hugh Town
St. Mary's

The tempo of our visit snowballed after that. We had barely come to terms with our first twitch before we were swept up into the adrenalin rush of the arrival of a 'mega'. A mega is an *extremely rare* migrant bird that has only been sighted in Britain less than a handful of times. Twitching is all about communication, and our new-found friends practically bristled with short-band radios, mobiles and pagers and a shout went up on the airwaves whenever a rare bird was spotted anywhere on the islands.

This time it was a Sykes's warbler visiting the UK for only the *fourth* time. It had been spotted at the other end of the island. There was another mad scramble – this time for taxis. Our seven-man team of crew and birders crammed into a cab and were driven at breakneck speed across the island by a feisty lady taxi driver, who told us that, while there were only 18 kilometres of road on the island, on 'mega-bird' days she had clocked up as many as 450 kilometres. We piled out at the new location. Our luck was still holding – once again we got crippling views of ... yes, you've guessed it, yet another small brown bird! This Sykes's warbler, we quickly learned, hadn't been blown off course because its migration is from northeast Arabia or Afghanistan to the Indian subcontinent, it was simply lost. We were all starting to relate to that – out of our elements and in a very strange place.

After two great 'ticks' in as many hours, it did occur to us that perhaps this twitching lark just wasn't that difficult. As it turns out, we were exceptionally lucky. After two days on the Scillies, our list was minimal – but, hey, two of those were megas! The first thing we did when we got back home was to add in all the British birds we'd already seen. That makes the list up to ... Oh my goodness, we've turned into twitchers!

The red-eyed vireo – a very rare sight for a British birder

The Scilly Isles – a haven for exhausted migratory birds

5 Forest of Bowland, Lancashire and North Yorkshire

Getting there:

The area is circled by the M6, A65 and A59. Leave the M6 by junctions 32 to 35, signs will show forest entrances. There is a regular Bowland Transit service between Clitheroe and Settle.

Tel: 01772 534140

Email: bowland@env.lancscc.gov.uk

Opening times: Forest open daily. Visitor Centre Easter–September 9.30am–6pm (Monday–Friday), 9.30am–6.30pm (Saturday–Sunday); October–Easter 10am–5pm (daily).

Charging policy: Not applicable.

Disabled access: Disabled access at Centre. Picnic tables suitable for wheelchair access.

The hen harrier – what a sight!

Find out more

Bowland Visitor Centre
**www.lancashire.gov.uk/
environment/countryside/sites/
bbvc.asp**

Forest of Bowland
www.forestofbowland.com/

Imagine it's growing dark. You're walking across a moor fringed with dense thickets of pine trees. There's a low mist blanketing the ground and creeping coldly and damply towards you. Suddenly, you hear three blood-curdling screams. You would be forgiven for thinking that someone was being murdered on those desolate moors. Instead, this is the 'triple whistle' of a male sika deer in rut.

Sika are notoriously difficult to spot, and especially to see rutting as they prefer to parade their wares to females while hiding in thick woodland, but the Forest of Bowland is a good place to attempt to see them or, at least, hear them. Sika are medium-sized deer, smaller than red and, while the males are generally dark, the hinds tend to be a more delicate biscuit colour. They originate from Japan, were introduced to Britain by the Victorians and the strain of sika found in the Forest of Bowland came via Parnell Park in Dublin in the 1800s.

During September and October, sika start to rut and the classic signs to look out for are the aptly named 'thrashings', areas of moorland where they have tossed and flailed the grass and moss with their antlers, scent-marking the ground. They also fray the bark from small trees and gouge out pits in the peat to mark the boundaries of their territory. Larger pits become wallows – the stags urinate in them and then roll around in the mud, scent-marking and possibly making themselves more attractive to hinds (although female humans find the smell as enticing as a gents' toilet).

Another animal that seems to flourish in this richly diverse landscape is the hen harrier, a bird that was persecuted heavily by gamekeepers and egg collectors, but is starting to make a comeback. Part of the reason it has been so easily exterminated is that it nests on the ground. The moors at Bowland are also attractive to grouse and this represents a curious conservationists' dilemma; because, while harriers flourish best when living on a game moor preserved for grouse, they also happen to prey on these game birds. Fortunately, many conservation-minded gamekeepers now seem to be on the side of the hen harrier since research seems to indicate they don't have a long-term impact on the decline of the red grouse, so let's hope their numbers continue to rise.

Sika deer and young

6 River Tweed, The Scottish Borders

Getting there:

FishTweed c/o FishScotland, Stichill House, Kelso, Scotland TD5 7TB. The Tweed lies close to the A1, the A68 and the A7. All routes have minor roads interconnecting the length of the river.

Tel: 01573 470612

Email: Enquiry form at www.fishtweed. co.uk/pages/contactus.asp?dom= FishTweed

Opening times: Open daily. Salmon season February–November, no Sunday fishing.

Charging policy: To book a fishing trip or check prices, go to www.fishtweed. co.uk/pages/availability.asp?dom= FishTweed

Disabled access: A 'Wheelie Boat' exists for wheelchair users wanting to fish – ask for details when booking.

Atlantic salmon powering its way upstream

Find out more

River Tweed Fishing – Part of Fish Scotland
www.fishtweed.co.uk/index.asp? dom=FishTweed

River Tweed Commissioners
www.rtc.org.uk/

The River Tweed

It's a scene reminiscent of North America – salmon power themselves into the air, tails thrashing, underbellies glinting rose-pink; we half expect a grizzly to emerge and start scooping them up. But instead we are on the banks of one of the greatest salmon rivers in Europe, the Tweed.

Atlantic salmon undergo an epic voyage, starting from when they are a smolt, barely twelve centimetres long, they travel from the river where they hatched to Iceland, Greenland and the Faroe Islands, eventually returning to their own stretch of river to breed – a round trip of over 3,000 kilometres! On their return, they have to battle their way upstream until they reach their spawning grounds. The females then lay thousands of eggs in shallow depressions in the gravel and males release their 'milt' over them. By this stage, a male will have turned deep red or green to attract females – in this Scottish border country, it's called turning 'tartan'. He'll also grow a rather impressive hook or 'kype' on his jaw. No one knows how they navigate back to the small stretch of river they originally came from, but scientists think that out at sea they use currents, the stars and the earth's magnetic field. Once they get to their river they may be guided by a chemical memory that allows them to remember and recognise substances, including hormones, which could be present in the water in minute quantities.

We followed the salmon for a small part of this journey, from the mouth of the river at Berwick-upon-Tweed, 80 kilometres inland to the Ettrick, a tributary of the Tweed where at Philiphaugh there's a weir in the river the fish must leap over. Unfortunately, they can't because it's much too high, though it's dramatic if heart-wrenching to see them try. There is a fish ladder in the middle and if they get through it (and most do), they'll break an infra-red beam that triggers a computerised counting system. Not only does this help scientists at the Tweed Foundation to monitor the health of the salmon population, the salmon are also filmed, both for the counting process and to show the public. So, you can watch them leaping up the weir and getting through the fish ladder in person, or swimming underwater from a salmon's point of view from the visitor centre.

All this is necessary research because out of every 5,000 eggs a female lays, only five will reach adulthood. So the Ettrick needs a minimum population of 3,100 salmon to maintain a healthy fish population. Thanks to the Tweed Foundation's work, the river does appear to be healthy – an otter has even taken up residence right by the weir.

7 Loch of Strathbeg, Aberdeenshire

Getting there:

From A90 in the village of Crimond, take the turn beside Kirk, following the brown tourist signs to the nature reserve.

Tel: 01346 532017

Email: strathbeg@rspb.org.uk

Opening times: Open daily: visitor centre dawn–dusk; loch hides 8am–4pm. Closed Christmas Day and New Year's Day.

Charging policy: Not applicable.

Disabled access: Reserve and access routes are being upgraded to accommodate wheelchairs – ring for information.

Find out more

The Royal Society for the Protection of Birds
www.rspb.org.uk/reserves/guide/l/lochofstrathbeg/index.asp

Birds of Britain - Pink-footed Goose
www.birdsofbritain.co.uk/bird-guide/pink-footed-goose.htm

There are some sounds that completely sum up a season. In winter, we'd go for foxes mating; in spring, the dawn chorus; in summer, the buzz of insects in a classic upland meadow. In autumn, though, you're spoilt for choice. Some might go for the sound of the red deer stags defending their territories, or tawny owls hooting in misty woodland. However, the most memorable and real sound of autumn, many believe, is the return of geese to our shores.

There are some top locations to choose from, but we urge you to go to one that many will not have heard of before. The RSPB's Loch of Strathbeg reserve is a gem. Tucked away in the northeast of Scotland, it's the kind of place that birders talk about in hushed tones. If you want a complete goose experience, then this is the place to come.

Strathbeg is a scene of the great autumn migration: the return of pink-footed geese to the UK. Every year these geese leave their summer breeding grounds in Iceland and Greenland and head south – and for many, the Loch of Strathbeg is their first refuelling point. It's here that they gather and recover before dispersing onto other sites in the northwest of England and the north Norfolk coast.

Come here in October and your senses will be assaulted with the sound of up to 80,000 of these creatures honking away on a loch not much bigger than your average reservoir. There are so many birds here that in the early morning gloom you'd be forgiven for thinking that during the night the water had been replaced by land. But as the light lifts, you see that the landmass is actually tens of thousands of geese.

Now, you do have to be out early for this experience. The geese roost up for the night either on the loch, or more conveniently on a shallow lagoon right in front of the visitor centre. That's what we call good planning. Get there while it's still dark and you'll be able to creep up on them and witness a truly remarkable event that happens every day.

As darkness lifts, all you'll hear is the sound of geese communicating with each other. Then, as the sun breaks through, the full splendour is revealed: a sea of pink-foots all waiting for the right moment to go. These geese only roost on the loch, before moving off onto farmland to feed. Sometimes they go in small groups – maybe a thousand or so at a time. When we were there, they were spooked by a passing heron and we were rewarded with the sight and sound of a flypast that would put the Paris Air Show to shame.

What you get first is a whoosh of wings as the birds lift in the air. Then the cacophony begins. It's almost as if they're shouting, and we mean shouting: 'OK, boys, let's go!'. As they wheel around swarming in unison, the sky gets darker before they line up in the classic 'V' shape and head for their feeding grounds. Once in a while, though, they decide that this isn't the time to go and settle down again on the water. Then you've got the whole thing to look forward to again.

It's not only geese that roost up here in significant numbers. There are thousands of golden plover and lapwing, too. While the geese line up overhead, the waders wheel this way and that before setting down. If ever there was a case for an extra set of eyeballs in your head, then this is it.

The reserve is pretty quiet during the day – but you've got the return of the pink-foots to look forward to. They tend not to return en masse so, as the light falls, you'll see squadrons of geese filling the sky, their bellies full from a day's foraging. By the end of October, geese numbers will have dropped markedly – but get your timing right and you'll be rewarded with a memory that'll stay with you for a very long time.

The beautiful pink-footed goose

The RSPB's Loch of Strathbeg Reserve

8 Ashridge Estate, Hertfordshire

Getting there:

The estate is just off the B4506, between Berkhamsted and Northchurch, and Ringshall and Dagnall.

Tel: 01442 851227

Email: ashridge@nationaltrust.org.uk

Opening times: Estate open daily. Visitor centre 12pm–5pm (daily).

Charging policy: Not applicable for estate. Monument: adult £1.30, child 60p.

Disabled access: Visitor centre fully accessible, grounds partly accessible (map provided). Portable induction loop and large print guides available.

Find out more

National Trust
**www.nationaltrust.org.uk/main/
w-vh/w-visits/w-findaplace/
w-ashridgeestate/**

Ashridge Estate, The Chilterns
**www.chilternsaonb.org/site_details.
asp?siteID=20**

Fungus
http://fungus.org.uk

Early one morning, as we walked along a ride with Ashridge mansion glimmering in the distance through the thick autumnal mists, a large fallow buck suddenly stepped out in front of us, snorting and pawing. Scraping his antlers down a tree, he almost took off one of the branches and then started to toss and twist his head through the bracken, scooping up the fronds. Male fallow deer have scent glands on their faces and he was advertising his presence by rubbing them along the bark of the tree. The bracken was to enhance his already large and impressive antlers.

October is a great time to see fallow deer because this is when the rut takes place, and Ashridge Estate is one of the best locations in England because of its high density of deer. The males signal to the females their suitability as a mate by continually groaning. A cross between a pig's grunt and a lion's growl, these calls are incredibly atmospheric as they resonate through the woods.

The bucks show themselves off to the does by displaying in open clearings – at Ashridge the rides and fields within the woods are often used by the deer, which means you can get within a few metres of the males. It's really only the 'grand bucks' – males over seven years of age – who tend to be the most serious contenders. When they do get into a fight, they lock horns and shove each other backwards and forwards until one emerges as the victor. It's not such a feat of endurance as you might see with red deer – the bucks aren't into such marathon duels as their red counterparts and, although they can hurt each other, they don't tend to injure one another as much because their antlers are flatter and without the sharp tines of their cousin.

The does are much shyer – we saw them flitting shadow-like through the woods on either side of us. You have to be both

Fly agaric – stunning but inedible

lucky and quiet to see them and you only have a few days to observe their behaviour during the rut because they are only in season for a short time; males, however, carry on regardless. The best time of day to see them is early morning or late evening.

Even if you miss the deer, the estate is a wonderful place for a walk. Because of its rich diversity of trees, Ashridge is a fantastic spot for fungi. There are around 3,500 species in the UK, several hundred of which have been recorded at Ashridge. Apparently you can find field mushrooms the size of dinner plates – or, at least, that's what they said in the local pub! We found parasol mushrooms and puffballs within minutes, both of which are delicious sautéed with a bit of olive oil and garlic.

Some of the less edible species are fascinating, like the bird's nest fungus, which really does look like a nest cradling a clutch of creamy eggs – the spore packets. Fly agaric is, of course, the one many of us recognise from cartoons and fairy tales. It's bright red with white spots. The reindeer-herding Koryak were a shamanistic tribe who used to dry and eat the toadstools; their reindeer loved them too and it's reported that poorer members of the tribe drank rich men's or reindeer's urine after they'd eaten fly agaric as a substantial portion of the drug would pass through into the urine! We wouldn't recommend that, but if you are certain that a mushroom is edible, then it is OK to pick it. Because the mushroom itself is effectively the fruit and, as the fungi are made up of thread-like 'mycelium' found below ground, picking the mushrooms won't destroy the organism. It is a good idea to leave a couple behind, however, to shed their spores to propagate the next generation of woodland fungi.

Autumn woodland on Ashridge Estate

Parasol mushroom

Opposite: A large male fallow deer

9 The Monach Isles, Scotland

Getting there:

Contact local tourist office in North Uist for local charters.

Tel: North Uist Tourist Office – 01876 500321
Scottish Natural Heritage – 01870 620238

Email: Enquiry form at www.snh.org.uk/nnr-scotland/contact.asp

Opening times: Open daily. Landings depend on weather.

Charging policy: Charges apply for boat travel.

Disabled access: Telephone North Uist Tourist Office with exact requirements.

Find out more

Scottish Natural Heritage – Monach Isles
www.snh.org.uk/nnr-scotland/reserve.asp?NNRId=6

BBC Science and Nature – Grey Seal
www.bbc.co.uk/nature/wildfacts/factfiles/277.shtml

Destination Scotland – Western Isles
www.destination-scotland.com/guidetoscotland/region.asp?region=23

If you were to try and travel as far northwest as possible while still remaining within the UK, then only the lonely outpost of St Kilda would beat the Monach Isles for isolation. The five low-lying islands that form the Monachs are located twelve kilometres from the southwest coast of North Uist in the Western Isles. Following due west from these islands, there is no land for over 3,000 kilometres until Newfoundland is reached on the eastern seaboard of Canada.

Despite North Uist being only a short flight from Glasgow, the last few miles across to the Monachs can be problematic, since gale-force winds are thought to blast the islands for at least 160 days a year, making any crossing potentially rough and landings difficult.

During the summer months, the lime-rich grasslands on the Monachs become blanketed with flowers, making this a lovely time to visit. It is in the autumn, however, that the really famous Monach spectacle unfurls, as the white sandy beaches play host to the largest breeding colony of grey seals in Western Europe. Having spent the previous ten months at sea, over 30,000 grey seals return to the islands each September, hauling themselves on to dry land in order to pup and mate before slipping back into the Atlantic again.

The colony of grey seals on the Monach Isles has not always been so huge – the population only began to steadily increase when the island became deserted as the last families departed in 1943. The seal population is now thought to have stabilised, with some 9,000 pups born each autumn.

After having spent three days champing at the bit on North Uist while we waited for the wind to abate, we awoke on our fourth and last morning before our return flight to Glasgow to find that at last the wind had dropped. This meant that we would have just six hours to get over onto the islands, and grab as much seal footage as possible, before the boat had to pick us up for the trip back to Uist.

As we drew closer to the isles, the unmistakeable torpedo-shaped blobs of grey seals could be seen on the beaches. Upon arrival, it was shoes off and trousers up as we waded onto the beach, and, as the nearest grey seals bolted into the water, no doubt indignant at our arrival on their island, very large flocks of turnstone and sanderling wheeled past us. Both these diminutive waders are species that breed around the Arctic Circle, their presence indicating that autumn had well and truly arrived in northwest Scotland. As both species settled back down onto the beach behind us, it was particularly fun to watch the sanderling rushing in and out with the surf – reminding us of wind-up clockwork toys!

Sanderlings searching for food in the surf

While grey seals are present on almost all of the beaches, the best beach for getting incredibly close views is on the north coast of the main island of Ceann Ear. After crossing the island, we crawled up the last sand dune separating us from the seals and peered over the top to find that we were no further than five metres away from the nearest pup! Strewn along the beach were the cows and their single young white pups, most of which looked at least a week old. In fact, the beach was so overcrowded beach that some cows had been driven inland and down into the dune slacks to deliver their young.

As the mothers attended to and fed their cubs at the water's edge, it was a picture of harmony. Interestingly, hardly a male was to be seen on the beach – it seems they had chosen to bide their time on a separate 'bachelor beach' until the females were in season and ready to mate, the cue for the big boys to turn up and the aggression to start. But, until then, it was just us, the cows and the pups – we could have stayed there all season if only we hadn't had a pressing date with the boat.

Opposite: Flock of turnstone

10 North Uist, Scotland

Getting there:

Ferries from Uig to Lochmaddy; flights from Glasgow to Benbecula or flights to Stornoway from Glasgow, Edinburgh and Inverness (there are daily flights between Stornoway and Benbecula).

Tel: Balranald Nature Reserve – 01463 715000
Lochmaddy Tourist Office – 01876 500321

Email: info@visitscotland.com
enquiries@uistonline.com

Opening times: Open daily.

Charging policy: Not applicable.

Disabled access: Circular nature trail is not suitable for wheelchair use.

Find out more

RSPB
www.rspb.org.uk/reserves/guide/ b/balranald/index.asp

Caledonian MacBrayne
www.calmac.co.uk

RSPB – Corn Bunting
www.rspb.org.uk/countryside/ farming/advice/birdsonfarms/ cornbunting/index.asp

Seemingly light years away from the hustle and bustle of city life, but in reality only an hour's flight from Glasgow, North Uist in the Western Isles is a wonderful place to both get away to and go birding at any time of the year. The island is a stunning blend of beaches, traditional 'machair' farmland, freshwater lochs and dark moorland hills.

North Uist has one of the most intricate landscapes in the whole of the UK – the eastern two-thirds of the island is characterised by literally thousands of freshwater lochans, giving the impression when seen from above of a giant waterlogged sponge. The land in the west of the island is dominated by coastline, sandy beaches and the low-lying and fertile machair. These sand-based grasslands, which have been farmed in a very low intensive manner for generations, are the reason why North Uist is such a top spot to see farmland birds, species that are rapidly disappearing from large tracts of the UK's mainland.

Balranald Nature Reserve, managed by the RSPB on the west coast, is a fine example of a reserve that is still managed along traditional crofting lines, whereby a small piece of tenanted land is used for cropping and grazing by a family and passed down through the generations. Mechanisation is limited on the island, and very little pesticide is applied, meaning that the machair is chock-full of flowers, insects and birds.

Most visitors to Balranald would generally consider the summer months the optimum time to visit, when the flowers are out in force and there is the best chance of seeing the rare bumblebees and, of course, the corncrake. But we found autumn to be much underrated, as this is the time when the farm birds begin to form flocks on the machair in readiness for winter.

As soon as we arrived at the reserve, the first farmland birds to fall under our scrutiny were a small flock of corn buntings bathing away in a puddle of water. This is a bird that has seen its population fall by 85 per cent in the last 25 years, and has largely retreated to its stronghold in Eastern England, but here on North Uist the population is considered to be in good health. During the autumn, the birds are able to take advantage of a seasonal bonanza in the form of the giant conical haystacks that the crofters build after the harvest to dry the hay.

As we walked out onto the reserve's machair, most of the hay had been cut, leaving stubble, which is the perfect habitat for skylarks. Everywhere we walked over the machair we pushed up flocks of skylarks, fluttering up in front of us with their 'chirruping' flight call as they went. Like the corn bunting, the skylark is a farmland bird that has seen its population halve in the last quarter of a century across on the mainland, but from the numbers we encountered here it looked like they had moved out to the Western Isles, lock, stock and barrel! Small flocks of twite were also seen in the stubble too, and all these small birds meant plenty of food for birds that eat birds. In one afternoon we were able to get good views of peregrine, merlin and hen harrier all looking for an unwary skylark or twite!

Skylark, a farmland bird

At the reserve office, the warden Jamie Boyle excitedly informed us that a snowy owl had been located on the north of the island and, although it wasn't strictly a farmland bird and therefore not really in our remit, it was definitely something we couldn't refuse! Arriving at a massive dune complex near Huilish Point, we abandoned the car and started walking along the beach while Jamie scouted ahead to try and locate the bird. Five minutes later, he returned with the unbelievable news that the bird in question was sitting on the beach on the other side of the sand dune right in front of us!

The massive snowy owl

Crawling over the top, we were immediately confronted with a massive female snowy owl checking us out with her lovely lemon-coloured eyes. Much more heavily streaked than the male, she was still surprisingly well camouflaged against the white sand. While snowys have never bred on North Uist in living memory, occasional ones have been known to visit the island during the summer before flying back north in the autumn. We were just glad she'd decided to stay around!

Eaval, the southeast point of North Uist

November

The slow inexorable slide to winter quickly gathers speed in November. As the weather takes a grip on the wildlife, what may appear to be the quietest month for wildlife watching, has more than few surprises up its sleeve.

Whether it is large flocks of black-tailed godwits on the Dee, huge numbers of pink-footed geese in Norfolk or simply vast pre-roost flocks of starlings swirling around the Somerset Levels, November is the time to see birds seeking the company of their own kin as they come together for warmth, protection and to be sociable.

Woodlands can be rewarding as, when the leaves drop from the trees, all manner of birds' nests and squirrel dreys are suddenly revealed. Ivy also shows prominently in November, with its late flowers providing a last burst of nectar for any insects having survived the frosts, and the evergreen holly produces an abundant food supply for our winter thrushes. Salmon rivers are a great place to try and catch the return of these fish after an absence of at least four years, as they leap over weirs and waterfalls on the way back to their breeding grounds.

1 Lough Foyle, Northern Ireland

Getting there:

Access to the reserve is off the A2 westwards between Limavady and Londonderry. The seawall offers excellent views over the Lough.

Tel: RSPB Nature Reserve – 028 9049 1547
Tourist information centre – 028 7126 7284

Email: rspb.nireland@rspb.org.uk

Opening times: Open daily.

Charging policy: Not applicable.

Disabled access: Full wheelchair access to the Tourist Information Centre.

Find out more

RSPB
www.rspb.org.uk/reserves/guide/l/loughfoyle/

Lough Foyle Ferry
www.loughfoyleferry.com/

Birds of Britain – Whooper Swan
www.birdsofbritain.co.uk/bird-guide/whooper-swan.htm

People travel halfway round the world for great wildlife experiences, sometimes ignoring even better ones that are right on their own doorstep. Why go to the Arctic wastes to see great birds, when, if you wait until autumn, they'll come to you?

That's why of all the bird hot spots in the UK, we'd put Lough Foyle right up there with the very best. This stretch of water, which has Northern Ireland on one side and the Irish Republic on the other, is a great place to see migrating brent geese and whooper swans. These are two top travellers that undertake epic journeys. They make a lot of effort to get here, so it'd be rude not to check them out!

We're big fans of whooper swans. Not only are they great to look at, but they've got a top call too. They get their names from their whooping cry – a really evocative sound of the wild. When you hear that half-whoop, half-honk you know that autumn is definitely here, and winter is just around the corner.

Lough Foyle is one of the best places in the UK to see these terrific birds. They come year after year, following in the wing beats of their ancestors who made the same journey long before man shaped this part of the world. These migrants use the lough as a feeding station. They arrive in mid-autumn exhausted after their long journey to escape freezing temperatures in Iceland. As a holiday destination for whooper swans, Lough Foyle can't be beaten. This is a seaside hotel for weary travellers where the restaurant never closes.

The whoopers roost and graze on farmland close to the lough. Stand at Longfield Point at first light, and you'll hear them mumbling to other members of their family group. Then, if you watch closely, you'll see their heads frantically going up and down – a sign that they're about to fly. Get ready, within seconds they'll be up and off.

In contrast to the superficially similar mute swan, you'll know you've got whoopers overhead by their almost silent wing beat. These are expert stream-lined flying machines with bodies designed to cope with the miles of migration.

The whoopers aren't the only long-distance travellers who've come to the lough. This is also a great place to see a bird that's been dubbed 'super-goose'. Brent geese might only be the size of a mallard, but they can certainly travel. They come from the Canadian Arctic – a 4,000 kilometre trek that involves dodging predators, hunters and a flight over the Greenland ice cap.

The little beauties at Lough Foyle are pale-bellied brent geese, which are lighter, and some might say a bit more dapper, than their dark-bellied cousins, which have bred in northern Russia and Siberia. The pale-bellied's main food source is eel grass. Get yourself in position and wait for an incoming tide and these little chaps will be pushed towards you as the eel grassbeds become covered with seawater.

These two star guests are backed up by a supporting cast in the form of massive flocks of wigeon, bar-tailed godwit and redshank. At peak times, there can be 25,000 ducks out there and 15,000 waders. On farmland nearby, flocks of finches, larks and buntings come in to feed and that in turn brings out merlin, sparrowhawk and peregrine. You might even get a glimpse of a golden eagle that's drifted over from Donegal.

But if you tire of staring out across the water, have a look around the farmland. Vast swathes of land have been reclaimed from the sea and there's also a network of drainage channels with their own wildlife – look in the ditches behind the sea bank for great crested grebe, little grebe and heron. Check out these channels, too, for a beautiful spiral shell known as the tower shell. There's nothing unduly remarkable about these shells, but they're colourful and can occur in great numbers – they're the perfect souvenir of what should be a cracking visit.

Bar-tailed godwit, feeding

Male wigeon

Lough Foyle – a great wildlife experience

2 Helford River, Cornwall

Getting there:

At Helston, head for RNAS Culdrose on A3083 (signposted Lizard). Turn left at the roundabout on to B3293 for just under 1 kilometre, follow signposts to the head of the river.

Tel: Helford Voluntary Marine Conservation – 01872 273939
National Seal Sanctuary – 01326 221361

Email: petomp@bioscope.demon.co.uk
seals@sealsanctuary.co.uk

Opening times: Seal sanctuary open year round (exc. Christmas Day) from 10am. Closing times vary.

Charging policy: No charge to visit the estuary. Seal Sanctuary: adult £9.95, Child £7.95. Group rates apply.

Disabled access: Wheelchair access to Seal Sanctuary. Some boat trips along the estuary can accommodate wheelchairs.

Find out more

Helford Voluntary Marine Conservation
www.helfordmarineconservation.co.uk/river.htm

Seal Sanctuary
www.sealsanctuary.co.uk/corn1.html

Cornwall Wildlife Trust
www.cornwallwildlifetrust.org.uk

In Daphne du Maurier's novel, *Frenchman's Creek,* the imperious Dona St Columb leaves her husband in London and heads to Cornwall with her children, where she falls in love with a French pirate-philosopher. The creek itself, the setting for piracy, smuggling and illicit love, is an inlet off the Helford River. This area is known as the 'soft side' of the Lizard Peninsula, a world away from the jagged cliffs and rugged coastline. A gentle setting, here you'll find tiny villages tucked alongside sub-tropical gardens and watery woodlands.

The estuary is rich in marine life; indeed, there's been an oyster fishery here since Roman times. The oysters are traditionally harvested from 1 November, so this is a good month to visit if you're a shellfish lover. The oysters themselves are wild and propagate naturally. They breed during the summer as the relatively warm water triggers them to release their spawn. The larvae spend ten to twelve days swimming freely – and are wolfed down by a myriad of predators – before settling down. The oyster then never moves from this spot again. During their lifetime they may change sex and even spend a period as hermaphrodites. They're dredged when they're about three to four years old.

The Helford estuary is a fantastic place to go rockpooling, one of those pastimes that instantly sends you back to your childhood. As well as tiny fish, crabs and delicate, coral-like seaweeds, you might find lumpsuckers. These grey-blue, scaleless, somewhat flabby fish, which measure about 30 centimetres long, have a large sucker on the undersides, which they use to attach themselves to rocks to cope with the tide surges; their eggs are often sold commercially as caviar. These are solitary fish, but in January the males will start defending territories. Once they've persuaded females to lay eggs for them to fertilise, they'll guard and aerate the clutch.

While you're rockpooling, or when the tide comes in and covers them, you can also birdwatch – and one

The Helford Estuary in Cornwall

particular species to look out for in autumn is the little egret. This small, white heron with yellow feet looks as if it would be much more at home on the wetlands of Botswana. The first ones to arrive in the UK came in 1957 and the bird began breeding here in 1996. Some remain all year round; others migrate here in autumn and winter from the Continent. There are now around 1,600 birds overwintering in the UK; their numbers may have increased due to global warming. Our sound recordist, originally a marine biologist, has a theory about their yellow feet. He says that yellow light waves are cut out under water at certain depths, making yellow objects difficult to see. So when the birds are hunting, fish can't see their feet, which means the egrets stand a better chance of catching them. Sounds plausible, but then why don't all herons have yellow feet? It's good to know there are still a number of mysteries in the natural world!

As well as visiting some gorgeous gardens when you're down here, you could also go to Gweek, which was once a Roman port and is now home to the National Seal Sanctuary. It was set up in 1958 by Ken Jones when a baby seal washed up on the beach near his house in St Agnes. Ken built a small pool to help the seal recover and later also used it to rehabilitate oiled birds. By 1975 he was dealing with so many sick and injured seals, as well as the birds, that he moved his sanctuary to Gweek. Now it has nursery and convalescence pools, as well as a hospital for injured marine creatures. Most of the seals are successfully released back into the wild, but some never recover and they remain in the seal sanctuary. Ken also has other animals, like Californian and Patagonian sea lions, and occasionally the odd dolphin and turtle needing a helping hand.

Oysters – November is a good month if you're a shellfish lover

Opposite: The little egret

3 Seal Sands, Cleveland

Getting there:

Teesmouth NNR is midway between Hartlepool and Redcar, approximately 5 kilometres northeast of Middlesbrough. Road access is via the A178. Car parking at Cowpen Marsh (on the A178). Nearest train station: Seaton Carew.

Tel: Teesmouth Field Centre – 01429 264912

Email: fieldcentre@teesmouth. freeserve.co.uk

Opening times: Open daily

Charging policy: Free activities for schools and groups; book in advance.

Disabled access: An easy-access footpath connects the Cowpen Marsh car park with two accessible observation hides.

Find out more

Teesmouth National Nature Reserve
www.english-nature.org.uk/special/ nnr/nnr_details.asp?nnr_name= &C=7&Habitat=0&natural_area= &local_team=0&spotlight_reserve= 0&X=&NNR_ID=153

Teesmouth Field Centre
www.teesmouth.freeserve.co.uk/

Some of the best wildlife experiences can be had in the most unexpected of places. Take Seal Sands near Hartlepool. It wouldn't win many awards in a beauty contest, sandwiched as it is between a nuclear power station and the vast expanse of heavy industry at the mouth of the River Tees, but one thing we've learned over the years is that wildlife isn't bothered by what a place looks like. That's just something that troubles the most fickle of mammals, the human. It's what's happening on the ground that matters. Here you'll find a vast array of wildfowl and waders, and the only regular spot on this part of the east coast where common seals breed. There's a full range of habitats from sand dune to saltmarsh and from mudflat to grazing marshland. It's this mosaic of landscapes that brings in a handsome range of species.

Life at Seal Sands hasn't always been a rosy picture. Wildlife must have loved this spot before the heavy hand of man made an impact. At one time, there were more than a thousand seals here – and it was the abundance of this creature that gave this corner of the northeast its name. Years of pollution, dredging and neglect made it tough for these animals to hang on and by the 1930s the seals had gone. The first greys came back in the 1960s, and in the 1980s common seals returned too. Numbers have slowly built up and there's now a mixed group of around 100 seals in the area. It is now part of Teesmouth National Nature Reserve run by Natural England.

The great thing about the seals here is that they are remarkably easy to see. There are two places where you're likely to find them. At low tide, try the hide with disabled access that looks out across the sandbank and you'll see the seals simply lounging about in front of you. Alternatively, if there's a particularly high tide, the seals may have been pushed up into Greatham Creek, which runs underneath the A178 linking Hartlepool with the industrial areas on the River Tees. A good viewpoint to see the seals is from the bridge that crosses the creek. Wildlife watching certainly doesn't get much easier than this.

Seal identification can be confusing when you get grey and commons together. However, there are more common seals here, and they're generally smaller than the greys, with dog-like facial appearance, as opposed to the 'Roman' nose profile of the grey seals.

Seal Sands is somewhere to come all year round. Visit in autumn, though, and there's the added bonus of migrants moving in from all over Europe and the Arctic, which come to the reserve to feed on the rich mudflats jam-packed with microscopic food. This is the largest area of inter-tidal mudflat between Lindisfarne to the north and the Humber to the south so expect to see up to 24,000 waders and about 4,000 wildfowl. Brace yourself too for lots of lapwing, shelduck and dunlin. In addition, in autumn and early winter all sorts of birds could get blown in so be prepared to have your identification skills tested as this place has turned up the odd rarity!

Don't forget to check out the industrial architecture for signs of wildlife, too. The abundance of waders brings in the hunters, and you may well spot a peregrine using one of the steel structures close to the reserve as an impromptu cliff face. You'll know these superb predators are on the hunt when the birds erupt in panic. Short-eared owl and merlin also are regular visitors throughout the winter too.

Once upon a time, locations with heavy industry would have been the last place you'd have gone to find wildlife. At Seal Sands there's a real variety of species and they're here in significant numbers. So come on, what are you waiting for? This is a place where beauty is definitely more than skin deep.

Grey seal

Wildlife and industry as neighbours at Seal Sands

4 Magdalen College, Oxford

Getting there:

Magdalen College, OX1 4AU. From the M40 or M4 take either the A40 or the A34 into Oxford. Access to the College is from Longwall Street, High Street or Rose Lane. Nearest train station: Oxford.

Tel: 01865 276000

Email: Enquiry form at www.magd.ox. ac.uk/enquiries/visiting.shtml

Opening times: Open daily. October–June 1pm–6pm (or dusk, whichever is earlier); July–September 12pm–6pm. Closed 22 December–31 December.

Charging policy: Adults £3, children and concessions £2. Residents of Oxford free.

Disabled access: Guide dogs allowed, accessible by wheelchair.

Hedgehog uncurling among the leaves

Find out more

Magdalen College, Oxford
www.magd.ox.ac.uk/

British Hedgehog Preservation Society
www.britishhedgehogs.org.uk

Deer-UK – Fallow Deer
www.deer-uk.com/fallow_deer.htm

The incredibly skittish fallow deer at Magdalen College

The College of St Mary Magdalen – pronounced 'maudlin'– was founded nearly 550 years ago. As you can imagine it's steeped in history with famous alumni including Oscar Wilde, but it is also home to some great wildlife. When we visited in November, the college was bathed in the most magnificent golden 'marmalade' light and surrounded by glorious autumn colour.

The college has spacious grounds, and, most importantly for us, it also has its own deer park called the Grove. This meadow contains a herd of 60 fallow deer – that's a 'fallow' for every 'fellow' in the college. A myth says that when one of the fellows dies a deer is culled – which makes you wonder what happens when one of the deer dies!

We'd come for a lesson in photographing deer, but, even dressed in camouflage gear, this was surprisingly difficult as the deer were incredibly skittish. As dusk started to fall, we were grateful to go off in search of a slightly more approachable creature – the hedgehog.

While many of us have vivid childhood memories of finding hedgehogs in our gardens at home, these creatures are becoming increasingly rare as roads continue to take a heavy toll. Late autumn is almost your last chance of seeing them before they go into hibernation. Our evening got off to a good start as it didn't take us long to uncover a sleepy female burrowed deep beneath a pile of leaves. Hedgehogs are one of our most primitive mammals, and have remained largely unchanged for at least 15 million years. As we gently pulled Mrs Tiggywinkle out of the leaves, she took on the typical defensive posture – rolling up into a ball and erecting all her spines, which can number between 5,000 and 7,000. As we held her gently and she started to uncurl, we were able to lay to rest a common childhood myth. Hedgehogs are not swarming with fleas – in fact, they have no more than a squirrel – it's just that the spines are widely spaced, allowing us to see the parasites more easily on the skin.

If you want to help out a hedgehog in winter this year, resist the temptation to put out bread and milk for them – as many of us used to do. The best way to ensure their survival is to leave a pile of wood and leaves in a corner of your garden for them to hide in. They will certainly be grateful for the sanctuary it provides.

5 Welney, Norfolk

Getting there:

Located 19 kilometres north of Ely, 42 kilometres north of Cambridge and 53 kilometres east of Peterborough. Access the Wetland Centre from the A10 either at Littleport or Ten Mile Bank.

Tel: 01353 860711

Email: info.welney@wwt.org.uk

Opening times: Open daily, except Christmas Day. See website for opening times.

Charging policy: Adult £4.50, Concession £3.70, Children £2.70, Family Ticket £12.00.

Disabled access: Wheelchair access to the centre, main observatory, birdwatching hides and reedbed boardwalk. Guide dogs welcome.

Whooper swans taking off

Find out more

Wildfowl and Wetlands Trust – Welney
www.wwt.org.uk/visit/welney/

Welney Community Website
www.welney.org.uk/

RSPB - Bewick's Swan
www.rspb.org.uk/birds/guide/b/ bewicksswan/index.asp

Welney RSPB Reserve at sunset

In 1630, to prevent flooding of the River Great Ouse upstream in Bedford and beyond, the Dutch engineer Cornelius Vermuyden constructed two diversion channels, the Old Bedford River and the New Bedford River (or Hundred Foot Drain). During the summer, the Ouse Washes (as they are now known) are managed as grazing pasture, but every autumn the sluice gates are opened to allow the central strip in between these two drainage ditches to flood, creating the perfect overwintering habitat for the largest inland concentration of wildfowl in Britain, many of which will spend the winter at the Wildfowl and Wetlands Trust reserve at Welney.

The reserve is famous for its Bewick's swans, which like to roost on shallow freshwater lakes or marshes and feed in the surrounding farmland. So perfect is the habitat for these Russian visitors that the Ouse Washes are home to the largest flock of Bewick's anywhere in the UK.

Another close relation of the Bewick's, which is attracted to the wetland habitat at Welney, is the whooper swan, and during the day both species can be seen feeding out on the neighbouring fields, hoovering up waste crops such as the tops of sugar beet.

The wetlands at Welney are worth visiting at any time of the day, as there is always something to see. However, if your time here is limited, late afternoon is definitely the time to choose as this is when the reserve hosts its superb floodlit feeding spectacle.

Sitting in the comfort of the heated observatory as the sun goes down, the first sight to be unveiled before your eyes is the spectacle of thousands of swans returning to the Washes in the classic 'v' formation, silhouetted against a red setting sun. It is then that the excitement really begins. As the sky fades to black, the area in front of the observatory stays bright, lit by floodlights and covered with swans; the large white birds contrast with the black water.

Then the noise becomes almost deafening as hundreds of wild swans honk and clamour, and push forwards as scoops of food are thrown out by the reserve wardens. It was a spectacular and simply unforgettable experience.

6 Ashton Court, Bristol

Getting there:

Ashton Court Estate, Ashton Court, Long Ashton, BS41 9JN. Access the estate from A369 Clanage Road, through Clifton Lodge, or from the B3128 near Long Ashton.

Tel: 0117 9639176

Email: cheri_seddon@bristol-city.gov.uk

Opening times: 8am–dusk (daily).

Charging policy: Not applicable, excluding some events.

Disabled access: Access for wheelchair users and facilities for the disabled.

Find out more

Ashton Court
www.forestofavon.org.uk/ashtoncourt.html

Visit Bristol
http://visitbristol.co.uk/site/things_to_do/p_23881

BBC – Going out in Bristol
www.bbc.co.uk/bristol/content/goingout/2004/parks/ashton/ashton.shtml

The Ashton Court Estate consists of over 340 hectares of woods and grassland with the most sublime views over the city of Bristol. Only a few minutes walk from the famous Clifton Suspension Bridge and just a couple of kilometres from the city centre, this is one of the finest places to leave behind the hustle and bustle of the city without ever actually leaving it!

Today, Ashton Court is probably best known for its balloon fiesta and the Ashton Court Festival, but it should also be known as a great spot to watch some cracking wildlife.

Dawn is a particularly good time to be in any forest, but if you are in a mixed wood or parkland in autumn then it is a very good time to listen out for tawny owls. October and November are the months when the male proclaims his territory and starts to court the female with the instantly familiar 'hooo-hoo-hooo!' call. So after an early rise and at the unearthly hour of 5.30am, we positioned ourselves on the edge of part of the wood on the Ashton Estate to await the hooting. Barely had we placed the camera on the tripod, when two birds began making their presence felt. With one male calling away to our left and a female responding with her 'kee-wick!' call to our right, it was like watching a tennis match with all the lights turned off!

Males become territorial at this time of year, and they can easily be persuaded to come to investigate what they consider to be an intruding male. So when one of us put our hands together to create a hoot of sorts, it was no surprise that within a matter of 30 seconds the local male tawny owl had come to investigate what all the commotion was about. With his beautiful mottled plumage, round face and huge black eyes, this can be a fierce adversary. Don't forget, this is the bird that was made famous for robbing the celebrated photographer Eric Hosking of his left eye while he was working near an active nest! We were therefore a touch relieved to see the owl fly off when it realised that we were not even worth bothering about.

Ashton Court

Ashton Court is famous for some very old oak trees, including the 'Doomsday Oak', which has been designated as one of the 'Fifty Great British Trees' to commemorate the Golden Jubilee of the Queen in 2002. Thought to be over 900 years old, though still very healthy, the tree is certainly showing its age as a number of branches are propped up and the trunk is riddled with holes.

It was in the hole of another very old oak, near the entrance to the park, that we were able to catch up with another species of owl. The little owl is not in fact a native bird, but was introduced into several locations in Southern England during the latter half of the 19th century. So well has the little owl settled into life in the UK, that today pairs are thought to number around 6,000 with some birds reaching as far north as Southern Scotland. Looking at the owl perched in the old oak, with its yellow eyes and seemingly permanent fierce expression, it seemed totally at home.

The little owl with its fierce expression

While few visitors will see the owls at Ashton Court, many people do come especially to view the captive herd of red deer, which have been associated with the site ever since the estate was enclosed in 1392. Unlike in the wild, the deer at Ashton Court are surprisingly easy to see with only a large deer fence separating them from the public. The male deer are a magnificent sight, partly due to the supplementary food they receive – many of the ones we saw were surprisingly stocky with the most incredible headgear, often consisting of up to 14 points on their antlers – a rare sight in the wild. It was certainly a very surreal experience hearing the primeval males bellow in the early morning light with the awakening city of Bristol as a backdrop!

Opposite: Red deer and their headgear

7 Old Moor, South Yorkshire

Getting there:

From junction 36 of the A1, take the A61 north (Barnsley), or from junction 37, take the A635 south (Barnsley). Follow RSPB Old Moor signs.

Tel: 01226 751593

Email: old.moor@rspb.org.uk

Opening times: Open daily. Visitor centre open November-January 9.30am-4 pm (gates close 4.30pm), February-October 9.30am-5pm (gates close 5.15pm). Closed Christmas Day and Boxing Day.

Charging policy: RSPB members, Passport to Leisure and Rothercard holders free; adults £2.50, children £1.20, concessions £2, family ticket £5.

Disabled access: Wheelchairs and an electric scooter for free hire (booking recommended). Wheelchair accessible viewing areas at each hide.

Find out more

RSPB - Old Moor
www.rspb.org.uk/reserves/guide/o/oldmoor/index.asp

Birds of Britain - Golden Plover
www.birdsofbritain.co.uk/bird-guide/golden-plover.htm

Picture a gritty, northern industrial landscape surrounded by busy urban roads, call-centres and bustling business parks, with a backdrop of rumbling traffic and wailing police sirens – it doesn't exactly sound like a perfect wildlife experience does it? But don't be misled, because at Old Moor near Barnsley the RSPB have created a little pearl of a wildlife reserve, and if you visit in November, as we did, you'll discover that it's as good a place as any to see wildfowl, and in autumn in particular there are wading birds in their thousands.

Walking through the gates you feel as if you're entering a different world. Yes, you can still hear the traffic thundering in the background, but it soon fades to an unobtrusive backtrack as you take in the wonderful wildlife habitat around you. Our landscape has been shaped by the hand of man for centuries, but this part of England in particular bears the stamp of the Industrial Revolution. As recently as the 1950s there were 30 coal mines in this area, employing over 30,000 people. When the coal-mining industry collapsed in the 1980s, much of the area was left barren and ruined, but as always nature took over. The mining resulted in large areas of subsidence that over the years have gradually filled in with water, and with a bit of careful land management the shallow lakes and pools have turned into real magnets for wildlife.

Old Moor is located in one of the most populated parts of Britain. It's a stone's throw from Barnsley, Rotherham, Doncaster and Sheffield, and is a popular location for local wildlife enthusiasts as well as visitors. It's one of the RSPB's newest reserves and has first-class facilities – there are 5 hides, some of which are huge, offering different views out across the wetlands. We chose to go to Wath Ings hide, which is furthest from the visitor centre, but before we were even halfway there we had our first views of waders en masse. It was a flock of golden plover, coming in overhead.

There's a resident population of golden plover that do breed in the UK, but in the autumn they are joined by thousands of migrants from Iceland and Scandinavia. They are a gregarious bird and like to flock together. As we watched them, they wheeled round in a tight flock, caught the sunlight, and were instantly turned to a shower of glittering gold. Immediately, they banked over in a uniform flying display, caught the sun again on their undersides and turned into a fluttering cloud of white snowflakes, before seeming to funnel down onto the ground and out of sight. It was quite magical. By the time we'd arrived at the hide, desperate to get some good, close-up views, the flock had all landed and were standing out on the shallow mudflats, but they

were being joined by smaller flocks all the time. As we watched, individual golden plover seemed to drop out of the sky like stones and join their brethren on the ground. They had been silent in the air, but once on the ground they set up a clattering call of 'tooee-tooee!' The reason they had caught the sun so beautifully was because their autumn plumage is much paler than earlier in the year. In spring, they have a black belly and neck, but always they retain the beautiful gold speckling from which they take their name. After watching the golden plover for some time, we noticed a couple of unusual things: first, they were all standing facing the same direction, into the wind, presumably so that the wind didn't ruffle their plumage, and also because it makes for an efficient, low-risk take off in case of emergency. (We watched them take off synchronously when a kestrel flew over, and, think about it, if they were all facing in different directions and took off at once there would be no end of mid-air collisions.) Secondly, there didn't seem to be a lot of activity on the ground, apart from a few skirmishes when one bird got too close to another and a bit of bathing activity; they seemed to be, well, just standing there as if they were waiting for something to happen. In fact, they were resting up. The golden plover feed at night on the surrounding grasslands, and essentially roost-up on the mudflats during the day.

Occasionally when you're filming you get a bit of special treatment. We met local lad and well-known poet Ian McMillan at the reserve and he presented us with a special poem called *Golden Plovers over Old Moor* to remember Old Moor by:

Hide at the RSPB reserve at Old Moor

Golden Plover flock

> This used to be coal country, now it's bird country,
> These are wetlands, not blacklands any more;
> And we can see the skies thick with seams of golden plover
> Landing like a promise on the waters of Old Moor
> And crowding to the Wintering through the wide sky's open door …

There's much more to see at Old Moor, including huge flocks of lapwing, one of the quintessential sights and sounds of the British countryside. No other bird has that broad-winged, black and white flapping flight, feathery black crest and distinctive 'peewit!' call. But there were also teal, shoveler, dunlin, snipe and redshank – the list goes on and on, but perhaps it's best if you just go there and see it all for yourself.

8 Lindisfarne, Northumberland

Getting there:

From the A1 at Beal, Holy Island is signposted east (8 kilometres). Nearest train station: Berwick-upon-Tweed. A public bus service runs from the station to the island (frequency depends on season and tide).

Tel: Lindisfarne Centre – 01289 389004

Email: lindisfarne-heritage-centre@ uk2.net

Opening times: Varies with tides and weather conditions. Check before travelling.

Charging policy: Castle: Adult £5.20, Child £2.60; Garden only: £1

Disabled access: Lindisfarne Castle partly accessible, Heritage Centre accessible. Braille and large print guides available.

Find out more

The Holy Island of Lindisfarne
www.lindisfarne.org.uk/

National Trust – Lindisfarne Castle
**www.nationaltrust.org.uk/main/
w-vh/w-visits/w-findaplace/
w-lindisfarnecastle/**

As you approach Lindisfarne, you soon realise why this is a special place for both humans and wildlife. Jutting out into the North Sea off the Northumberland coast, it's long been a place for contemplation. Dominated by the dramatic ruins of the medieval priory, a reminder of when this spot was an important centre for Christianity, it's no wonder they also call this place Holy Island. Of course, birds and animals don't care too much for all that. What they're after is the food and safety this island provides.

This is the only place in England where you'll find pale-bellied brent geese that have migrated from Spitsbergen to the north of Norway. These mallard-sized, black and white beauties are a joy to watch. The brent goose is much smaller than other black geese and has a shorter, thicker neck. Once you've got your eye in, you won't confuse them with Canada or barnacle geese. What brings the brents here is the eel grass that reveals itself when the tide is out. Get your timings wrong and you'll be disappointed. On a low tide, the birds will be so far away that even with a scope they'll be specks in the distance. If you're here on an incoming tide, then the birds will be pushed towards you as they munch on the remaining eel grass before it gets covered with water. There's something about eel grass that drives these birds barmy. We've never tasted it ourselves, but if you're a brent goose then this stuff is like scoffing high tea at The Ritz.

Brent geese are not alone in finding this a great place to hang out. They're joined in significant numbers by pink-footed and greylag geese, together with grey plover and redshank. Altogether, it's a rich mixture of goose and wader in one location.

You can see these birds from the mainland – but of course island life is best. So check the tide timetables and get yourself across onto Lindisfarne itself. Please don't try and chance your arm and dash across the causeway which connects the island to the mainland. The locals tell lots of stories about foolish visitors who've got their timings wrong and have been forced to watch from the rescue tower as their brand new car drifts away on the fast-moving tide. Assuming you've made it in one piece, keep your eyes peeled for short-eared owls and merlin hunting across the dunes that make up much of the island. Seeing these birds is a real treat.

Once you're ensconced on Lindisfarne, we recommend something that might seem foolish to a grown up, but is in fact a favourite pastime of the *Nature's Calendar* team. Whenever we're at the coast, rockpooling is one of our top activities. And Lindisfarne is a better location to do it than most. Firstly, the views under the shadow of Lindisfarne Castle are stunning. Secondly, the creatures you're likely to discover are pretty good too.

What makes Lindisfarne so good for finding sea creatures is that this is a boulder shoreline, so your hunt for animals is really about turning stones over and seeing what's lurking underneath. Come in mid-autumn and you'll be able to catch quite a few creatures before they head off to spend the winter in deeper waters.

We've had some amazing finds over the year – from scorpion fish and sea hares to velvet swimming crabs – and pipe fish. Again, choose an outgoing tide and you'll be rewarded with some cracking finds. Remember, though, to put any discoveries back where you found them. Also, if you're turning over stones, always make sure you put them back the same way. It's not much fun if what you consider to be your roof suddenly becomes your basement!

A flock of Brent geese feeding

Lindisfarne castle, a Tudor fort and then private residence

9 Westonbirt, Gloucestershire

Getting there:

From the M4, junction 18, take A46 north towards Stroud, then A433 for approx 5 kilometres. From the M5, junction 13, take A419 towards Stroud, then the A46 (Bath) and A4135 (Tetbury). Take the A433 (approx 5 kilometres).

Tel: 01666 880220

Email: westonbirt@forestry.gsi.gov.uk

Opening times: Open daily 9am–dusk (or 8pm, whichever is earlier).

Charging policy: Dependent on time of year – check website for details. Concessions and group rates available.

Disabled access: Electric scooters and manual wheelchairs must be booked in advance

Find out more

Forestry Commission
www.forestry.gov.uk/westonbirt

Great British Gardens
www.greatbritishgardens.co.uk/
westonbirt_arboretum.htm

Garden Action - Japanese Maple
www.gardenaction.co.uk/
plantfinder/japanese_maple-1.asp

At over 240 hectares, containing around 3,700 different types of tree and a grade one listed landscape, Westonbirt justifiably deserves its grandiose title of the 'National Arboretum'. Ask many people to pick two natural history phenomena that remind them of autumn, and the chances are they'll mention leaves turning colour and the arrival of seething ranks of mushrooms and toadstools. Believe us, this is one of the best places to see both!

The arboretum was created by a man of means called Robert Holford, who first started planting trees on this site in the 1820s. Successive owners then expanded and added to the collection, using seeds brought back by plant hunters during the Victorian age of exploration and discovery. In the 20th century, with no one to care for the arboretum, it became run down and by World War II it was in a very sorry state. Westonbirt was handed to the Forestry Commission in 1956 and since then, and with much effort, the arboretum has slowly been turned round to the major visitor attraction it is today.

The main interest for people wishing to see the vivid colours of autumnal leaves is the famous display of Japanese maples in the Old Arboretum, northeast of the visitor centre. But Westonbirt also has a huge area comprised mainly of native trees in the Silk Wood, to the south and west, and what better place to carry out our fungal foray.

In the company of Justin Smith, a man with a passion for fungi, we picked an area underneath some huge statuesque beech trees to see what was around. Underneath the dense canopy of golden-yellow leaves, we were astounded at the variety of fungi we were able to find without any difficulty at all. Fungi, it has to be said, are a bewilderingly difficult group to identify at the best of times, with thousands of species to choose from, and many species changing their colour and shape with age. So it is best to have an expert with you, or at least be certain of your identification before you pick for the table.

In half an hour, we were able to clock up an impressive tally of 15 species in a very small search area. The edible highlight of the foray was, without doubt, the penny bun, a wonderfully named, stout-looking mushroom with a bulbous stem, russet-coloured cap and a system of pores and tubes replacing the more familiar gills. This is a fungus noted for its taste - young specimens are delicious raw in salad, and large mature fungi are very strongly flavoured even when cooked. The contrast could not have been greater between the penny bun and another fungus barely two metres away. The deadly panther cap is a fungus often

Autumnal maple foliage at Westonbirt arboretum

A close-up view of the vivid red of the Japanese maple leaves

associated with beech. It too has a white stem and russet-coloured cap, but across the surface of the cap are numerous white, warty fragments. This was definitely a toadstool that should be photographed and then left to its own devices!

To appreciate the best autumn colours that Westonbirt has to offer, it is advised to cross back into the Old Arboretum and take an amble through the Acer Glade. This glade contains the National Japanese Maple Collection, a species that turns the most incredible vivid red colour towards the end of October. This beautiful and diverse tree has as many as 500 different cultivated forms, many of which are represented within the Old Arboretum.

The reason why the leaves are thought to turn these incredible colours is because as day length shortens, the dominant green leaf colour, represented by chlorophyll, begins to break down, leading to the other background colours in the leaves showing through before the leaf eventually falls. Why the Japanese maple should turn a colour so much more vivid than any of the other trees in the rest of the collection is anybody's guess; we say, turn off your mind, breathe in the lovely autumnal air and revel in the colour!

Penny bun fungus – noted for its taste

10 Abbey Farm, Norfolk

Getting there:

Abbey Farm, Flitcham, King's Lynn, PE31 6BT. On the A148 King's Lynn to Cromer road, turn north on to the B1153. At Flitcham village, turn right to Abbey Road. Abbey Farm is under 1 kilometre on the right, the bird hide is signposted further on.

Tel: 01485 609094

Email: organics@abbeyfarm.co.uk

Opening times: Open daily.

Charging policy: Not applicable.

Disabled access: Access paths and the viewing facilities are suitable for wheelchair users.

Find out more

Visiting Abbey Farm
www.abbeyfarm.co.uk/visiting.shtml

RSPB - Pink-footed Goose
www.rspb.org.uk/birds/guide/p/pinkfootedgoose/index.asp

British Garden Birds - Tree Sparrow
www.garden-birds.co.uk/birds/treesparrow.htm

If you had just flown here from Iceland or Greenland, you might be grateful for a bit of sustenance – even if it was just a beet top. Pink-footed geese breed out on the Arctic tundra before flying to Scotland, Lancashire and Norfolk. Around 100,000 come to Norfolk and up to 20,000 visit Abbey Farm at Flitcham near Sandringham.

This organic farm actively encourages the geese by leaving out beet tops in the fields – the beets themselves are harvested for sugar. Ironically, the sugar beet industry has been criticised for reducing biodiversity and grubbing out hedgerows to grow vast fields of these tubers to satiate our sweet tooths – yet they have been a boon for the pink-footed geese and have really helped to increase their numbers. The birds roost out on the coast and then fly to the farm at dawn to feed – it's a spectacular sight, as there are so many it can take over an hour for them to arrive. As their name suggests, they are easily recognisable by their pink legs and pink bills. They are a bit daintier than other geese – larger than a mallard but smaller than a swan. They are also incredibly noisy, making a musical yelping as they darken the skies on their way to the beet fields. They fly in typical goose formation, in a loose 'V'. Pink-footed geese aren't a protected species and are quite shy – they can cause problems by feeding on fresh, young winter barley and some farmers do shoot them. Abbey Farm isn't open access, although there are public footpaths through it. Instead, you'll need to watch the geese from the road: the farm has set up bales of hay to act as hides, which, as well as keeping visitors out of the working parts of the farm, also means the geese aren't disturbed.

Because the farm is managed organically with an emphasis on encouraging wildlife, they have recorded a large number of birds here – 180 species in total. One uncommon bird, which is encouraged by being fed in winter and given nest boxes, is the tree sparrow. Most of us can probably remember the days when both species of sparrow were common: now house sparrows have grown increasingly rare and the more timid tree sparrow is in even greater danger; it has declined by a massive 95 per cent over the last 25 years. Intensive farming over the past 30 years has significantly reduced insect levels and it's likely that large areas of farmland no longer provide enough seasonal variety of invertebrates for tree sparrows to feed their young during the breeding season.

The tree sparrow is slightly smaller than the house sparrow, with black-spotted cheeks and a chestnut crown, and its tail is almost permanently set at a jaunty angle. Instead of hanging round houses, it prefers open farmland, hedgerows, trees and small isolated woods. In late autumn, small flocks will form where there's abundant food – especially over stubble or weedy turnip and beet fields. Research carried out by the RSPB has shown that the sparrows prefer nest boxes near wetlands – they feed their young on insects and like to give them a high proportion of aquatic invertebrates.

Abbey Farm leek harvest

They grow their own vegetables at Abbey Farm and this has encouraged legions of hares to come and munch on their tender cos lettuces. Now they fence off the vegetables but, because they also grow legumes, like lucerne and vetch, which fix nitrogen and increase soil fertility naturally, there's plenty for the hares to munch. Traditionally people like to look for hares in spring when they are easier to see boxing, but seeing large numbers feasting on winter vegetation is still a real treat.

If you want a more intensive dose of farmland wildlife, you can go and stay on the farm and help weed in return for free camping and as many vegetables as you can eat!

Pink-footed geese flock feed at Abbey Farm

December

Though it is tempting to 'hibernate' indoors as you prepare for the season's festivities, a walk in December will give surprising views of animals letting their guard down.

In December the urban red fox makes its presence known. The Vixen is only in season for a few days so the dog fox needs to keep track of her movements both by smell and by constantly communicating his desires though his 'wow-wow-wow' bark and listening out for her blood-curdling response.

December will bring some of the year's best birdwatching in your own garden as the tits and finches carry out a circuit of the best eating joints in the area. The same happens in the countryside with linnets, yellowhammers and skylarks, as they eke out an existence in stubble fields and along hedgerows.

Loose bark or dense growth of ivy can give views of hibernating insects. Of course, December and Christmas also bring the mistletoe on its favourite host tree, the apple and visiting an orchard can bring wonderful sightings of overwintering blackcaps, which adore mistletoe berries.

1 The New Forest

Getting there:

There are three main routes in from the M27 junction 1 (busy in Summer), the A35 from Southampton, and the A31 from Bournemouth. Nearest train stations within the forest: Ashurst, Beaulieu Road, Brockenhurst and Sway.

Tel: Lyndhurst Visitor Information Centre – 02380 282269
Lymington Visitor Information Centre – 01590 689000

Email: information@nfdc.gov.uk

Opening times: Open daily.

Charging policy: Not applicable.

Disabled access: Three wheelchair-friendly trails – guide at visitor centres.

Find out more

New Forest Official Website
www.thenewforest.co.uk/

New Forest National Park Authority
www.newforestnpa.gov.uk/

New Forest Pony Breeding and Cattle Society
www.newforestpony.com/

Every year, as winter approaches, a remarkable event takes place in the New Forest, and, if you're lucky enough to witness it, it will become something you will always remember. It's a spectacle that makes you wonder at the forces of nature that cause an animal to know when it is time to head to its breeding grounds. This is the time of year when the sea trout leave their saltwater habitat and head for the shallow, freshwater streams of the New Forest to spawn.

These fish are not tiddlers either, weighing up to 9 kilos and over 70 centimetres long. Such is their determination to get upstream to their spawning grounds that they will swim and thrash through the shallower areas of certain forest streams with their backs practically clear of the water. Year after year they relentlessly head for the spot where they themselves were born – and yet, despite their size, are rarely noticed.

Once at her birthplace, the female fish uses her tail to scrape a shallow hollow on the bottom of the stream. This is known as a 'redd' and is the location where she will lay her eggs and the male trout will fertilise them. You can identify the males because they are wearing their best and brightest colours to impress the ladies, their sides glowing a golden yellow. No one knows why this species of trout decides to spend most of its life out at sea, rather than in the rivers, but when you see a brown river trout alongside its oceanic cousin, it's obvious that the richer pickings are to be had out at sea.

Much of the other wildlife in the New Forest can be a whole lot easier to spot than sea trout, where it's generally a case of waiting for a good dose of rain to fill up the meandering streams and then hanging over the side of a bridge and hoping. That said, spawning goes on for several weeks and once you've spotted your first trout you can be pretty sure of seeing others.

If you do miss the spawning trout, you are virtually guaranteed to see ponies and deer in the New Forest

Male red deer in the New Forest at sunset

and one thing that can't run away – the famous Knightwood Oak. At over 400 years old, this oak tree is said to be the oldest tree in the forest and has been a visitor attraction since Victorian times. Look closely in the Knightwood enclosure and you might find another venerable tree called the Eagle Oak. This became notorious in 1810 when a New Forest keeper shot the last sea eagle from its branches. Keepers are still employed by the Forestry Commission to manage the deer and other animal and plant life, but these days shooting birds of prey is very much off the agenda, meaning you've got a good chance of spotting birds such as buzzard, goshawk or, in the summer months, the rare honey buzzard.

The New Forest is full of history and traditions. More than 900 years ago it was designated as a royal hunting ground by William the Conqueror – whose own son, William II, was killed here. No one knows whether it was an accident or part of a plot by his younger brother Henry who went on to seize the throne. You can still visit the spot where Sir Walter Tyrell is supposed to have killed the King with a stray arrow. It's marked by the Rufus Stone near the village of Minstead. If you want to find out more about the history of the forest, there's a great local museum at Lyndhurst.

If you're prepared to wait until the end of winter to visit the New Forest, one of the other seasonal spectacles is the migration of toads and frogs to the forest ponds. In February, as soon as there's a bit of mild weather, they begin to make their way to the water to breed – just like the trout, these creatures are driven by instinct. And, please, if you're driving to see them, take a little extra care when using the forest roads as the frogs and toads have no conception of the green cross code!

Though difficult to spot, the sea trout head to the New Forest to spawn

....

Opposite: Famous New Forest ponies

2 Donna Nook, Lincolnshire

Getting there:

Access from the main A1031 coastal road. Parking at Stonebridge, Howden's Pullover, Sea Lane, Saltfleet and Saltfleet Haven. Public access is also possible at Merrikin's Pullover, but no parking.

Tel: 01507 526 667

Email: info@lincstrust.co.uk

Opening times: Open daily.

Charging policy: Not applicable.

Disabled access: Access on natural sandy tracks though the dunes – difficult but not impossible for wheelchairs with assistance.

Find out more

Lincs Trust
www.lincstrust.org.uk/reserves/nr/reserve.php?mapref=15

English Nature – Donna Nook
www.english-nature.gov.uk/special/nnr/nnr_details.asp?nnr_name=&C=26&Habitat=0&natural_area=&local_team=0&spotlight_reserve=0&X=&NNR_ID=260

Photographing Grey Seals at Donna Nook
www.wildsight.co.uk/articles/donna-nook.html

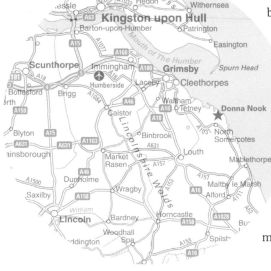

At first glance, an active bombing range might not be the place you associate with one of Britain's most famous winter wildlife spectacles, but the presence of the RAF has given Donna Nook's grey seal population welcome protection. Since the colony became established in this remote corner of the Lincolnshire coastline in the 1970s, the population has boomed.

Britain is a very special place for the grey seal. Its incredibly convoluted coastline has some superb wildlife beaches which play host in late autumn and early winter to around 50 per cent of the entire population of *Halichoerus grypus*, or, as its Latin name translates, the 'hook-nosed sea-pig'. While most breeding grey seal colonies are located off remote Scottish islands, Donna Nook is much more accessible, as it is only a short drive from the Lincolnshire market town of Louth.

Out of all the grey seal colonies, Donna Nook is the latest one to get into full swing, with September being the peak time for colonies in England and Wales, October in Scotland and November on the east coast. The large bull seals are the first to arrive back and typically arrive at Donna Nook in early November, coming ashore to set up territories and wait for females to turn up. The males are Britain's largest mammal, with the biggest weighing in at an incredible 300 kilos. The smaller females, or cows, arrive shortly after and are herded into the harems by the bulls. Here they will give birth to a single, cream-coloured pup. The young pups are suckled for three weeks during which time their weight will triple, and they gradually lose their pale coat. Once the pups are weaned, the females become available for mating, which gives rise to some fierce competition among the bulls. The most dominant bulls are called 'Beach Masters', who try to hold their harem against all challengers. Fights can be vicious and bloody with the action peaking by mid-December. By the end of January, it's all over and the seals are back out at sea until their return ten months later to start the cycle all over again.

On arrival at the reserve, the first thing we noticed was the chestnut-paling fence that ran the entire length of beach, which is designed to keep visitors and seals apart – and for good reason. While the young pups are harmless and indeed vulnerable, a cow keen to protect her pup will inflict a nasty bite if approached too closely and earlier warning hisses are ignored. The big bulls are even more dangerous, and could catch the unwary off guard as they are capable of moving at surprising speeds across the beach. In spite of the

fence, the seals are still very close and we were able to film the most
wonderful shots of different aged pups studded along the entire
length of the beach. Invariably the pups were attended by their
mothers and seemed to spend the majority of the time either
snoozing, or latched onto their mother's nipples, extracting the
incredibly rich milk which apparently consists of 60 per cent fat; no
wonder the pups grow so fast!

Grey seals (and the RAF) on Donna
Nook beach

This scene of peace and harmony was, of course, frequently
brought to an end by the brooding malevolent males, who would
occasionally arise from their seeming slumbers and hurtle after any
interloping males that tried to encroach on their harem. While we
saw plenty of disagreements between males, we didn't witness a full-
blooded fight, which happens only occasionally when two very well-
matched bulls meet. We did manage to film a particularly large male
having his wicked way with one of his females. This was not
particularly pleasant viewing and certainly not for the squeamish or
faint-hearted!

Grey seal pup latched to its mother's
nipple

For the plane enthusiast, too, Donna Nook is a real treat and we
regularly had to stop the filming as another fighter jet screamed over
the beach on a practice dummy run. Not that that this interruption
bothered the seals, though, who seemed totally oblivious to the
noise. While the colony grows from strength to strength, it's good to
know that nothing is going to mess with the seals at Donna Nook as
they have friends in high places.

3 The Cairngorms, Scotland

Getting there:

From the A9 trunk road at Aviemore, take the B970 all the way to the Cairngorms (about 14 kilometres).

Tel: Cairngorms National Park Authority – 01479 873535

Email: enquiries@cairngorms.co.uk

Opening times: Open daily.

Charging policy: Not applicable.

Disabled access: Limited disabled access to mountainous areas.

Find out more

Cairngorms National Park Authoriy
www.cairngorms.co.uk/

Cairngorm Mountain
www.cairngormmountain.com/

The Cairngorm Reindeer
www.reindeer-company.demon.co.uk/

Wildlife Scotland
http://wildlife.visitscotland.com

The Cairngorms in Scotland is Britain's premier mountain range, in scale, altitude and sheer wilderness. The range is stunningly beautiful, but, with mountains mostly above 1,200 metres, it does have a severe climate. Despite the harsh conditions in winter, look closely and you'll find wildlife aplenty – golden eagles, snow buntings and mountain hares as well as two other extremely hardy mountain specialists. The best-known, and perhaps best-loved, of these is the reindeer and they're relatively easy to see.

From the Cairngorm Reindeer Centre near Aviemore, you can head off with a herder onto the hillside to find them. After a covering of snow, the mountains are crispy white, and as you listen to the herder calling the deer in a loud yodel, you might believe you're in Switzerland, and Heidi and her goats are about to turn up, along with the reindeer.

The animals soon appear over the hills, knowing the herder has a sackful of barley and sugar beet. It's a supplement to their natural diet and, to the reindeer, it's the equivalent of a bagful of sweets.

There are about 130 reindeer in the Cairngorm mountains and they are Britain's only free-ranging deer herd. Our native reindeer died out over 8,000 years ago. These are descendants of a herd re-introduced to Scotland in 1952. From top to toe, they are perfectly adapted to life in the frozen north. Their broad, cloven hooves splay out like snow shoes to stop them from sinking, and their coats work like duvets. Their entire body is covered, including their noses. (Only their eyes are exposed.) And the hairs are hollow, filled with air, which is great insulation when the temperatures spiral down.

Reindeer are unique among deer in that both the males and females have antlers. Males drop their antlers in early winter, but females keep them throughout the season, so that they can protect their young from predators that have long been lost from the British Isles.

There are daily visits to the herd, weather permitting, leaving from the Reindeer Centre at 11am. During the winter months, this is dependent on whether they can be found, as they really are free ranging. They're not camera shy, so you'll be able to take some great snaps, but be warned. One or two deer don't like mobile phones. If they hear your phone ring, you might get more attention than you bargained for!

Another creature that's as tough as boots, and survives in the mountains, is the ptarmigan. In the 18th century, these birds were found as far south as the Lake District, but they're now confined to the Scottish Highlands and the main concentration is in the Cairngorms.

CairnGorm Mountain itself is as good a place as any to find them. Ptarmigans are high-altitude grouse and are seldom found below 600 metres. So, you can either put on your hiking boots and make the trek to the mountain top, or take the easy way by joining the winter skiers on the funicular railway. Check the forecast first at the mountain centre next to the main car park, as blizzards aren't the best conditions for searching for these creatures. Not that blizzards worry them.

On the snowy white peaks, you're looking for a creature that's... snowy white; not easy. But that's the point – in winter, the ptarmigan's plumage undergoes an ermine-like transformation. Hunkered down in the snow, a peregrine falcon or an eagle sweeping overhead has to be especially sharp eyed to spot one. There's a bit of black around the eye and tail, and the male also has a splash of red above the eye, but otherwise the ptarmigan is pure white.

The birds are renowned for their hardiness and, as you cast your eye around the barren, snowy waste, you cannot fail but wonder at their extraordinary ability to survive the rigours of this environment. Their survival is down to several factors: they have especially dense plumage and thick feathering on their feet, the equivalent of miniature snow shoes, and they survive by burrowing into the snow to find shoots. Even so, it still seems a miracle that they make it to spring. If ever snow creeps across the earth, the ptarmigan is likely to be the last bird alive.

Reindeer – well-adapted to the harsh winter climate of the mountains

Mountain hare in its winter coat

The rugged scenery of the Cairngorms

4 Fountains Abbey, North Yorkshire

Getting there:

Located 6 kilometres west of Ripon –
close to the A1 and A61. From Ripon,
follow the tourist signs along the B6265
to Pateley Bridge.

Tel: 01765 608888

Email: info@fountainsabbey.org.uk

Opening times: Open daily. Abbey and
Water Garden November–February
10am–4pm, March–October 10am–5pm.
Deer Park during daylight.

Charging policy: Adult £5.50, Child £3,
Family £15, group rates. National Trust,
English Heritage members and under 5s
free.

Disabled access: Most areas are
wheelchair accessible, minibus service
to take visitors to different parts of the
property. Large-print and Braille guides.

Blue tits spend the winter searching for
the next meal

Find out more

Fountains Abbey
www.fountainsabbey.org.uk/

National Trust
www.nationaltrust.org.uk/main/
w-vh/w-visits/w-findaplace/
w-fountainsabbeyandstudleyroyal
watergarden/

A stunning, though very cold, location

Visit this stonking location on a crisp, frosty day and you
will certainly be impressed. The setting blows your socks off.
A gorgeous monastic ruin set in a small wooded valley, with
the odd ornamental garden thrown in. Apparently the fact that it's
in a valley is important as it creates a milder microclimate, ideal
for wildlife. Well, that's the theory! The image we captured of a
lone duck standing on a thick sheet of ice revealed a different
story.

During our trip we were fortunate to see a number of birds,
including goldcrests, blue tits and great tits, but what we were
particularly after was the dipper as it searched for food in the stream
that runs through the abbey grounds. These are busy little birds,
spending two-thirds of the day foraging. They are also fun to watch
and are Britain's only songbird that feeds underwater. It's amazing
to think that these little creatures have developed in this way through
some magical process called evolution.

The dippers weren't the only ones on the hunt for an easy
underwater meal. At one of the Abbey's many lakes, we watched a
mute swan elegantly reaching below the surface in search of some
vegetation to eat; nothing strange there. But what happened next
took us by surprise. Close to the swan was a group of little grebe
that were watching their much larger neighbour with great interest.
Every time the swan put its neck under the water to feed, the little
grebes dived down. They weren't in competition, instead they were
after the invertebrates that were being disturbed by the swan as it
foraged.

The other 'must do' at Fountains Abbey is deer watching, or deer
feeding if you fancy helping out at one of the National Trust's
organised events. And, if you have artistic talents, try sketching the
backsides of the three deer species to be found in the grounds – red,
sika and fallow. We did precisely this, proving the key to species
identification is all to be found at the bottom end of the beast.

5 Morvern Peninsula, Scotland

Getting there:

Take the A884 just east of Strontian to Lochaline on the Sound of Mull. About 5 kilometres before Lochaline is a left turning to the 14th century ruins of Ardtornish Castle.

Tel: Ardtornish Estate Office – 01967 421288

Email: tourism@ardtornish.co.uk

Opening times: Open daily.

Charging policy: Charge for ferries and specific activities.

Disabled access: Variable depending on terrain.

Otters – most easily seen very early or at dusk

Find out more

Ardtornish Estate
www.ardtornish.co.uk/main.htm

WWF – Otters
www.wwf.org.uk/core/wildlife/fs_0000000027.asp

Wildlife Scotland
http://wildlife.visitscotland.com

Castle Stalker and the Morvern Peninsula

The otter is a creature many people dream of seeing. And why not? They look great with their broad muzzles and small ears, and their slim, streamlined bodies. And the success of books like *Ring of Bright Water*, an account of living with an otter in Scotland, and *Tarka the Otter*, set in Devon, have planted them firmly in our affections.

Perhaps people's desire to see them also stems from the fact that they're so difficult to see. They're shy and elusive and often nocturnal. But if you want to up your chances of spotting them, the west coast of Scotland is a top spot.

The Morvern Peninsula is one of those off-the-beaten track places, sparsely populated and relatively untouched by modern life. In this beautiful landscape of mountain, woodland and lochs, you can see golden eagle, sea eagle, red deer, pine martens ... and otters.

Otters are semi-aquatic, inhabiting the banks of rivers, lakes and rocky coasts feeding on fish, crustaceans, and water birds. During the 1950s otter populations plummeted in many lowland areas, mostly because of river pollution and habitat destruction. Happily, now their numbers are recovering.

On the Morvern Peninsula, it's best to look for them along the seashore and the edge of the many sea lochs. The pristine waters are full of food for them, and, because there's little pressure from humans, many hunt during the day.

Otters are most active at dawn or dusk. To increase your chances of seeing them, avoid wearing bright colours, sit quietly and keep your eyes peeled along the shoreline.

When fishing, their tail makes a splash as they dive below. From a distance, you might confuse them with a seal, but otters always arch their back before they dive. Underwater, their webbed feet and powerful rudder-like tail propel them speedily along. They're capable of closing their ears and nostrils, and air forced out of their coat leaves a trail of bubbles rising to the surface.

We were rewarded with a brief but exciting close encounter. Suddenly and quite unexpectedly, a female otter emerged from the water onto the bank and moved rapidly towards us. Then, just as quickly she slipped back into the water.

6 Holkham Estate, Norfolk

Getting there:

Five kilometres west of Wells-next-the-Sea on the A149. Two stops on the Norfolk Coasthopper bus route from King's Lynn and Hunstanton to Sheringham. Nearest train station: King's Lynn (approx 37 kilometres)

Tel: Site Manager – 01328 711183
English Nature – 01603 620558

Email: nature.reserve@holkham.co.uk

Opening times: Grounds open daily to walkers and cyclists except Christmas Day. Closed to vehicles at weekends (November-April, except Easter). For Hall opening times, see website.

Charging policy: Free entry to the grounds. Hall: Adults £7; Children £3.50. Group rates available.

Disabled access: Access to hall via metal ramp and stair lift. Acoustiguide and Braille guides.

Find out more

Holkham Hall and Estate
www.holkham.co.uk/cms/

Holkham Nature Reserve
www.holkham.co.uk/naturereserve/

English Nature - Holkham
www.english-nature.org.uk/special/nnr/nnr_details.asp?NNR_ID=86

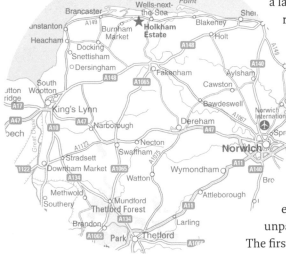

Holkham Estate on the North Norfolk coast is quite simply the jewel in the crown of an area famous for nature reserves. The 4,000 hectare Holkham National Nature Reserve forms part of the much larger Holkham Estate, home to the Earl and Countess of Leicester, who, it has to be said, must enjoy the birdwatching from their ancestral windows!

The reserve is as windswept as it is dramatic and consists of an incredibly diverse array of habitats – from tide lines, creeks and saltmarshes to shady pinewoods, pastures and arable fields. If you combine the fact that the reserve has a far-flung feel to it with the reality that very few people live within its borders, it is perhaps no surprise that it proves a magnet for huge flocks of winter birds.

During the last few decades, Holkham has become simply the best place to see pink-footed geese in the world. Although not sociable birds when seen nesting in the Icelandic river gorges or the Greenland tundra, when seen on their wintering grounds they're the living embodiment of the phrase: 'birds of a feather flock together'. Moving south in October to escape the winter at more northerly latitudes, the pink-footed geese often form the most enormous flocks, consisting of anything up to 40,000 birds, centred in and around the estate. These large concentrations of birds last into April, before the flocks disperse back to their breeding grounds.

Now, being able to track down the geese in and around the huge estate depends on local knowledge. Between dawn and dusk, the geese have only one thing on their mind and that is food. The best place to try and locate them while feeding is in the numerous sugar beet fields dotted in and around the Holkham Estate. With the help of local expert birder Paul Laurie, who knows the movements of the flocks as well as anyone in Norfolk, we managed to track down a large flock of 'pink-feets' feeding away on the harvested remains of sugar beets.

When approaching a flock of up to 5,000 geese feeding away, you have to do so in the full knowledge that there are potentially 10,000 eyes on the lookout for predators, and they scare easily. As well as being keen to avoid causing any unnecessary disturbance to the birds, the last thing we wanted was to scare the birds away, because an empty sugar beet field doesn't make for gripping television! Therefore, the technique we employed was to move carefully and quietly, using hedges and cars to break up our human outline. By employing this simple field-craft, we were soon treated to unparalleled views of the geese grazing away on the beets. The first thing we noticed about these dainty geese was that 'pink-footed' is not their best name. It has to be said that the feet are indeed pink, but for us the most noticeable feature is without doubt the lovely chocolate-coloured head and neck, topped off by a petite pink bill. Maybe 'chocolate-headed goose' would be a much more appropriate name, we mused!

Although it was lovely to see the geese happily grazing away, the ultimate goose experience at Holkham is to see the enormous skeins as they fly over the estate to roost on the Bob Hall's Sand Banks at dusk. Getting the best possible views of this wonderful wildlife phenomenon can be a hit-and-miss affair because the precise roosting location is dictated by the tide and the best spot to watch depends on where they have been feeding during the day. We plumped for a position just off the A149 west of Holkham village, and as the sun dipped below the horizon a dark moving cloud of birds could be picked out in the far distance – we had chosen well! As soon as the enormous flock was spotted, the next thing we appreciated was the sound, as a flock of what we estimated to be 15,000 geese, incessantly calling 'wink-wink!' ran the gauntlet of our camera as they headed out to the coast. The long shallow Vs of the birds as they traced across the sky in huge skeins, one after the other, was simply awe-inspiring.

Pink-footed geese feed on the fields

The windswept Holkham Estate

7 Slimbridge, Gloucestershire

Getting there:
Leave the M5 at junction 13 or 14 and follow signs for reserve. Nearest train station: Cam/Dursley. Sustrans bus route 41 or Sunday service from Gloucester.

Tel: 01453 890333

Email: info.slimbridge@wwt.org.uk

Opening times: Open daily 9.30am–5.30pm (5pm November–March). Closed Christmas Day.

Charging policy: Members and children under 4 – free, Adults £7.50, Concession £6.15, Children (4–16 years) £4.35, Family £20.35 (all include Gift Aid).

Disabled access: Excellent access throughout the centre, including bird hides, restaurant and toilets. Hearing and guide dogs allowed by prior arrangement.

Find out more

The Wildfowl and Wetlands Trust – Slimbridge
www.wwt.org.uk/visit/slimbridge/howto.asp

Birds of Britain – Bewick's Swan
www.birdsofbritain.co.uk/bird-guide/bewick-swan.htm

British Garden Birds – Starling
www.garden-birds.co.uk/birds/starling.htm

Slimbridge is internationally known throughout the birding world as the headquarters of the Wildfowl and Wetlands Trust. It was set up by the visionary Sir Peter Scott in 1946 after he realised that thousands of geese, swans, waders and ducks depended on the shores of the Severn Estuary during the winter months. However, a much lesser known fact is that during the winter the reserve plays host to very large numbers of common starlings – not very impressive, did you say? Well, wait until you hear what they do!

With currently just over a million breeding pairs in Britain, the starling is quite comfortably one of our commonest breeding birds. Despite a reduction in the number of pairs over the last 30 years, it is still abundant enough to be thought of as a ubiquitous species. In winter, the population of our resident starlings are boosted still further by huge influxes from Poland and Russia.

It has to be admitted that during the winter months most people visit Slimbridge not to look at a small black and speckled bird, but to admire the collection of wildfowl from around the world – or just gaze at the spectacle of thousands of wild birds using the estuary to feed and roost. Without doubt, the most celebrated visitor to the reserve is the Bewick's swan. These diminutive cousins of our resident mute swan arrive in Gloucestershire from their breeding grounds in the Russian tundra, a flight that marks the halfway point of an annual return journey consisting of over 4,000 kilometres. It was once again Sir Peter Scott who first realised that individual Bewick's could be identified by the pattern of yellow and black on their bill, a discovery that heralded nearly 40 years of research into the species which still continues today.

One of Slimbridge's undoubted highlights during these cold, dark months is the dusk floodlit feed from the Peng Observatory. Here, visitors are entertained while one of the reserve staff takes a stroll out in front of the hide with a wheelbarrow load of grain to feed the birds. While this attracts a huge variety of ducks, geese and swans every evening, the Bewick's swans are undoubtedly the star attraction as they trumpet to their family members on arriving at the lake, before jostling for position during the free handout. Once the feed has taken place, many of the birds simply leave, or settle down for the night, and many of the visitors also take this as a cue to leave – but don't be so hasty!

Closely following on the heels of the feed, we witnessed a small flock of starlings arrive and begin circling the lake. It was not long before a flock formed of around 50 starlings, which is thought to serve as a 'flag' for other small flocks of starlings, who have spent the day feeding out in the surrounding countryside to join them. In a short space

Swans and ducks at Slimbridge at sunset

of time, the flock had moved from a cast of hundreds to thousands as the birds swirled above the lake in a tight flock creating the most mesmerising shapes, twisting one way and then the other. As the smaller flocks arrived and became absorbed by the 'mother' flock, we attempted to count the numbers of birds: 'count the number of wings and divide by two', one wag said! The best guess we could come up with was over 20,000.

The behaviour then suddenly changed as the flock spiralled down to the reedbed and several hundred birds peeled off the bottom and disappeared into the reedbed by the side of the lake, before the rest of the flock lifted again. This behaviour then reoccurred a number of times while yet more birds disappeared into their reedbed roosts, in a manner that could only be described as the birds being drawn to the reedbed like iron filings to an enormous magnet. This performance carried on until there wasn't a bird to be seen in the sky. And the reason for this behaviour? Well, it is thought that a large flock confuses and confounds potential predators such as sparrowhawks and peregrines, and reduces the chance of them being eaten to about 20,000 to one!

Slimbridge ... what a place and what a sight! In half an hour we had just enjoyed two exciting winter spectacles for the price of an admission ticket!

Starlings flock at Slimbridge

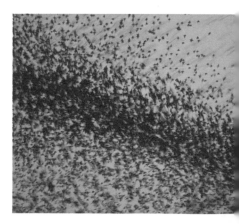

8 Poole Harbour, Dorset

Getting there:

Enter Poole from the A250, the A35 or the A31 and follow signs for the town centre then the harbour. Boat service to Brownsea from Poole Quay and Sandbanks, also Bournemouth and Swanage.

Tel: National Trust – 01202 707744

Email: brownseaisland@nationaltrust.org.uk

Opening times: Brownsea Island open daily late March–late October – see website for exact times.

Charging policy: Brownsea Island: adults £4.40, children £2.20, group rates.

Disabled access: Island tracks are rough in places – map of accessible route available. Braille guide. Contact operators about boat trips.

Find out more

National Trust – Brownsea
www.nationaltrust.org.uk

Poole Tourism
www.pooletourism.com/

Dorset Wildlife Trust – Brownsea Island
www.wildlifetrust.org.uk/dorset/reserves/brownsea.htm

Poole Harbour is the second biggest natural harbour in the world, a huge estuary with five large islands and four rivers running into it: the Frome, the Piddle, the Corfe and the Sherford. It's a sight of national and international importance for wetland birds too. Winter is a spectacular sight with over 30,000 migrants flooding the harbour – and it's very cosmopolitan, with waders and waterfowl from Canada, Greenland and Continental Europe. You might wonder why they come here. However, for the brent geese from Siberia, spending the winter months in Poole is the equivalent of us going to Barbados for our summer holidays. The harbour is comparatively warm, compared to the Siberian wastes, the water won't freeze and there are plenty of shellfish, crustaceans and juicy lugworms for them. The flocks tend to roost in the saltmarsh and lagoons at Brownsea Island.

One of the most exciting birds to see at this time of year is the avocet – you could spot up to 1,400 of these elegant, black and white birds with their needle-sharp bills and long, powder-blue legs. Seeing so many is fantastic, especially considering that this bird became extinct as a breeding bird in the UK during the 19th century due to the drainage of our marshes, hunting and collection of both its eggs and feathers for fishing flies. In fact, the bird was adopted as the RSPB's logo in the middle of the last century because of their commitment to helping the species recover.

Brownsea Island is well worth a visit. 'I had no idea I had such a delightful spot in my kingdom', said the Prince Regent on a trip to the island in 1818. Brownsea has been pillaged by Viking raiders and blitzed by Nazi bombers; in the 19th century, china clay was mined there. Today, this 200 hectare island with pinewoods, heathlands and saltmarshes is a National Trust reserve and, between spring and early autumn, a good place to get close to wading birds, deer and a small population of red squirrels. Although the original deer were roe, fallow were introduced, and it was here that a Japanese population of sika deer was also introduced in 1896. Brought over as ornamental animals, no one realised that they could swim. During a fire that swept the island in 1934, many of the deer escaped and swam to the mainland. During the 1970s some swam back to Brownsea, and they have grown in numbers ever since. Sika deer are sometimes hard to spot and if you don't see any at Brownsea, you might stand a better chance on the western shores of Poole Harbour at the Arne Nature Reserve. The sika, with no natural predators and cast-iron stomachs and lips, have really flourished here and this is where you'll find the largest concentration of them in the UK, all 7,000 of them, so you're virtually guaranteed to see one or two!

Arne is lovely: a great expanse of heath combined with old oak woodland, it sits on the edge of Poole Harbour, so in winter you'll get another view over all those wading birds and wildfowl, as well as being able to see Arne's rarer inhabitants like the Dartford warbler, which is resident all year round. If you come back in spring, you might see migrants such as swallows and martins, wheatears, cuckoos, willow warblers, blackcaps and chiffchaffs. In summer, sandwich and common terns start feeding just off the shores of the reserve and you might hunt out green tiger beetles, and silver-studded blue butterflies. Early waders, like whimbrels, greenshanks and spotted redshanks start arriving and the sika begin producing young. By autumn, the winter migrants are starting to build up once more, including black-tailed godwits, dunlins, avocets and grey plovers. The late autumn passage of migrants includes redstarts, whitethroats and spotted flycatchers. In fact, it sounds like Heathrow airport - only more colourful and with no need for passports!

Avocet – the logo of the RSPB

Winter sunset from Brownsea Island

9 Gigrin Farm, Powys

Getting there:

From Rhayader, take the A470 south, signpost to the farm is under 1 kilometre on the left hand side.

Tel: The Red Kite Centre – 01597 810243

Email: Chris@gigrin.co.uk

Opening times: Open daily except Christmas Day. Visitor Centre 1pm–5pm (daily).

Charging policy: Adults £3; OAP £2.50; Children (16 or under) £1.

Disabled access: Three hides are wheelchair friendly with ramps and internal access. Parking directly outside the hides is possible.

Find out more

Gigrin Farm
www.gigrin.co.uk/

Red Kites at Gigrin
www.gigrin.co.uk/redkite.html

RSPB – Red Kite
www.rspb.org.uk/birds/guide/r/ redkite/index.asp

It's sometimes easy to become blasé about a promised 'wildlife spectacle'. But the red kite feeding frenzy at Gigrin Farm in mid-Wales is above and beyond what is promised and, believe us, it is worth driving a long way to see.

Gigrin Farm used to be just a normal 80 hectare upland sheep farm. Run by the Powell family, it lies about 300 metres above sea level, with wonderful panoramic views over the Elan and Wye valleys – but that is not what makes it special. Since 1994, it has been the official RSPB red kite feeding station.

It all began several years ago, when the farmer noticed a number of birds of prey hanging around his fields, particularly during the lambing season. They were red kites, which, being carrion feeders, were gathering in the hope of picking up stillborn lambs, bits of afterbirth and the like. The farmer was seeing what then amounted to a very rare sight. Red kites used to be widespread in Britain until the 18th century, scavenging on the refuse-rich streets of our medieval cities, but the cleaning up of cities, and their relentless persecution by gamekeepers and farmers, brought the red kite almost to the edge of extinction in this country. By the end of the 18th century, only a handful of red kites survived in the remote hills of mid-Wales. Farmer Powell was of a different mind, he thought the birds beautiful and started to feed them daily when he went out to check his sheep. He noticed that year on year the numbers were gradually increasing. Today, if you visit the farm in December, as we did, you can expect to see a couple of hundred red kites arrive for the feeding event. The significance of feeding is that it helps to develop strong, healthy birds that will breed more successfully and produce strong, healthy young which are more likely to survive.

On arriving at the farm, it seemed like we were doomed to disappointment – oh, the birds would be there all right, and they would come to feed, but we just weren't going to get to see them. The farm and surrounding valleys were swathed in thick fog. This was going to be more frustrating than a wildlife 'no show'; the wildlife was actually there, but we were unable to film it. We pottered around the farm looking at the various feeding stations set out for small birds: they're lovely to look at at this time of year in their breeding plumage, all puffed up against the cold. The hour approached and we assembled, as gloomy as the weather, at the feeding site. Through the swirling mist we could see the ghostly outlines of huge birds in the shadowy trees. Well, the red kites were out in force – but it wasn't exactly going to make riveting television. But then the

gods of filming smiled on us: the sun came out, the mist lifted like the opening curtain going up at a concert, and what a stage set met our eyes. It wasn't just red kites that had come to the party; the trees were crowded with buzzards, crows and jackdaws as well. It was like a scene from a Wild West movie, when the vultures gather, waiting for the hapless cowboy to die of thirst. The farmer went into the field and started shovelling bucket loads of beef off-cuts from local butchers out of his tractor. And then it started ...

We had seen red kites a couple of times in the wild, but only ever circling high overhead with that characteristic deeply forked tail. We knew they were big, beautiful, charismatic birds, but seeing them within a few metres was a revelation. Big? They've got a wingspan of nearly two metres and looked huge. Beautiful? Seen close, their plumage is a glorious combination of deep, glossy, chestnut-red, with dramatic white patches under the wings, accessorised with glaring bright yellow eyes and talons. Charismatic? They came hurtling down like bullets, wings held sharply back, talons out, and snatched the 'prey' off the ground while still in flight. Then they went wheeling and twisting up into the sky to eat the tasty morsel on the wing. There was such a noise too: 'mewing' of the kites and buzzards, 'cawing' of the crows, 'jack-jacking' of the jackdaws, flapping and bickering, all accompanied by the sound of the huge beating wings of the kites. Once in the air, the kites would chase each other – we saw several drop their scraps of food only to have them snatched out of the air by a pursuer. It was a bit much to take in all at once. But it was, in truth, a genuine feeding frenzy, and a spectacular wildlife spectacle.

Gigrin Farm in winter

The spectacular sight of a flying red kite

10 Old Country House Farm, Herefordshire

Getting there:

Old Country Farm, Mathon, Malvern. From Worcester take A4103 for 17 kilometres, then B4220 towards Ledbury. After leaving Cradley, turn left at the top of the hill for Mathon then right for Coddington. Farm is under ½ kilometre on right. Nearest rail station: Colwall (pick-up by arrangement with the owner).

Tel: 01886 880 867

Email: ella@oldcountryhouse.co.uk

Opening times: Limited opening hours, by appointment only – please call to make a reservation.

Charging policy: Accommodation charges apply, details when booking.

Disabled access: Limited access, though improvements are being made to the orchards.

Find out more

Old Country House Farm
www.oldcountryhouse.co.uk/

BBC Food – Apple Orchards
www.bbc.co.uk/food/food_matters/
appleorchards.shtml

RSPB – Fieldfare
www.rspb.org.uk/birds/guide/f/
fieldfare/index.asp

Looking to escape for a few days in winter to an ornithological treat in a forgotten corner of an underrated county? Then you could scarcely do better than the rural hamlet of Mathon, nestling in the lea slopes of the Herefordshire Malverns.

Old Country House Bed and Breakfast is a 600-year-old family home, which owns and nestles next to two of the finest orchards you'll find for many a mile. The presence of apple trees on this site is thought to date back to the 17th century, with the orchards consisting of apples of a 'bittersweet vintage variety' used for cider making. The orchard is full of wonderful and ancient varieties with evocative names such as 'Yarlington Mill', 'Strawberry Norman' and 'Chisel Jersey'.

Even though many of the apples are regularly harvested in early winter for the thirsty cider drinkers around the country, the sheer quantity of fruit means that there's still a bountiful supply leftover for hungry winter wildlife. The moment we entered the first orchard we were immediately assaulted by the harsh 'chack-chack-chack!' call of the fieldfare. Although a handful of pairs of this bird do breed in Scotland, it is in winter when this bird makes its presence known, as over a million immigrants arrive in Britain from Scandinavia to gorge themselves on the winter fare of berries and fruits provided by our hedgerows and orchards. The fieldfare usually wanders around in nomadic flocks in a constant search for food, but here it seemed like the entire Herefordshire population had decided to camp around Mathon for the whole winter, so abundant were the pickings to be had!

Normally the fieldfare is a bird that quickly flushes when approached, so we decided the best technique to get wonderful views of the feeding flocks was to get tucked into one of the hedgerows which surround the orchard on all sides. This method breaks up the human outline and, if we sat quietly, would hopefully mean that the birds would soon be so intent on gorging themselves that they'd be blissfully unaware of a camera crew sticking half out of a hedge barely ten metres away! We positioned ourselves close to a particularly beautiful tree that had dropped most of its precious cargo onto the ground, and in no time fieldfare began fluttering down to feed on the fallen apples.

It was not until we had fully inspected the flock that we realized there was certainly more than one species of thrush in among the throng. Dotted in between the fieldfare, the occasional redwing was spotted, another winter visitor to our shores from Scandinavia. Noticeably smaller than the fieldfare, the clear white stripe above the eye and red patch on the flanks of this bird are instantly recognisable. Also present at the fruit-fest

Fieldfare feeding on fallen apples

Mistletoe on one of its favoured hosts – the apple tree

The orchard at Old Country House Farm

were small numbers of more familiar year-round residents – the blackbird and mistle thrush. It was only after closely studying the flock for a while that we realised there was a distinct pecking order with the fieldfare very much the bully boy! Constantly they would drive off the blackbirds and redwings from particularly tasty apples – as if there wasn't enough to go round, we thought! Interestingly, though, the fieldfare seemed to have developed an *entente cordiale* with the bigger and bulkier mistle thrush, perhaps realising that despite the fieldfares' superiority in numbers they might well be biting off more than they could chew taking on the mistle!

Of course, the wildlife interest in the orchard was not just confined to the birds. Many of the apple trees were festooned by that most festive of plants, the mistletoe. These golden evergreen globes, which seem suspended in the branches of favoured hosts, such as apple trees, are actually hemi-parasites. The plant makes a living partly off the tree, into which it sinks its specialied roots, but also off food produced by its own chlorophyll. It is, of course, only the female mistletoe bushes that would interest romantics, as the male plants do not possess the instantly recognisable white berries. But competing for these sought-after berries with the Christmas kissers at this time of the year are wintering blackcaps, which also become irresistibly drawn to this sticky winter bounty.

Old orchards are under threat in Britain through changes to agricultural practices and because the large retail stores are increasingly sourcing their fruit from overseas. This has meant that as traditional fruit growing becomes uneconomical, many examples of this wonderful habitat have been disgracefully bulldozed to oblivion.

The Best of the Rest
– Where Else to Watch Nature

England

Avon/North Somerset – Avon Gorge
Instantly recognisable and spectacular limestone gorge that has exceptional wildlife value, supporting two species of whitebeams found nowhere else in the world and a host of other botanical rarities. Famous for its nesting peregrines and healthy populations of greater and lesser horseshoe bats. Contact Mandy Leivers, 0117 903 0609 or mleivers@ bristolzoo.org.uk; web: www.bristolzoo. org.uk/about/conservation/wild/ avongorge

Avon/North Somerset – Chew Valley Lake Created in 1953, covering over 485 hectares, Chew Valley is the largest freshwater body in southwest England. Most of the man-made lake is open water; the margins are exposed mud, reedbed, scrub and wet woodland. Large numbers of wildfowl and a gull roost in winter, but spring and autumn can be fruitful as it's an important migration site. Public viewing areas, but access to hides needs a permit from Bristol Water at Woodford Lodge, 01275 332339. Web: www.bristol-water.co.uk/leisure/ birdwatching-information.asp or www.cvlbirding.co.uk

Bedfordshire – The Lodge
Headquarters of the RSPB and doubles as a reserve that comprises woodland, heathland and acid grassland. Located on relict heathland, much of which has been plantation and is currently being converted back to heathland. The site contains an impressive array of woodland birds including all three woodpeckers. Contact 01767 680551 or thelodge@rspb.org.uk; web: www.rspb.org.uk/reserves/guide/ t/thelodge/index.asp

Berkshire – Windsor Great Park
Originally a Norman royal hunting estate and still owned by the Crown, the site is an enormous 2,020 hectares of deer parkland and woods and has the largest collection of mature, over mature and ancient oak and beech trees remaining in Europe.The oldest trees are thought to be more than 1,000 years old and the Park is wonderful

for beetles. Contact 020 7851 5000; web: www.thecrownestate.co.uk/1651_the_ windsor_great_park

Cambridgeshire – Grafham Water At the western end, 149 of the 627 hectares of this huge reservoir are managed by the Wildlife Trust for Beds, Cambs, Northants and Peterborough. Blackcap, garden warbler and nightingale can all be heard singing from the scrub in spring but winter is a real treat: gadwall, wigeon and shoveler can be seen in good numbers with nationally important numbers of great-crested grebes. Contact 01480 811075 or grafham@wildlifebcnp.org; web: www.wildlifebcnp.org/reserves/ reserve.php?reserveid=49

Cambridgeshire – Nene Washes Lying just nine and a half kilometres from Peterborough, the Nene Washes in the Cambridgeshire Fens contain impressive floodplain meadows. Regularly flooded by the River Nene in winter, the reserve plays host to Bewick's swans and large numbers of duck. In the spring, impressive numbers of waders breed, including black-tailed godwit, snipe and ruff. Contact 01733 205140; web: www.rspb.org.uk/reserves/ guide/n/nenewashes/index.asp

Cornwall – Marazion Marsh Cornwall's largest reedbed, with a view across to St Michael's Mount. Come in spring and listen to the songs of breeding sedge, reed and Cetti's warblers. However, August and September are the times to look for two rarities in the reedbed: the aquatic warbler and spotted crake. Bittern now also regularly over-winter. Contact 01736 711682 or marazion.marsh@rspb.org. uk; web: www.rspb.org.uk/reserves/ guide/m/marazionmarsh/index.asp

Cumbria – Haweswater The fells and valleys around Haweswater reservoir are famous as the territory for the only pair of English golden eagles, which attempt to nest most years at the head of the reservoir. A good range of upland birds including raven, peregrine and ring ouzel can also be seen. Contact 01931 713376 or haweswater@rspb.org.uk; web: www.rspb.org.uk/reserves/guide/h/ haweswater/index.asp

Derbyshire – Dovedale Created over thousands of years as the River Dove carved its way though a massive limestone plateau. Wildlife interest centres on lily-of-the-valley and herb Paris in limestone woods, and limestone bedstraw and hutchinsia in the grasslands. Dipper and grey wagtail also frequent the river. Web: www.peakdistrict-nationalpark.info/ studyArea/factsheets/08.html# dovedale or www.nationaltrust. org.uk/main/ w-vh/w- visits/w-findaplace/ w-ilampark/w-east_midlands-places-southpeakestate/w-east_midlands-places-dovedale.htm

Devon – Exe Estuary The Exe Estuary between Exeter and Exmouth is over nine and a half kilometres of tidal mudflats, making it the most important estuary for wildfowl and waders in southeast England. The best time to visit is in winter when brent geese, black-tailed godwit and up to 600 avocet feed on the mudflats or roost at the Bowling Green Marsh RSPB Reserve at high tide. Contact 01392 824614; web: www.rspb.org.uk/reserves/guide/e/ exeestuary/index.asp

Devon – Yarner Wood One of three adjacent sites in East Dartmoor Woods and Heaths (with Trendlebere Down and Bovey Valley Woodlands). The sites are an excellent example of western oakwoods that are abundant in mosses, lichens and liverworts. The birds reflect the habitat with pied flycatcher and redstarts particularly common as well as wood warbler and spotted flycatcher. Contact 01392 889770 or somerset@ english-nature.org.uk; web: www.englishnature. org/special/nnr/nnr_details.asp?nnr_ name=&C=0&Habitat=0&natural_area= &local_team=0&spotlight_reserve=1&X= 1&NNR_ID=219

Dorset – Arne Reserve One of the best locations to see lowland heathland in the UK. All six species of reptile can be seen and May is the time to listen out for the Dartford warbler at dawn and nightjar at dusk. Many species of moth, butterfly and dragonfly can be seen during the summer months. Contact 01929 553360 or arne@ rspb. org.uk; web: www.rspb.org.uk/ reserves/ guide/a/arne/index.asp

Dorset – Durlston Country Park 113 hectares of predominantly sea cliffs and chalk downland close to Swanage. There are orchids such as early spider and autumn lady's tresses but the real interest is in the butterflies, especially in August, with great views of Lulworth skipper and chalkhill and Adonis blues. Contact 01929 424443 or info@durlston.co.uk; web: www.durlston.co.uk/

Durham – Moor House, Upper Teesdale NNR One of the most famous sites in the UK with a whole range of arctic-alpine plants such as spring gentian, mountain everlasting and alpine bistort. But this huge National Nature Reserve of almost 7,400 hectares also possesses a fine range of upland birds such as black grouse, and breeding waders like curlew, golden plover, lapwing and snipe. Spring is the best time to visit; it can be very bleak in winter. Contact 01833 622374; web: www.english-nature. org. uk/special/nnr/nnr_details.asp?NNR_ID =159 or www.durham.gov.uk/ durhamcc/ usp.nsf/pws/Durham+Wildlife+Sites+- +Moorhouse+Upper+Teesdale+National+ Nature+Reserve

East Sussex – Ashdown Forest Although plenty of forest can be seen across its 2,600 hectares, Ashdown Forest is considered the largest tract of heath in southeast England. A great location for deer-watching with native roe deer alongside the introduced muntjac, fallow and sika. Healthy populations of specialist heathland breeding birds can also be seen during the summer. Contact enquiries@ ashdownforest.co.uk; web: www. ashdownforest.co.uk

Essex – Epping Forest A huge public open space near London at almost 2,500 hectares. The habitats have been managed for over 1,000 years by man and his grazing stock, and the forest is internationally known for its ancient pollards of oak, beech and hornbeam, which make it a boon for fungi and insects. Web: www.cityoflondon.gov.uk/ corporation/living_environment/open_ spaces/epping_forest.htm

Essex – Fingringhoe Wick Lying on the Essex coast just eight kilometres from Colchester, former gravel workings have resulted in a freshwater lake, mature secondary woodland, reeds and scrub. This Essex Wildlife Trust reserve is one of the best places in the UK to try and glimpse nightingale in late May and June and, in winter, large numbers of dark-bellied brent geese and some sea duck can be seen. Contact 01206 729678 or fingringhoe@essexwt.org.uk; web: www. essexwt.org.uk/centres/Fingringhoe.htm

Gloucestershire – Lower Woods An extensive 283 hectares of semi-natural ancient oak woodland and grassland, with woods situated on damp, clay soils and made up of distinct woodland blocks separated by ancient wide trenches. The woodland flora is particularly rich and contains violet helleborine and wild service tree. During the summer butterflies fly along the rides and a small population of nightingales breed in the dense scrub. The site is jointly managed by the Gloucestershire and Avon Wildlife Trusts. Contact 01452 383333 or info@ gloucestershirewildlifetrust.co.uk; web: www.gloucestershirewildlifetrust. co.uk/ or www.avonwildlifetrust.org. uk/

Greater London – Kempton Nature Reserve A former reservoir in the middle of suburbia but now an 18 hectare nature reserve managed by Thames Water. Winter populations of gadwall and shoveller; also waders on passage. Access is by permit, public open days or guided walks. Contact 07747 640361 or steven.long@thameswater.co.uk; web: www.englishnature.gov.uk/text_version/ special/lnr/lnr_projects_details.asp?ID= 86&r=London&k=

Greater London – Tower Hamlets Cemetery Park Opened as a cemetery in 1841 and closed for graves in 1966, the park became neglected, until its value for wildlife led to it being designated a Local Nature Reserve in 2001. Twenty species of butterfly have been recorded in the park and foxes are commonly encountered. Contact Ken Greenway, 07904 186981; web: www.towerhamletscemetery.org/

Hampshire – Martin Down NNR Consisting of 342 hectares of chalk downland and scrub and home to an exceptional array of rare and threatened species: 12 orchid species have been recorded on site; bats are abundant; birds such as turtle dove and quail, though rare elsewhere, can be regularly seen or heard here. Invertebrates are exceptional too. The site is jointly owned and managed by Natural England and Hampshire County Council. Contact 01380 726344 or wiltshire@english-nature.org.uk; web: www.english-nature.org.uk/special/ nnr/nnr_details.asp?NNR_ID=109

Hampshire/West Sussex – Langstone and Chichester Harbours Huge, complex estuary of extensive tidal mudflats and saltings. One of the most important sites in Britain for wintering waders and wildfowl, and supports internationally important numbers of grey plover, sanderling, dunlin and brent geese. Rare grebes can also be seen in the harbour in winter. Web: www.conservancy.co.uk/ out/bird_watching.asp

Herefordshire – Lugg Meadow A fine example of ancient hay meadows that date back to the Doomsday Book, managed by the Herefordshire Nature Trust. Historically, the meadow was split into narrow strips, grown to produce a hay crop and then thrown open for communal grazing – perfect management for a rich flower meadow. Over 20 grass species have been recorded and star plants include meadow saffron and adder's tongue. Contact 01432 356872 or sholland@ herefordwt.cix.co.uk; web: www. wildlifetrust.org.uk/hereford/reserves/ luggmeadow.htm

Hertfordshire – Therfield Heath A large reserve, managed by the Herts and Middlesex Wildlife Trust, and one of the largest remaining tracts of chalk downland in eastern England. The site is well known for its colony of pasque flowers which bloom around Easter, and has many characteristic base-rich loving plants in late spring and summer including squinancywort and horseshoe vetch. Contact 01727 858901 or info@hmwt.org; web: www.wildlifetrust.org.uk/herts/

Humberside – Blacktoft Sands An RSPB reserve on the south side of the Humber Estuary at the confluence of the Rivers Ouse and Trent. The tidal reedbed is the largest in England and ideal for specialist breeding birds such as marsh harriers and bearded tits. A series of artificial lagoons attract a variety of waders in spring and late summer. Contact 01405 704665 or blacktoftsands@rspb.org.uk; web: www.rspb.org.uk/reserves/guide/ b/blacktoftsands/index.asp

Kent – Bedgebury Pinetum Owned and managed by the Forestry Commission and has the finest collection of conifers in the world. It is an excellent place to look for seed-eating specialists such as crossbill and hawfinch and has a healthy population of dormice that can sometimes be seen on ranger-led tours. Contact 01580 879820 or bedgebury@forestry. gov.uk; web: bedgeburypinetum.org.uk

Kent – Cliffe Pools These flooded clay pits on the south bank of the River Thames represent the newest of the RSPB reserves in Kent. The site consists of a mixture of saline lagoons, freshwater pools, scrubby grassland and saltmarsh, and is particularly famous for its waders, which pass through and use the pools as a high tide roost in winter. Tel: 01634 222480; web: www.rspb.org.uk/reserves/guide/c/cliffepools/index.asp

Kent – Dungeness The Dungeness RSPB reserve occupies nearly 1,000 hectares, forms part of the Dungeness National Nature Reserve and is one of the largest expanses of shingle in the world. The site has an active bird observatory and is famed for its migrants in spring and autumn. Freshwater pits in some of the hollows formed by gravel extraction are important gull and tern colonies in the summer. Contact 01797 320558 or dungeness@rspb.org.uk; web: www.rspb.org.uk/reserves/guide/d/dungeness/index.asp

Lancashire – Gait Barrows NNR A complex mosaic of limestone habitats including limestone pavement, yew woodland, fen and reedbed. Most significant is the limestone pavement with specialist plants such as dark red helleborine and angular solomon's seal. The site is very important for a rich variety of invertebrates and supports rare butterflies such as high brown and Duke of Burgundy fritillary at different times through the summer. Permits from Natural England: contact 01539 531604 or northwest@ english-nature.org.uk; web: www. english-nature.org.uk/Special/nnr/nnr_ details.asp?nnr_name=&C=0&Habitat=0&natural_area=&local_team=0&spotlight_reserve=1&X=1&NNR_ID=65

Lancashire – Morecambe Bay Formed as a result of a complex system of five estuaries and is now simply the most important inter-tidal area in Britain attracting up to 200,000 waders in winter. Of international importance for pink-footed geese, shelduck, pintail, oystercatcher, grey plover, knot, dunlin, bar-tailed godwit, curlew, redshank,

turnstone and ringed plover. There are numerous places to watch the bay from and the RSPB has a reserve at Hest Bank, from which the birds are best viewed at high tide. Contact 01524 701601; web: www.rspb.org.uk/reserves/ guide/m/morecambebay/index.asp

Leicestershire – Eyebrook Reservoir On the border between Leicestershire and Rutland, the reservoir was completed in 1940 and consists of 162 hectares of open water with gently shelving banks. In winter you can see large numbers of wigeon, golden plover and a fine gull roost. Very cold weather can bring in smew, scaup and even sea duck. Web: www.lros.org.uk/eyebrook.htm

Lincolnshire – Gibraltar Point NNR 430 hectares of sandy and muddy seashores, sand dunes, saltmarshes and freshwater habitats extending for almost five kilometres along the Lincolnshire coast, from the southern end of Skegness to the entrance of the Wash. Botanically rich and varied and containing a range of calcareous loving plants such as pyramidal orchids and lady's bedstraw. The introduced sea buckthorn dominates parts of the reserve, and its berries in autumn are fine food for visiting thrushes. Contact 01507 526667 or info@lincstrust.co.uk; web: www. lincstrust.org.uk/reserves/gib/index.php

Merseyside – Hilbre Island The largest of three islands at the mouth of the Dee Estuary (Middle Eye and Little Eye can only be reached on foot from the mainland at low tide), which are a stopping-off point for birds migrating along the west coast in spring and autumn. Many are caught for research in the nets at the Bird Observatory. Flowers such as bluebells and thrift are splendid in spring too. Permits are needed to cross onto the Islands. Contact 0151 648 4371/3884; web: www.wirral.gov.uk/er/hilbre.htm

Norfolk – Cley Wonderful reserve managed by the Norfolk Wildlife Trust and one of the best-known sites to watch birds in the the UK. With 176 hectares of reedbeds, pools and grazing meadows, there is always something to look out for – from bitterns in summer to snow buntings in winter. It is also regularly host to rare birds. Contact 01263 740008 or admin@norfolkwildlifetrust.org.uk; web: www.norfolkwildlifetrust.org.uk/big%205/cley.htm

Norfolk – Strumpshaw Fen This fine RSPB reserve in the heart of the Norfolk Broads consists of reedbeds, grazing marshes, alder and willow carr and open water. In spring and summer, the fen meadows bloom with over 200 species of recorded wild flowers, including six orchids. It is great for reedbed specialists such as marsh harriers and bittern, and don't forget the localised swallowtail butterflies and Chinese water deer. Contact 01603 715191 or strumpshaw@rspb.org.uk; web: www.rspb.org.uk/reserves/guide/s/strumpshawfen/

Northamptonshire – Titchmarsh Reserve Centred in the Nene Valley in the middle of a complex series of gravel pits, Titchmarsh has a variety of wetland habitats and a heronry – the herons return to their nest sites in February. Later in the year you can see banded demoiselles and red-eyed damselflies, and large numbers of wintering wildfowl on the lake. Contact 01604 405285 or northamptonshire@wildlifebcnp.org; web: www.wildlifebcnp.org/reserves/reserve.php?reserveid=116

Northumberland – The Farne Islands Located off the coast between Bamburgh and Seahouses, this collection of 28 rocks is one of the most important bird sanctuaries in Britain. Over 65,000 seabirds are thought to nest there, with huge numbers of puffins, guillemots and kittiwakes. Watch out for the dive-bombing terns on Inner Farne and Staple Island! During the season, boats leave daily from Seahouses. Contact 01665 720651; web: www.nationaltrust.org.uk/main/w-vh/w-visits/w-findaplace/w-farneislands/

Nottinghamshire – Clumber Park Originally home to the Dukes of Newcastle and now owned by the National Trust, Clumber consists of over 1,500 hectares of woods, open heath, farmland and a large lake. A variety of woodland birds can be seen, but, with persistence, the star attractions are honey buzzards and hawfinch, which both breed in the woods. Contact 01909 476592; web www.nationaltrust.org.uk/main/w-vh/w-visits/w-findaplace/w-clumberpark/

Oxfordshire – Warburg Nature Reserve A superb flagship reserve of the Berks, Bucks and Oxfordshire Wildlife Trust. It is a mixture of chalk grassland and ancient woodland, with an astonishing 2,000 recorded species of plant, animal and fungi. The habitats make it an excellent place for butterflies and it has a number of rare orchids. Introduced red kites are frequently seen over the reserve. Contact 01865 775476 or info@bbowt.org.uk; web: www.bbowt. org.uk/content.asp?did=23596

Somerset – Ebbor Gorge Near to its more famous Cheddar cousin, but less well-known, Ebbor Gorge is a largely wooded valley at the southern end of the Mendip Hills. Elm trees survive in the bottom of the valley, and in the open areas silver-washed fritillaries are common in the summer. The numerous caves are also wonderful for lesser horseshoe bats. A National Nature Reserve managed by Natural England. Contact 01823 283211 or somerset@english-nature.org.uk; web: www.english-nature.org/special/nnr/ nnr_details.asp?nnr_name=&C=35& Habitat=0&natural_area=&local_team= 0&spotlight_reserve=0&X=&NNR_ID=57

Somerset – Westhay Moor NNR In the heart of the Somerset levels and two kilometres northeast of Westhay village, the site is a mosaic of open water, reedbed, raised mire, fen and wet grassland. Managed by the Somerset Wildlife Trust, during the summer the site has the usual range of wetland birds, plants and insects. It is one of the best locations in England to see otter, and the real spectacle in November and December is the enormous starling roost, with latest estimates as high as six million birds. Contact 01823 652400 or mark.blake@somersetwildlife. org; web: www.somersetwildlife.org/ reserve_4.php

Staffordshire – Blithfield Reservoir At over 320 hectares, this is the largest reservoir in the West Midlands and an important site in spring and autumn for wader passages and in winter for wildfowl: wigeon and teal in addition to smaller numbers of Bewick's swans, goosander and the occasional rare gull. Several parts of the reserve are visible from public areas or permits can be obtained through the West Midlands Bird Club, PO Box 1, Studley Warwickshire, B80 7JG; www. westmidlandbirdclub. com/blithfield/ index.htm

Staffordshire – Chartley Moss NNR Chartley Moss is the largest example of a floating bog or schwingmoor in Britain. The site has a fine array of acidic and bog-loving plants including cranberry,

cowberry, bilberry and common sundew. Insects abound in the summer; the star attraction is the white-faced darter dragonfly. The site is privately owned and leased to Natural England with access by permit only. Contact 01733 455101 or enquiries@english-nature.org.uk

Suffolk – Landguard Point A shingle spit, south of Felixstowe at the mouth of the River Orwell. The bird observatory is housed in disused military buildings and is famous for attracting a host of rare migrants in spring and autumn. In summer ringed plover and little tern breed on the shingle, and black redstart around the docks. The site is managed by the Suffolk Wildlife Trust. Contact 01473 748463/01394 673782 or landguardbo@ yahoo.co.uk/landguard@suffolkwildlife. cix.co.uk; web: www.lbo.org.uk/ or www. suffolkwildlife.co.uk/nr/sites/land.htm

Suffolk – Walberswick NNR Just south of the village of Walberswick on the Suffolk coast and consisting of heathland, grazing marsh, hay meadows, woodland and the largest single block of freshwater reed in Britain, this is an incredibly diverse site for species of flowering plant, insects and birds, many of which are rare or localised. Notable birds include bittern, marsh harrier, bearded tits, and special plants such as frog-bit, southern marsh orchid and bog pimpernel. Contact 01284 762218 or Suffolk@english-nature.org.uk; web: www.english-nature.org uk/About/ teams/team_photo/Walberswick.pdf

Surrey – Staines Reservoir Just 27 kilometres west of the centre of London and close to the M4 and M25 motorways, Staines is the best known and most accessible of all the London reservoirs. These two concrete-banked bodies of water contain large concentrations of wildfowl in winter, black-necked grebes and little gulls are regular through the spring and summer and it is a good place to watch migration in action. Contact 01895 833375; web: www.colnevalleypark. org.uk/stainesmoor

Surrey – Thursley Common NNR One of the largest fragments of lowland heath in the UK, it contains good breeding populations of Dartford warbler, hobby and woodlark and also the highest number of recorded dragonflies in the country. It was badly burnt in 2006. Let's hope this site recovers. Contact 01273 476595 or sussex.surrey@english-nature.

org.uk; web: www.englishnature.gov.uk/ Special/ nnr/nnr_details.asp?nnr_name= &C=39&Habitat=0&natural_area=&local _team=0&spotlight_reserve=0&X=&NNR _ID =158

Warwickshire – Brandon Marsh An 81 hectare nature reserve on the banks of the River Avon just southeast of Coventry. Once an active sand and gravel quarry, the site is now a series of pools and wetlands, with nature trails, bird hides and a centre complete with tea room and shop. You can see waders and wildfowl in winter and on passage, and wetland breeding species like kingfisher, Cetti's warbler and water rail. Contact 02476 302912 or enquiries@ wkwt.org.uk; web: www.warwickshire-wildlife-trust.org.uk/Brandon/brandon. htm

West/North Yorkshire – Fairburn Ings The shallow lakes and marshes are created by the mining industry and subsidence, but the site – in the middle of an extensive industrial area and only a few miles from the centre of Leeds – has been restored into an oasis for birds. Flocks of duck can be seen in the winter, including smew, and large numbers of migrants in spring and autumn. Reedbeds alive with reed warblers mean it is a great place to look for cuckoo in the spring. Contact 01977 603796 or fairburnings@rspb.org. uk; web: www.rspb.org.uk/reserves/ guide/f/fairburnings1/about.asp

Wiltshire – Bentley Wood Large mixed woodland that is nationally recognised for its importance as a butterfly site, containing all the woodland species confined to central and southern England. Also the most famous site for the purple emperor (on the wing in mid-July). Woodland flowers and both dormice and glow-worms too. Managed by the Bentley Wood Trust; Grid ref: ST 259 292; OS Map: 184

Wiltshire – Lacock Abbey Founded in 1232 and converted into a country house in about 1540, large parts of this wonderful abbey have remained intact. The gardens and grounds were designed with nature in mind. In late summer up to 1,000 pipistrelles emerge from various exits below the roof above the famous Fox Talbot window and a number of other bat species can be seen during an evening in the grounds. Contact 01249 730459; web: www.nationaltrust.org.uk/ main/w-vh/w-visits/w-findaplace/w-lacockabbeyvillage. htm

Worcestershire – Wyre Forest About 50 per cent broadleaf and dominated by sessile oak, the forest is one of the most important areas on ancient woodland in the country. The woods have an impressive range of woodland birds, are a real stronghold for adders and grass snakes, slow-worms and common lizards, and are also an exceptional place for the rapidly declining butterfly, the pearl-bordered fritillary amongst others. Contact 01299 266929 or liz.bunney@forestry.gsi.gov.uk; web: www.forestry.gov.uk/website/Wild Woods.nsf/LUWebDocsByKey/England WorcestershireNoForestWyreForestWyre ForestVisitorandDiscoveryCentre

•••••••••••••••••••••••••••••••••••

Northern Ireland

County Down – Carlingford Lough This small inlet, thought to be a sunken valley carved out by a glacier, forms the border between Northern Ireland and the Irish Republic. Inter-tidal areas are limited but large numbers of pale-bellied brent geese still overwinter here; in the summer four species of terns, including the rare roseate tern, breed on the disappearing Green Island and nearby Greencastle Point. Web: www.ehsni.gov. uk/biodiversity/designated-areas/spec_ protect/spec_protect_carlingfordlough.htm

County Fermanagh – Pettigoe The Pettigoe Plateau covers 1,270 hectares and is one of the largest expanses of blanket bog in Northern Ireland. The site is part of an extended cross-border site which supports over a hundred wintering Greenland white-fronted geese and breeding hen harrier, merlin, dunlin, and common tern. Other breeding species include lapwing, curlew, and snipe. Web: www.ehsni.gov.uk/biodiversity/designate d-areas/spec_protect/spec_protect_ pettigoe.htm

•••••••••••••••••••••••••••••••••••

Scotland

Argyll – Loch Gruinart On the island of Islay, 19 kilometres off the southwest coast of Scotland, this RSPB reserve sea-loch, saltmarsh, wetland, farmland and moorland is the winter residence of 70 per cent of the world's Greenland barnacle geese and 40 per cent of the Greenland white-fronted goose population. Contact 01496 850505 or loch.gruinart@rspb.

org.uk; web: www.rspb.org.uk/reserves/ guide/l/lochgruinart/index.asp

Borders – St Abb's Head NNR Nineteen kilometres north of Berwick-upon-Tweed and home, between April and August, to 60,000 seabirds. The Head is also good for migratory seabirds in autumn when shearwaters and skuas are to be seen moving south. Divers and sea duck can also be seen on the sea during the winter. Contact 01890 771443; web: www.nts.org. uk/web/site/home/visit/places/Property. asp?PropID=10024&NavPage=10024& NavId=5115

Clyde – Lochwinnoch RSPB Reserve One of the few remaining areas of substantial wetland in west Scotland, comprising Aird Meadows to the northeast and Barr Loch to the southwest. Aird Meadows has a mosaic of lily ponds, sedge beds, willow scrub and woodland and holds breeding sedge, grasshopper and garden warblers. In winter Barr Loch holds a small population of whooper swans and a large population of wild greylag and winter duck. Contact 01505 842663 or lochwinnoch@rspb.org.uk; web: www.rspb.org.uk/reserves/guide/l/ lochwinnoch/index.asp

Dumfries & Galloway – Carstramon Wood A wonderful oak wood to see and hear the 'western trio' in mid-May: redstart, pied flycatcher and wood warbler. The woodland floor is also carpeted with bluebells. Managed by the Scottish Wildlife Trust. Contact 0131 312 7765; web: ww.swt.org.uk/wildlife/reserves.asp

East Lothian – Aberlady Bay Nineteen kilometres east of Edinburgh, on the south shore of the Firth of Forth, Aberlady consists of intertidal mud, giving way to sand-dunes. Winter is the best time to see pink-footed geese and large rafts of winter waders and wildfowl. The site also has the reputation of attracting rarities in autumn. Contact imt.aberlady@ic24.net; web: www.aberlady.org/Nature%20reserve. html

Flintshire – Point of Ayr This RSPB reserve at the Mouth of the Dee estuary has sand-flats and dunes – great places to watch waders and wildfowl. A colony of little terns breed just west of the point and, in late summer, thousands of common, sandwich, little, arctic and maybe even a roseate tern or two will gather on the beaches before migrating

south. Contact 0151 336 7681; web: www.rspb.org.uk/reserves/guide/p/ pointofayr/index.asp

Highland – Bridge of Grudie A stunning wet peat bog reserve pitted with small pools on the banks of Loch Maree. This is an excellent place for rare Scottish dragonflies such as the azure hawker and northern emerald; other northern specialists to look for include the large heath butterfly and creeping lady's tresses orchid. Grid ref: NG 966 678; OS Map 19

Highland – Glen Affric This glen has been called the most beautiful in Scotland and contains one of the largest blocks of Caledonian pinewoods, in addition to lochs, moorland and mountains. Look for Scottish mammal specialities such as pine marten, red squirrel and otter and, of course, localised birds such crested tits, Scottish crossbill or the now rare capercaillie. Contact 01320 366322 or fiona.barnett@forestry.gsi.gov.uk; web: www.forestry.gov.uk/website/recreation. nsf/LUWebDocsByKey/ScotlandHighland NoForestGlenAffric

Highland – Rum The Isle of Rum is a National Nature Reserve, purchased by what is now Scottish Natural Heritage in 1958. It is an excellent place to look for both species of eagle and a unique mountain-top colony of Manx shearwaters. The outstanding spectacle is in autumn when the red deer stags rut. Contact 01687 462026; web: www.snh.org.uk/nnr-scotland/reserve. asp?NNRId=22 or www. isleofrum.com/isleofrumreddeer.html

Northeast Scotland – Corrie Fee NNR An outstanding example of the landscape and habitat of the Cairngorm mountains. Scotland's newest NNR is superb walking country and also one of the best sites for arctic-alpine plants such as the rare woolly willow and alpine woodsia, and upland birds like the golden eagle and peregrine. The site is managed by Scottish Natural Heritage. Contact 01575 530333 or shona.hill@snh.gov.uk; web: www.snh. org.uk/scottish/taysclack/CFnnr.asp

Perth & Kinross – Loch of Lowes A 98 hectare site managed by the Scottish Wildlife Trust. Plays host to a breeding pair of ospreys that are easily viewable from the observation hide (April–August). Fallow and roe deer can regularly be seen, and on the loch is a range of aquatic plants such as bogbean and both yellow and white water-lilies. In winter a large number of wild greylag geese roost on the loch. Contact 0131 312 7765; web: www.swt.org.uk/wildlife/reserves.asp

Shetland – Fair Isle Situated between the Orkney and Shetland Isles, Fair Isle is Britain's most isolated inhabited island. In summer this 765 hectare rocky outcrop is a wonderful place to see towering seabird colonies with arctic and great skuas breeding on the moorland tops near the cliffs. In autumn the site is internationally renowned for the high number of rarities that use the isle as a stopover, including many firsts for Britain. Accommodation is available at the bird observatory. Contact 01595 760258 or fairisle.birdobs@zetnet.co.uk; web: www.fairislebirdobs.co.uk/

. . . .

Wales

Anglesey – Cemlyn Bay This wonderful brackish lagoon on the north coast, which was sealed off from the sea by a shingle ridge, has small islands that are home for up to four species of breeding terns in summer. The Point is good to look out for Manx shearwaters and harbour porpoise. Managed by the North Wales Wildlife Trust. Contact 01248 351541 or nwwt@cix.co.uk; web: www.wildlifetrust.org.uk/northwales/cemlynwebpages/cemlynindex.html

Anglesey – South Stack Situated on the western extremity of the island, this reserve contains heathland, cliffs, offshore stacks and caves. The heathland and adjacent farm fields are good places to look for a real feature – choughs. Over 4,000 seabirds, including guillemots, razorbills and puffins, nest on the cliffs from late spring and through the summer. Contact 01407 764973 or south.stack@rspb.org.uk; web: www.rspb.org.uk/reserves/guide/s/southstack/

Caernarfon – Great Orme A massive limestone headland lying immediately north of Llandudno on the North Wales coast, three kilometres long, one and a half kilometres wide and rising 207 metres from the sea. In addition to seabirds that nest on the cliffs, the base-rich nature of the rock supports a variety of wildflowers, including rare species such as dark-red helleborine. Butterflies abound, including a local variety of silver studded blue. Contact 01492 874151; web: www.greatorme.org.uk/greatorme.html

Carmarthenshire – National Wetland Centre Wales Located on the north shore of the Burrey Inlet and one and a half kilometres east of Llanelli, this relatively new Wildfowl and Wetlands Trust Reserve attracts an excellent range of wintering wildfowl, waders and raptors and passage birds in spring and autumn. The habitats consist of mud-flats, saltmarsh, reedbeds and man-made lagoons. There is an impressive little egret roost in the winter. Contact 01554 741087 or info.llanelli@wwt.org.uk; web: www.wwt.org.uk/visit/llanelli/

Ceredigion – Tregaron Bog One of the few remaining examples of a raised peat bog in Britain, Tregaron Bog was formed by the slow filling of a shallow lake after the last Ice Age. Now it contains plants adapted to the acidic conditions, such as all three species of sundew, bog rosemary and cotton sedge. Also one of the best places to see original Welsh red kites. Contact 01974 298480; web: www.ccw.gov.uk/places/index.cfm?Action=Reserves&ID=16&lang=en

Denbighshire – Gors Maen Llwyd With 280 hectares of heather moorland, blanket bog and lake, this is the largest of the North Wales Wildlife Trust's reserves. It is particularly attractive in August when the heather is in flower and the paler pink of cross-leaved heath can be seen in wetter areas. The lake hosts goosander and breeding common sandpiper and is a good place to spot ravens and raptors. Contact 01352 810469 or nwwt@cix.co.uk; web: www.wildlifetrust.org.uk/northwales/GorsMaenLlwyd.html

Glamorgan – Gower Coast NNR Some of the finest sea cliffs in the whole of Wales, extraordinarily rich in lime-loving plants with some real rarities. At Worm's Head the breeding colonies are packed with guillemots, razorbills and kittiwakes (April–July). Managed by the Countryside Council for Wales. Contact 01792 634960; web: http://countryside.wales.info/National_Nature_Reserves.asp

Mid Glamorgan – Kenfig Dunes NNR Considered one of the last remnants of a sand-dune system that once stretched along the coast between the River Ogmore and the Gower Peninsula, this site near Porthcawl consists of wetland, sand-dunes and scrub. It attracts a wide range of wildfowl, waders and raptors in winter and on passage, and the rare fen orchid can be seen in the dune slacks in early summer. Contact 01656 745940; web: www.ccw.gov.uk/places/index.cfm?Action=Reserves&ID=27&lang=en

Montgomeryshire – Lake Vyrnwy The largest man-made lake in Wales is surrounded by wonderful heather moorland, deciduous woodland, conifer plantation, mountain streams and crags. Breeding species on the moorland include hen harrier, merlin, red grouse and short-eared owl, and a whole suite of woodland species can be seen in both forest types. The streams and reservoir both hold kingfisher, grey wagtail and dipper, with numerous waders and wildfowl on migration and during the winter. Contact 01691 870278 or vyrnwy@rspb.org.uk; web: www.rspb.org.uk/reserves/guide/l/lakevyrnwy/index.asp

Pembrokeshire – Grassholm One of three principal islands off the western tip of Pembrokeshire and the only gannet colony in Wales. With an estimated 32,000 pairs, increasing steadily, it is now the UK's third-largest colony behind St Kilda and Bass Rock. It is not possible to land on the island but boat trips are organised during the breeding season. Web: www.rspb.org.uk/wales/action/grassholm.asp

Further Reading

Beebee, T and Griffiths, R (2000), *Amphibians and Reptiles*, HarperCollins Publishers Ltd, London.

Blamey, M, Fitter, R and Fitter, A (2003), *Wild Flowers of Britain & Ireland*, A & C Black Publishers Ltd, London.

Brooks, S and Lewington, R (2002), *Field Guide to the Dragonflies and Damselflies of Great Britain and Ireland*, Revised Edition, British Wildlife Publishing, Dorset.

Chinery, M (2005), *Complete British Insects*, HarperCollins Publishers Ltd, London.

Cocker, M and Mabey, R. (2005), *Birds Britannica*, Chatto & Windus, London.

Harding, P and Tomblin, G (1998), *Collins How to Identify Trees*, HarperCollins Publishers Ltd, London.

Harrap, A and Harrap, S (2005), *Orchids of Britain and Ireland*, A & C Black, London.

Harrap, S and Redman, N (2003), *Where to Watch Birds – Britain*, Christopher Helm, London.

Holden, P and Cleeves, T (2006), *RSPB Handbook of British Birds*, 2nd edition, Christopher Helm, London.

Marren, P (1999), *Britain's Rare Flowers*, T & AD Poyser, London.

Mabey, R (1997), *Flora Britannica*, 2nd edition, Chatto & Windus, London.

Morris, P, Alderson, K, Beebee, T, Chapman, N and Harris, S (1984), *Field Guide to the Animals of Britain*, Reader's Digest Association Limited, London.

Phillips, R (2006), *Mushrooms*, Macmillan, London.

Rose, F (1989), *Colour Identification Guide to the Grasses, Sedges, Rushes & Ferns of the British Isles and North-Western Europe*, Viking, London.

Svensson, L and Grant, PJ (1999), *Collins Bird Guide*, HarperCollins Publishers Ltd, London.

Thomas, J and Lewington, R (1991), *The Butterflies of Britain & Ireland*, Dorling Kindersley, London.

Waring, P & Townsend, M (2003). *Field Guide to the Moths of Great Britain & Ireland*. British Wildlife Publishing, Dorset

Index